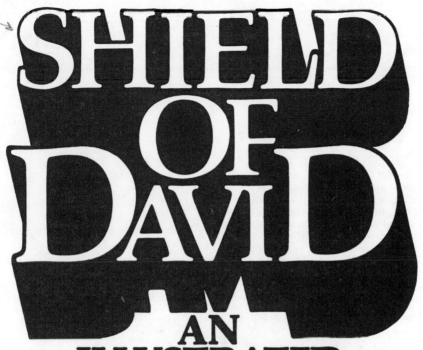

SHIELD OF DAVID

AN ILLUSTRATED HISTORY OF THE ISRAELI AIR FORCE

Murray Rubenstein & Richard Goldman

PRENTICE-HALL, INC., Englewood Cliffs, New Jersey

Shield of David: An Illustrated History of the Israeli Air Force
by Murray Rubenstein and Richard Goldman
Copyright © 1978 by Murray Rubenstein and Richard Goldman
Printed in the United States of America
Prentice-Hall International, Inc., London
Prentice-Hall of Australia, Pty. Ltd., Sydney
Prentice-Hall of Canada, Ltd., Toronto
Prentice-Hall of India Private Ltd., New Delhi
Prentice-Hall of Japan, Inc., Tokyo
Prentice-Hall of Southeast Asia Pte. Ltd., Singapore
Whitehall Books Limited, Wellington, New Zealand
10 9 8 7 6 5 4 3 2 1

Library of Congress Cataloging in Publication Data
Rubenstein, Murray.
    Shield of David.
1. Israel.   Chel ha-avir—History.   I. Goldman,
Richard Martin, joint author.   II. Title.
UG635.I75R8   358.4'0095694   78-851
ISBN 0-13-808907-8

CONTENTS

I
THE BEGINNING
1947–1949

II
THE CHEL HA'AVIR
COMES OF AGE
1949–1967

III
CLAWS OF THE LION
1967–1978

APPENDICES

AIR BASES OF
THE ISRAEL DEFENCE
FORCE/AIR FORCE

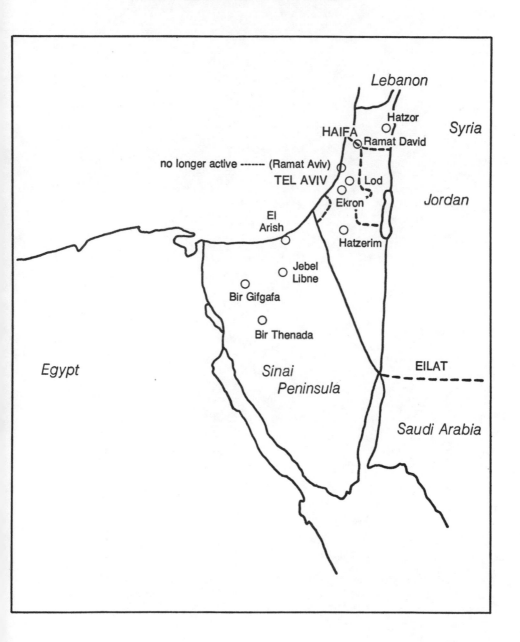

THE
BEGINNING
1947–1949

1
THE
LITTLE MOTHS

THE ISRAELI AIR FORCE, LIKE ISRAEL ITSELF, HAS BEEN IN existence for only thirty years. In that brief time it has fought four wars, emerging victorious from each. It is today perhaps the most battle-tested air force, and the most ready for combat, of any in the world. Its record in air-to-air combat is unsurpassed: Indeed, though his name is a closely guarded secret, it is an Israeli who is undoubtedly the world's highest-scoring jet fighter pilot. And certainly its performance against odds is in a class by itself. If ever the catch phrase "a legend in its own time" was deserved, it is merited by Israel's astonishing air arm.

The formal name of this famous organization is the Israel Defence Force/Air Force (IDF/AF). More commonly, it is called by its Hebrew name, *Chel Ha'Avir*. But its beginnings antedate both names—go back, in fact, to a time before there was even such a thing as the modern state of Israel. Many air forces have had a colorful origin, but none has been stranger or more dramatic than that of the *Chel Ha'Avir*.

Before picking up the thread of this story, we should pause briefly to remind ourselves of some relevant history. Contemporary Israel was born in 1948, as the result of lapse of the British mandate in Palestine. Britain had conquered Palestine in 1918, driving out the Turks, who had controlled the Holy Land for centuries. But long before the advent of the Turks, Palestine had been the ancient state of Israel, a state modern Jews wished to recreate as a homeland for all Jews, especially their oppressed brethren in Europe. The British, seeking support for their war effort, had made promises both to the Arabs of the Near East and to Jewish Zionists that England would

11

support postwar aims of each group. And, when World War I ended, both peoples pressed their claims.

For political, diplomatic, and strategic reasons, Britain, which was given a mandate to run and police Palestine, leaned toward the Arabs. And the Arabs, believing their "right" to Palestine had been assured, began to increase pressure on Jewish settlements in the Holy Land, even those which had been there for centuries. To protect themselves, Jews in Palestine formed community military defense groups called *Shomrim*.

In 1939 England blocked further immigration of Jews to the area and forbade Jews already there to have weapons. But the Jews, with the terrible example before them of the Nazi persecutions in Europe, and with the need for some place to resettle millions of refugees, refused to obey British regulations. Instead, Jews in Palestine created their own clandestine national defense force to protect their interests. They had no choice. England had broken its word to them and they could not rely on the protection of British soldiers when Arabs attacked their settlements.

After the end of World War II, this already intolerable situation deteriorated steadily. Britain's new socialist government had made plain its intention of pulling out of Palestine at the earliest opportunity. However much the Palestinians might applaud this in principle, it was clear that withdrawal of the British presence would inevitably be the signal for an all-out Arab attack on the Palestinian Jews, notwithstanding efforts by the United Nations to find a peaceful solution to the problem. More than ever, the Palestinian Jews felt a desperate need to arm themselves for the impending struggle, but the British continued to try to thwart all such efforts.

In 1947 the die was cast. The United Nations voted to divide Palestine into separate Arab and Jewish states, effective upon the termination of the British mandate. Since this termination was set to take place on May 14, 1948, the Jews could now predict to the day when the dreaded full-scale war would begin.

In fact, preliminary hostilities began almost immediately. The Arabs, determined to snuff out the Jewish state before it was born, poured infiltrators across the borders and began attacking Jewish settlements. Since the British did little to prevent these attacks, more than ever it became apparent to the Jews that salvation lay solely in their own hands. Now, almost overnight, the need for air power became critical to their survival, for it was only by air that the scattered settlements under Arab siege could be supplied with food, weapons, and medical supplies. From this dire necessity was born the

Sherut Avir ("Air Service"), an illegal, clandestine Jewish air force that would be called upon to supply the endangered Jewish settlements up until the time of the British withdrawal and to help defend the new state of Israel in the days that followed.

That such an air force could have been assembled under the watchful eyes of British authorities who had in no way relented in their policy of denying arms to the Jews is certainly one of the more extraordinary covert operations of recent times. What made it possible was, first, that the aircraft earmarked for the *Sherut Avir* had such decidedly unwarlike configurations that hardly anyone could have imagined they had military potential, and second, that the civil aviation establishment in Palestine was able to provide an adequate, if often precarious, cover to disguise what was really going on.

From the point of view of the *Sherut Avir*, the most useful civilian cover organizations were the clubs for sport flying enthusiasts. Two of these, the Carmel Club, founded by two glider pilots in 1932, and the Flying Camel Club, which since 1933 had been enrolling both Jewish and Arab members, had acquired an enviable patina of respectability. A third, the Civilian Flying Club, was a relative newcomer. Headquartered in an ex-RAF hanger at Ramleh Lydda (now Ben-Gurion) airport, it operated a few Taylorcraft and five old Polish lightplanes—two RWD-8s, two RWD-13s, and a single RWD-50. The Civilian Flying Club thus seemed innocuous enough; actually it flew more secret missions for the *Sherut Avir* prior to the British withdrawal than did any other group.

In addition to the clubs, there were two other civilian organizations that provided personnel and/or aircraft for the *Sherut Avir*. One was a curious organization called the Aviron ("Airplane") Company. Founded in 1936, it purchased and sold aircraft and also trained pilots in RWD-13s and a biplane Tiger Moth: It was to become one of the *Sherut Avir*'s principal procurement agencies. The other organization was the Palestine Air Service, Ltd., a small commercial airline that had been formed in 1937. Closely watched by the British, it was of more potential than immediate value to the *Sherut Avir*, but it was a useful training facility for pilots and ground crews.

As Arab violence against the Jews mounted, it became apparent that the inventory of planes available to the *Sherut Avir* was already inadequate to meet the needs of the beleaguered settlements, let alone to satisfy Israel's probable military requirements once the mandate ended. It was imperative that additional innocent-looking aircraft be procured—legally if possible, but procured in any event.

The hard-pressed Civilian Flying Club at Ramleh made some of the first of the new acquisitions. Their 55-horsepower Taylorcraft, though much used, were poor load carriers, and their little RWD-8 two-place monoplanes were so old as to be virtually useless; and since their sole five-place RWD-50 was painted white, it was of dubious value for covert nighttime operations. Thus the Club had been compelled to do most of its secret *Sherut Avir* work with its two high-wing, three-place RWD-13s (registered VQ-PAL and VQ-PAM). In 1947, however, the Club obtained permission to import two de Havilland D.H. 82A two-seat light training biplanes from Canada (registered VQ-PAU and VQ-PAV) and a third de Havilland from England. (The latter differed from the Canadian machines only in that it lacked a sliding hood; it was registered as VQ-PAN.) All three of these frail aircraft were destined to serve throughout the War of Independence.

Other types of planes dribbled in from various sources. Some additional Taylorcraft were recruited from private individuals and from the Aviron Company. (Three of these were operated by a "flying school" that was actually a part of the *Etzel* right-wing underground organization.) Aviron also made available a de Havilland Dragon Rapide, a fabric covered twin-engine biplane of prewar vintage. An attorney named Tzopeck donated a Republic Seabee single-engine amphibian. Even an Egyptian smuggler contributed to the *Sherut Avir*'s inventory—though not willingly—when the *Haganah*, Israel's underground army, commandeered his Fairchild F-24R Argus in the Negev.

But in quantitative terms, by far the most significant additions to the *Sherut Avir*'s invisible air force were British Austers. Looking like a typical high-wing two-place sport plane, the Auster was nevertheless driven by a relatively powerful 130-horsepower engine. Although there were two versions of the aircraft, the J/1 civilian version and the A.O.P. 5 military observation model, they were in fact, nearly identical. Several privately registered J/1 Austers had been flying in Palestine for some time, and the *Sherut Avir* made arrangements to recruit these. In addition, much to everyone's surprise, it was learned that the British government might be willing to sell two dozen old military Austers that it was preparing to send to the scrap heap. A representative of the Aviron Company immediately called on the appropriate authorities. The representative was permitted to take a brief look at a few battered aircraft and was informed that the lot could be purchased for £14,000. Almost as soon as the money had been handed over and the hulks carried away by truck, the British thought better of their decision and tried to cancel the transaction. But by then it was too late. The planes were quickly hidden, overhauled, and cannibalized, eventually producing several airworthy specimens. Like the civilian Austers, they were thenceforth usually painted yellow, so that from a distance they might be mistaken by the British for Taylorcraft.

Throughout 1947 and the early part of 1948 the *Sherut Avir* and other elements of the Jewish underground managed to maintain a generally successful defense of their homeland against the incursions of the Arab irregulars, but as the term of the British mandate drew toward its close, the thoughts of the Palestinian Jews turned increasingly to the more menacing problem of the coming war. The *Sherut Avir's* motley collection of planes had been barely adequate for the conduct of the guerilla, but it seemed hopelessly unready to fight a real war. The Jews still did not possess a single aircraft originally intended for combat. Their potential enemies, on the other hand, were all-too-well equipped. Egypt, for example, had late-model British Supermarine Spitfires, as well as formidable Italian Fiat and Macchi fighters. The Iraqi Air Force had Hawker Fury fighters, a type so advanced that it had been produced too late to see action in World War II. All told, Egypt, Iraq, and Syria possessed among them 131 military aircraft of all types. The Jews had a total of just 28.

Last-minute efforts by the Jews to persuade the British to relax their import restrictions proved fruitless, and in addition, several foreign governments, the United States among them, embargoed arms shipments to Palestine. Even relevant treaty relationships militated against the Jewish position. England, for example, was bound by a treaty with Jordan whereby if Jordan attacked Israel, the British would doubtless feel obliged to do nothing, but if Israel attacked Jordan, the British might well intervene on the Jordanian side.

The British began their evacuation of Palestine in May, often turning over fortresses and police stations—and sometimes even heavy weapons—to Arab irregulars as they went. On May 14 the new state of Israel was created. On May 15 it was invaded simultaneously by the armies of Lebanon, Syria, Iraq, Jordan, and Egypt, supported by large irregular forces operating in the Galilee and by military contingents sent from Saudi Arabia, Sudan, and Morocco.

Besides tanks, artillery, armored cars, and heavy machine guns, the Arab countries surrounding Israel had on May 15, 1948, an overwhelming superiority in air power. The enemy had collectively: 45 fighters, 29 bombers, 29 transports, 8 light aircraft and 20 trainers. (The 10 Egyptian "bombers" were C-47 transports fitted with bomb racks.)

ARAB AIR FORCES AND THEIR AIRCRAFT
ON MAY 14, 1948

Country	Fighters	Bombers	Transports	Light aircraft	Trainers	Total
Egypt	40	10	20	5	10	85
Iraq	5	4	6	3	5	23
Syria	0	15	3	0	5	23
						131

Israel had no fighters, 2 "bombers" (an antiquated Dragon Rapide and a Noorduyn Norseman single-engined cargo aircraft, both fitted with bomb racks), 22 transports (all of them small single-engined aircraft), 2 light aircraft (an Auster and a Fairchild), and 2 training planes. A more precise breakdown is as follows:

Austers (A.O.P. 5 and J/1 Autocrat)	19
Noorduyn Norseman	1
De Havilland Dragon Rapide	1
RWD-13	2
Beechcraft Bonanza	2
Fairchild F-24R Argus	1
Taylorcraft Model C	2
	28

Plainly such a tiny force was inadequate. The only question was whether it could hold out until reinforcements arrived. Now that the British were gone, Israel could purchase foreign aircraft legally (although, to be sure, the number of nations willing to sell was limited), but there was bound to be a dangerous hiatus in which the *Sherut Avir*'s battered little moths would be Israel's only defense in the air.

The Arabs understood this perfectly well and acted accordingly. Israel suffered her first air raid on the first day of her existence. Egyptian Spitfires attacked Tel Aviv and, more important, shot up Sde Dov airfield, damaging fully half the *Sherut Avir*'s entire complement of aircraft. More raids ensued on the following days, yet somehow the Israeli planes escaped destruction. One by one they were all patched up and made airworthy again.

It is entirely possible that if the Arab air forces had been more efficient and had wiped out the *Sherut Avir* in the first days of the war, Israel could not have endured. The Israeli Army was scattered and painfully ill-equipped, and aircraft were essential to distribute still-meager supplies to forces barely holding on. Often a single machine gun or planeload of ammunition spelled the difference between repulsing an attack and being overwhelmed. As it turned out, the *Sherut Avir* not only survived, but time and again made the vital difference.

There was still nothing the Israelis could do to fight off Arab air raids, but at least once during this period Arab raiders unleashed an unexpected whirlwind. On May 22, Egyptian Spitfires twice bombed and strafed the airfield at Ramat David. This was no small error, since the airfield was still occupied by No. 32 and 38 Squadrons of the RAF, whose planes were stationed there to cover the evacuation of the last remaining British troops. The first raid caught the British by surprise (they even imagined that the attackers might be Israelis), but when the raiders returned for the second attack the British were fully prepared and scrambled their fighters—also Spitfires—at once. Three Egyptian Spitfires were brought down; nine RAF Spitfires sustained varying degrees of damage on the ground and a Dakota was destroyed by a bomb. The incident did nothing to improve Anglo-Egyptian relations.

By this time the *Sherut Avir*'s planes had been organized into three squadrons. The Galil ("Galilee") was based at Yavneel; the Tel Aviv Squadron was stationed at Sde Dov, north of Tel Aviv; and the Negev Squadron operated from several bases in the south, including Dorot and Niram. Somewhat later, Ekron, which was to become the main fighter base, also became operational.

The primary missions of the squadrons continued to be supply and reconnaissance, but against all likelihood they also managed to add bombardment and ground attack to the list. On May 19 the Tel Aviv Squadron, flying its tiny aircraft in a series of night raids, pummeled Arab ground forces with grenades and homemade bombs. The technique—if that is the word—used in this operation set the pattern for most of the lightplane raids that followed. A man designated as "bombardier" would sit next to the pilot carrying a box of small bombs or grenades on his lap. Austers, called "Primuses" because their puttering engines sounded like Primus kerosene stoves, were especially favored for this kind of operation. When the enemy came in sight, the pilot would dive as low as possible and the "bombardier" would simply throw his stores out the window. The effect fell short of precision but seemed satisfactorily demoralizing to the Arabs.

More such raids were conducted against a Syrian staging area at Zemlach on May 20 and against the Gaza airfield and the village of Deir S'neid and Shaafat the following night. On the 22nd the fortress of Iraq Suweidan was bombed, as was Kafr-Hareb the following night. Gaza and a Jordanian salient at Latrun were hit on the 25th, Biddu on the 26th, Ramallah that same night. The *Sherut Avir's* moths were proving they could also be hornets.

On May 27 the *Sherut Avir* ceased to exist, for on that date Israel created its official air arm, the Israel Defence Force/Air Force or *Chel Ha'Avir*. The little planes, of course, soldiered on as before and, indeed, continued to operate well after new, more appropriate equipment began to arrive. From first to last, their story forms a special and uniquely heroic chapter in the history of the War of Independence.

The force of little planes received only one reinforcement in kind during the course of the war. In the early summer twenty American Piper Cubs, somehow spirited past the U.S. embargo, arrived in Israel. They were immediately put to work, many of them being assigned to the Negev Squadron. The Negev's second Commanding Officer, Hy Goldstein, now a glass manufacturer in Long Island, New York, remembers the period thus:

> We flew bombing raids in the Piper Cubs; we flew reconnaissance; we flew mercy missions; we flew wounded back from the Negev and we flew ammunition into the kibbutzim that were under siege. I was "Chaim" in Israel, second in command of the Negev Squadron. My commander at the time was Ralph Moster from Vancouver who was killed in the Kinneret. . . . We worked with the army—the army was responsible for us. In other words, anytime the army wanted to take a town, they'd give us a map that said tonight we're going to take this town. We'd bomb it for them. We used 20-kilo—40-pound—bombs. When we started flying, we carried them on our laps and then they put the bomb racks on the planes.
>
> There were seven planes in my outfit. There were thirteen men. The Egyptians claimed we had thirty or forty planes at times down there. They were trying to find us in the worst way, but never could. We pushed the planes into the brush at the different places where we stayed. Our main base was Kibbutz Dorot. The army had an airstrip there. . . . There was an airstrip at Niram. Also at Nevatim near Beersheba. All the kibbutzim had an airstrip—not airstrips really; we used to fly down there and land in the desert. We used to fly in supplies, orders, ammunition, food, reconnaissance, the army.
>
> One day I flew down to Nevatim and I was told that this one guy was wounded; he was shot when he was laying down and hit in the shoulder, so they wanted me to fly him back to the hospital. That was in Rechovoth. . . .

To do it, you just hope or wish or pray. The way we did it, we'd fly down about eight or ten feet off the ground. Close to the ground was our only defense. We used to fly around a house, or a tree, or any object. We would turn into them [Egyptian Spitfires]. They'd have to turn off. To hit you, they have to put their noses on to you. It was luck, mostly, I guess. We'd fly into wadis. Things like that. These were the only ways we had of getting away from them. We lost a couple of boys. Killed. Shot down by the Spits.

We did most of our bombing at night. The army would pick out the towns and give us the places to bomb. We bombed Faluja, Bet Hanun, Beersheba, Revivim when they had it—that whole area when the Egyptians had it.

I think the longest flight I made in a Piper Cub was in Aqir in the Negev and we went down to Sodom, then to Faluja and back on a reconnaissance for the army. We put a special tank in the plane. In fact, we drew straws for the flight because it was a suicide mission. All of our missions against Spitfires were suicide missions. There was no such thing as flying *against* Spitfires and coming back. That's what we did every day.

We ran into Spits pretty often. One day I was coming back from a reconnaissance. I had an army officer observer with me in the back seat. The sun gets awfully hot there in the desert. I got careless. I looked up and there was a Spitfire diving down on me. I took evasive action, put the stick forward and dived. He never pulled out of his dive. He went right into the desert near El Arish.

Ralph Moster and I were flying the day we took Beersheba. If the enemy had counterattacked, we would have lost Beersheba. We couldn't hold it. We flew over and we saw that the entire Arab army was in trucks. As we got back to Beersheba again, looking down on the ground, we saw explosions.

I had an army officer and Ralph had an army officer in his plane. Looking down, I saw explosions and I said to myself that it must be some ammunition blowing up. I looked up and a Spit was just pulling out of his dive. Egyptian Spit. I must have been only twenty feet from him. He never saw me until I saw him. We came together about ten feet from each other. He went one way, I went the other. He was as scared as I was, but he had ammunition and I didn't. So I dived. The only defense was to dive to the ground.

At the beginning of the War of Independence hundreds of Jewish volunteers flocked to the aid of the new state, many of them veteran airmen of World War II. One such was Boris Senior, a former lieutenant in the South African air force. Wealthy in his own right, he undertook to provide as many aircraft as possible for the fledging Israeli Air Force. After an abortive attempt to ship twenty fighter aircraft by sea to Israel, he purchased two Beechcraft Model 35 Bonanza aircraft. He and another pilot, Cyril Katz, decided to fly the aircraft the length of Africa to Israel, no small task for small single-engine aircraft with a range of only 750 miles.

Although British and South African authorities suspected what was afoot, they had no good grounds to intercede, since the Bonanza was as unlikely a candidate for a military aircraft as could be found. The two Bonanzas left Johannesburg, South Africa, and arrived at Pietersburg without incident, but were not so lucky on the next leg of the journey, to Lusaka, Rhodesia. En route, Cyril Katz had to make a forced landing, damaging his aircraft beyond repair. Senior returned for him, but he too damaged his aircraft beyond repair.

Undaunted, Boris Senior purchased another Bonanza. This time, he was successful in his trans-African flight. His last stop before Israel was at Luxor, in Egypt. He succeeded in convincing authorities there that he was a wealthy tourist and, after being feted by local officials, filed a flight plan for Beirut. Instead of flying there, he landed in the Negev Desert, where he was at first mistaken for an Englishman serving with the Egyptians. And it was in this round-about manner that Israel acquired a Bonanza.

The Bonanza was immediately incorporated into the Tel Aviv Squadron at Sde Dov, north of the Yarkon River. This airfield was then the main base of the Israeli Air Force. Most of the squadron was comprised of Piper Cubs.

On the morning of May 15, 1948, Egyptian Spitfires attacked Sde Dov, damaging three aircraft and wounding several men. In the afternoon they returned, but this time anti-aircraft fire struck one of the Spitfires. Belching smoke, it began to lose altitude; it headed for the coast and disappeared from view in the direction of Herzliya. The Tel Aviv base commander took off in the Bonanza in pursuit of the fighter aircraft. He found the Spitfire on the beach of Herzliya and landed nearby. The Egyptian pilot had already been captured by Is-raeli ground forces. The Spitfire became an Israeli fighter.

The Bonanza Boris Senior brought to Israel helped win another victory. On the morning of June 4 a three-ship Egyptian convoy headed north from the Gaza Strip. In the lead was the armed troop transport, *Amira Fauzia*, followed by a large landing craft and a cor-vette. The only Israeli warship available to intercept the flotilla was an immigrant ship, originally an icebreaker built by the United States. It had been hastily pressed into service little more than a week earlier.

The ship, named the *Eilat*, was armed with 65- and 75-mm field guns totally unsuited for naval warfare. At about 2:00 P.M., the *Eilat* intercepted the convoy. Almost immediately, the captain realized that he was hopelessly outgunned. The Egyptian corvette opened rapid and accurate fire, scoring hits on the *Eilat*. The damaged Israeli ship retreated and the Egyptian convoy headed toward Tel Aviv. If not stopped, a troop landing near that city would have taken pressure off an Egyptian armored column at nearby Ashdod and allowed a breakout toward the Israeli capital.

Then, at 3:15, three Israeli airplanes swooped down on the Egyptian ships. These "bombers" were the Bonanza, the fabric-covered de Havilland Dragon Rapide twin-engine biplane, and a small single-engine Fairchild. Without bombsights in the face of heavy anti-aircraft fire, the little airplanes launched a total of six attacks. They scored only a single hit. During the attack, the Fairchild was hit and went down; pilot and gunner were both lost. But the cowed Egyptian naval force turned about and fled.

The attack on the Egyptian naval force was probably the highlight of the Bonanza's career, but it continued to fight on to the end of the war, regularly flying missions that could never have been expected of a civilian touring craft. Once it even raided Amman. The small, 200-pound bombs probably did little physical damage but their effect on Jordanian morale was said to have been disproportionately great.

Speaking of the role the lightplanes played in the War of Independence, one veteran says, "As romantic as it all sounds, the war couldn't have been won against anyone but the Arabs." Certainly the Arabs' lack of discipline under air attack had something to do with the little planes' success. For example, as the same veteran points out, when an Arab motorized column came under grenade attack by Cubs or Austers, "all the Arabs had to do was get under their equipment and stay there; instead they just ran—frightened, disorganized, and leaderless." But of course there was more to it than that. It took courage of a high order to fly such frail, battered little planes at all, let alone to risk exposing them to the guns of prowling enemy Spitfires or to take them down through storms of small arms fire to make ground attacks. The success of the *Sherut Avir*'s aircraft can hardly be dismissed as an Arab gift.

By the time the *Sherut Avir* was transformed into the *Chel Ha'Avir*, the lightplanes had accomplished the first and most difficult part of their mission: They had survived. The first of the desperately needed new equipment were now beginning to appear on Israeli airfields. Two days before the birth of the *Chel Ha'Avir* the first Israel twin-engine Douglas C-47 transport plane had been made operational and had flown a bombing mission against Ramallah. A few days later the airfield at Ekron was opened and Curtiss C-46 Commando transport planes began ferrying in Israel's first fighter planes; they were in action before the end of the month. By early June the Israelis had acquired the capability of mounting major bombing attacks. Just before a UN-sponsored truce went into effect on June 11, a Douglas C-47 Dakota bombed Damascus, dumping more than two tons of explosives on the Syrian capital in a moonlight raid that lasted 30 minutes.

For the Israeli Air Force the ephemeral June truce marked the end of the beginning. Powerful new warplanes were now beginning to arrive in significant quantities, and the days when Israel's survival depended on a handful of gallant fliers in a ragtag collection of worn-out civilian planes were fading into history. To be sure, the lightplanes fought on until the end of the war, but in roles of steadily diminishing importance. Today hardly any of them remain in existence, but the memory of their service to Israel will remain bright for a long time to come.

2

THE
BIG BROTHERS

THE MIDDLE PHASE OF THE WAR OF INDEPENDENCE WAS bounded by two unsuccessful truces, both sponsored by the United Nations. The first lasted from June 11 to July 9. The second was invoked on July 18 but was never really effective, collapsing utterly on October 15 when Israel launched her big Negev offensive, "Operation Yoav."

During this period there was a comparative lull in air combat operations but certainly not a cessation. Hardly had the first truce ended before Israeli Messerschmitt fighters (about which more later) of 101 Squadron were involved in an aerial attack on Syrian AT-6 Harvards; one Harvard was downed, and one Messerschmitt, piloted by Lionel Bloch, disappeared in Syrian territory while pursuing another Harvard. A potentially more lethal dogfight took place on July 18 when 101 Squadron's Messerschmitts encountered some Egyptian Spitfires over Beersheba—the first time the two famous fighter types had done battle since the end of World War II. One of the Spitfires was brought down by 101 Squadron's commander, Modi Alon.

While fighter skirmishes continued to take place throughout the summer, bomber transport and reconnaissance activity also flourished. Three Boeing B-17 Flying Fortresses joined the *Chel Ha'Avir* on July 15 and within two days were bombing Syrian targets, including Damascus. Noorduyn Norseman transport planes were acquired and were employed in the dangerous task of supplying beleaguered Sodom. And continuous reconnaissance missions resulted in many hair-raising exploits. For example, on August 14, Egyptian Spitfires brought down the lightplane flown by Paltiel Maklef and

Monty Goldberg in the Gaza Strip. Surrounded by bedouins, the two men set their plane on fire and attempted to escape. They almost made it, but in the end were captured and interned by the Egyptians until the war's end.

But for the *Chel Ha'Avir*, far more important than the combat which took place between June 11 and October 15 was the impressive buildup of strength. This was truly the time when the modern Israeli air force was created. The new planes which were now beginning to swell the ranks of the *Chel Ha'Avir* were of course a vast improvement over what had gone before, but by any standards save those of necessity they were still a mixed blessing. Some were excellent, fully up to the tasks assigned them, but many others had inherent design problems or were so worn out that they became maintenance men's nightmares.

The new planes fell into two broad categories: the larger aircraft used as bombers and transports, and the fighter planes. Although these "big fellows" often acted together on operations, it is easier to consider them separately.

Perhaps the best way to suggest some of the problems the new planes brought to the *Chel Ha'Avir* is to begin with the saga of the *Bagel Lancer*. She was born into a very select family, for only eleven of her kind were ever built. She was a Douglas DC-5, one of a type originally intended to serve as a complement to Douglas's earlier DC-3, the most successful and widely produced airliner in the world. Unlike the DC-3, the DC-5 was a high-wing design, intended primarily for short hauls. It had tricycle landing gear—then still something of a novelty on large planes—and could carry sixteen to twenty-two passengers and a crew of three. But almost as soon as DC-5 production had started, it stopped. World War II had begun and America's aviation industry had new and pressing priorities. The DC-5s were shunted aside as Douglas Aircraft Corporation's El Segundo Division turned all its efforts to manufacturing Dauntless dive bombers.

It seemed that the eleven DC-5s were about to enter the relatively enormous limbo of forgotten aircraft, but one, at least, still had a curious destiny to fulfill. She was Douglas No. 426 or, as the U.S. Army Air Corps called her when she was turned over to them, a type C-110, serial number 44-83232. She did not enjoy any significant service with the air corps, however, for she was almost immediately sold to the Dutch airline, KLM. She joined KLM West Indies at Curaçao on May 5, 1940, five days before the German invasion of Holland. On May 19, *Zonvogel* (Hummingbird), as the Dutch had now christened her, was hastily transferred to Batavia in the Dutch East Indies to join the small fleet of planes operated by Koninkijke Nederlandsch-

Indische Luchtvaart Maatschappij (KNILM), the Royal Netherlands Indian Air Lines Company.

There, under the registry PK-ADC, *Zonvogel* operated peacefully until December 1941, when the Japanese attacked. After making a series of emergency flights to evacuate civilians to Australia, she was taken over by the Allied Directorate of Air Transport and assigned to No. 31 Squadron at Brisbbane. Then in March 1942 she was leased to Pan American Airways which, on behalf of the U.S. government, used her to shuttle cargo and passengers throughout the Pacific for the remainder of the war.

In September 1946, barely airworthy, she was sold as scrap to Australian National Airways. But ANA saw some residual virtue in her and somehow managed to keep her flying (now under the registry VH-ARD) until 1947, when she was again sold, this time to a little outfit named New Holland Airways, which promptly renamed her *Bali Clipper*.

NHA was, among other things, in the unlikely business of ferrying Italian emigrants to Australia. How the company's mechanics managed to restore the battered DC-5 to a condition in which she could make this long haul is a matter as mysterious as it is admirable, but that is how she finally came to the attention of an Israeli purchasing agent in Sicily. In June 1948 she joined the *Chel Ha'Avir*, which gave her her last, most mellifluous, and certainly most famous sobriquet.

Now virtually a flying wreck, the *Bagel Lancer* was immediately pressed into service flying supplies to troops in the Negev Desert and the Galilee. Possibly because of unauthorized alterations made during the course of her long career, her center of gravity had by now shifted so far forward as to make her excessively stable. "We (both pilot and copilot) had to plant our feet on the console for additional leverage whenever we wanted to maneuver her," one pilot recalls. Yet the *Bagel Lancer* flew transport and even bombing missions straight through to the end of the war, a valiant old ruin who made an outstanding contribution to her adoptive country. Needless to say, she was retired from active service the minute the war ended, but she was kept on as a kind of memento at the Aeronautical School at Tel Aviv until 1955, when she was at last broken up.

Of course, few of the larger aircraft then being acquired by the *Chel Ha'Avir* were in as bad condition as the *Bagel Lancer*. But unlike the DC-5, some of the newer planes had congenital defects that were almost as troublesome. One such was the lamentable Curtiss C-46 Commando.

On March 6, 1948, a C-46 purchased for an airline called Service

Airways left Teterboro Airport in New Jersey, its ultimate destination Czechoslovakia. In fact there was no such airline as Service Airways. The not-yet-born state of Israel was taking its first steps toward acquiring an airlift capability against the day when the inevitable war would begin.

The C-46 was a terrible airplane. The largest twin-engined transport of the Second World War, it had two 2,000-horsepower engines and a normal loaded weight of 45,000 pounds. The power was adequate only if both engines functioned. If one failed on take-off, the C-46 could not remain airborne. Despite its shortcomings, however, it was instrumental in the survival of Israel during the War of Independence.

On April 6, four C-46s, fully manned, were prepared to leave the United States from Millville, New Jersey, with a second wave of five to follow. Few problems developed for the first four; but with the second wave, which departed from Los Angeles and flew south via Mexico towards the rendezvous point in Panama, things didn't go so smoothly. On take-off from Tijuana, one of the Commandos crashed, killing Captain William Gerson, the pilot. The eight remaining Commandos rendezvoused in Panama but were grounded there by authorities. However, on May 8 they were allowed to leave, and they departed for Paramaribo, Dutch Guinea, then Natal, Dakar and Casablanca and, finally, Catania, in Sicily.

Before long, C-46 Commandos were shuttling between Zatec, Czechoslovakia and Israel, carrying arms clandestinely. All were weary planes, dogged by engine problems. One of them, en route from Zatec, had an engine failure over the Alps and made a forced landing at the Italian military airfield at Treviso, where its crates, marked "glass," were found to contain arms. After a few days the airplane was allowed to continue, but the arms were seized and were not returned until after the War of Independence. Shortly afterward, another C-46 came down at Rhodes because of engine failure and was seized by the Greeks.

In August 1948, Jewish settlements and Israeli army units facing Egyptian forces in the Negev Desert were in desperate need of resupply. The C-46s, because of their great cargo-carrying ability, were pressed into service for "Operation Dust," as it was called. In three weeks, six C-46 Commandos, plus five C-47 Dakotas and six Norseman "transports," completed 170 flights, carrying in 1,000 tons of equipment and 700 soldiers. By the time the operation was complete, on October 20, these aircraft had made 417 flights, bringing in 4,991 tons of arms and supplies as well as 1,700 troops. The major share of men and material was moved by the Commandos; they had flown as many as thriteen flights a night.

On December 19, C-46 Commandos were called upon to act as lead ships for the Spitfires—newly acquired by Israel—on flights between Czechoslovakia and Israel. Twelve Spitfires in two flights of six each, each flight led by a C-46, flew for 6 hours and 45 minutes, arriving safely in Israel. On December 22, a C-46 led 12 more Spitfires on a similar flight. Underpowered and unsafe, the aging C-46s were still useful to a beleaguered nation forced to risk everything to get as much equipment as possible in the shortest time.

The first C-54 transport used by Israel was not part of IDF/AF: it was chartered from an American company. After the conclusion of an arms deal with Czechoslovakia, Israel needed transports to fly the arms, particularly the disassembled Czech-built Messerschmitt fighter aircraft, from Czechoslovakia to Israel. Curtiss C-46 Commandos had been purchased with this in mind. But after Italian authorities temporarily impounded them in Sicily, it was not known whether the C-46s would be released in time to do the job. An American company, U.S. Overseas Airlines, was willing to charter a four-engine Douglas C-54 Skymaster and crew. The price was very steep, but worth it. On March 31, 1948, the first C-54 with a cargo of arms left Czechoslovakia bound for yet-to-be-created Israel. The plane flew nonstop to the abandoned airstrip at Beit Daras and there unloaded cases containing 200 guns, 40 machine guns, and ample supplies of ammunition.

A second charter trip was undertaken on May 20. This time the C-54 carried a dissembled Avia fighter from Czechoslovakia to Israel. Since Czech technicians would not be made available to reassemble the fighters until at least three of them had been delivered, the C-54 made an immediate second trip without rest for the weary crew. Luckily a third was not needed: C-46s became available to complete the transport job.

On May 15, 1948, two DC-4s—civilian versions of the C-54—were acquired and were used to ferry arms. These aircrafts were also used by Israel as bombers, and twice, DC-4s acted as lead ships for flights of Spitfires from Czechoslovakia. On the second occasion, on December 18, when a DC-4 led six Spitfires from Czechoslovakia, the flight ran into a snowstorm. Four of the Spitfires were forced to turn back, and two others crashed, killing their pilots, one of whom was Sam Pomerantz, an American aeronautical engineer who had conceived the notion of adding the long-range tanks to the Spitfires.

Then there was the Norseman, a large, high-wing, single-engine transport plane. Designed by R.B.C. Noorduyn, it was first flown in 1935. In World War II the United States ordered 759 of these big Canadian aircraft, assigning to it the designation C-64. Early in 1948 the United States Air Force declared 50 of the cargo planes, each capable of carrying a one-ton cargo, to be surplus. There was a United States embargo on sale of military hardware, but a buyer for an imaginary airline company was set up in Spain. The ruse worked, and twenty Norsemen were purchased by the Israelis. French authorities indirectly helped in moving them to Israel. Never averse to embarrassing the English, they turned a blind eye to the nature of the clandestine operation by permitting the Norsemen to land in France. The planes stayed there to await volunteer pilots from the United States, England, and South Africa who would fly them to Israel. A few Norsemen were also distributed to Dutch and Italian airfields.

Not all of the Norsemen escaped the watchful eyes of Arab agents. One of them took off for Israel from the airport at Urbe, near Rome. It was hardly airborne when it exploded in flight, a probable victim of an Arab time bomb. Killed in the crash were George "Screwball" Buerling—a non-Jewish volunteer and Canada's highest-ranking World War II fighter pilot—and Leonard Cohen, a brilliant pilot formerly with the RAF. Nevertheless, of the original twenty Norsemen, seventeen made it safely to Israel.

Once in Israel, the Norsemen proved ideal as cargo and supply carriers. Capable of lifting one ton of freight, the Norsemen could shuttle supplies and ammunition to outlying settlements in far greater quantities than could be managed by the small Austers and Pipers. With a landing speed of only 55 mph, these single-engined aircraft could get into fields that were impossible for larger C-46 and C-47 twin-engine cargo planes. The Noorduyn Norsemen in Israel, organized into a unit called "Wing 35," undertook the difficult and dangerous task of supplying Sodom. The field was small, the aircraft heavily laden, and they were usually fired on by enemy anti-aircraft guns. Crews often flew this route four or five times daily. On one of the flights a Norseman missed the short runway. The pilot applied his brakes, but the plane flipped over. However, the crew managed to crawl safely out of the damaged Norseman.

The Norseman was the right plane at the right time in the War of Independence. But these planes had weak points. They were fabric covered, and a fabric skin requires more care and protection from the elements. Also, the wing structure consisted of spruce spars, walnut packing pieces under fittings, and spruce ribs. In time "the structure just got tired," a former IDF/AF pilot commented.

At least as valuable as the Norsemen were the *Chel Ha'Avir*'s Douglas C-47 Dakotas. The Dakota, the military version of the DC-3 airliner, was probably the greatest transport plane of World War II, if not of all time. Two of the Israeli Dakotas had been acquired via Boris Senior, who persuaded a South African airline to make them available on loan. Three more were loaned by a Mr. Van Lir, a Dutch millionaire, and some others had been purchased as war surplus. Superbly dependable and versatile, used as transports, bombers, or anything else the needs of the moment required, the C-47s served the Israelis as handsomely as they had everyone else who had ever flown them.

Jewish agents in the United States succeeded in buying three worn Constellations and somehow managed to recondition them. Using a bogus airline as a cover name, they smuggled one of them to Panama. The other two were seized by United States government agents and not turned over to Israel until after the end of the War of Independence. The one that got away to Panama, RX 121, was used to shuttle arms to Israel from a secret base in Czechoslovakia. On its seventh arms-carrying mission, failure of the hydraulic system caused it to crash-land in Czechoslovakia, but it was eventually repaired and returned to Israel, where the two others later joined it.

In addition to the Norsemen, the C-46s, the C-54s, the Constellations, and the DC-5, a whole museum of aircraft carried the military freight and passengers for Israel during the War of Independence. Among these were a twin-engine Lockheed Hudson and Lodestar, an Avro Anson, and a Grumman Widgeon. Military air transport work did not have the "glamour" attached to it that fighter-*vs*-fighter dogfights always suggest, but without this Fighting Airline of antiques and near antiques, Israel could not have survived her first test.

Still, the transport wing of the *Chel Ha'Avir* also got more "glamorous" jobs as well. When not hauling military freight and passengers, many of the aircraft of this Fighting Airline served as bombers. To be sure, Israel had designated some of its aircraft as "real" bombers, but since most of these were hardly better suited for combat than the transports, distinctions tended to become blurred. "Bombers" often hauled freight, "transports" often dropped bombs, and nobody worried overmuch about formal categories of nomenclature or "primary mission."

The story of how Israel managed to acquire its three real military bombing planes in the first place is typically, a wild one. Agents had located four Boeing B-17Gs, surplus World War II military aircraft, and had purchased them as "transport" planes. Getting the planes out of the United States was no easy matter. To circumvent the embargo, they were flown first to Puerto Rico and a flight plan was filed indicating the planes were to go on to Brazil. Devoid of turrets, armament, and a good many important instruments, the aircraft were a mess, but the pilots got three of them to Israel.

Harvey Nachman, who took part in this daring operation, recalled the following:

> We cleared out of Puerto Rico for Brazil [actually they were headed for the Azores], because otherwise we would have needed an export declaration. . . . It was terrible because we had absolutely no navigational equipment. This was a B-17 that had been converted to carry cargo. The nose turret had been taken out and pieces of wood and plaster had been put over it. Bomb bays were sealed, and, where the top turret had been, there was a waist hole which you could take out.
>
> We had drift needles and altimeters and radio compasses that had a range of maybe 200 miles. That was it. We had to figure our position by dead reckoning, mostly from transferring indicated air speed to true air speed and we were getting some drift off the drift meter, but I recall some of the drift meters didn't work. The B-17 is unique in the fact that in the nose—where that little plexiglass nose is—you put a plotter on so you can read drift roughly [to the wind] two or three degrees.
>
> In order to get your course lines you had to shoot the sun, and in order to shoot the sun they had to rope me into the aircraft. (I don't know what they did in other planes.) Four men held me and they took off the top. I'd stay standing out in the slipstream and shoot the sun for maybe a half hour at a time and try to average it out.
>
> This kid, Cohen, was in Bean's plane, one of the three B-17s, also went out to read drift and fell out—he fell right through one of those turret holes. He screamed bloody murder. He was 10,000 feet above the ocean and close to dying. Luckily, the armorer—a guy from Canada by the name of Bill Lichtmann—heard him. He ripped down some heated suit cords that had been left lying in the plane and using them was able to grab him and pull him back into the plane.
>
> We got to Santa Maria in the Azores five minutes late and right on course. We went straight to the Azores (not Brazil, the country we had filed in the flight plan). When we got down, we heard that the American Ambassador had already left Lisbon to impound us, so we had to take off at dawn in the worst fog I've ever taken off in (including anything I ever had in England).

The B-17s went on to Czechoslovakia, where they picked up some equipment and bombs, although they were still without defensive armament.

> Our plane had no guns at all. All we had were a few 500-pound g.p. bombs. We chose targets ourselves from the maps I had gotten from an encyclopedia. We ran into a temperature and pressure inversion over the Mediterranean and, in order to save fuel, I decided to fly right down the coast of Yugoslavia and the Adriatic. . . . I flew off the northern tip of Albania. The three planes were flying in formation.
>
> They shot at us in Albania and when we got off the coast of Africa, the eastern side of Tunis, we split up. Our plane went down across the desert and they, the other B-17s, went straight across the Mediterranean.
>
> . . .[All three B-17s] had planned to hit Cairo between sundown and last light (which would have been perfect) but we got there after dark. [This] was even more perfect because the town was lit up like a Christmas tree.
>
> We hit the palace—I never got an accurate report on what we did—we must have done a lot of damage. We had a beautiful but harrowing ride out of Cairo. We dropped twelve 500-pounders. We hit the barracks of the big officer's school first and training camps and stuff. . . . You had to cause as much damage as possible to the enemy to make them feel that they were up against a losing proposition. It would shorten the war immeasurably. We left Cairo and headed up the Nile delta with army searchlights flashing on us all the way out.

During the balance of the War of Independence, the three B-17Gs bombed Egyptian targets in the Negev Desert, destroying fortifications and harassing enemy troop columns.

The B-17s were formed into their own three-plane squadron (the 69th, the *Maccabeem*, "The Hammers"), and were not considered part of the air transport section of the Israeli Air Force. But in a sense the C-47s, the C-46s, and all the rest of the Fighting Airline were just as much a part of the heavy bombing force of the tiny state as the World War II B-17 heavies. The only difference between the actual bombers and the transports was that, while both carried heavy loads, the latter sometimes didn't unload their cargo while airborne. They unloaded in the air only when they were carrying bombs over enemy targets—which they often did. For example, on one occasion acting as makeshift bombers, C-46 Commandos accompanied the three B-17s, Beaufighters, Spitfires, Avias, C-47 Dakotas, and lightplanes, and launched a surprise bombing raid against the Egyptian air base at El Arish. The strike hit a large number of aircraft, destroying them on the ground. Not all bombing missions of the transport service ended so successfully. On one, a C-47 Dakota flew north with two tons of bombs to strike Syrian positions at Mishmar Hayarden. Six bombs were dumped out the door, the seventh snagged its fins on the door of the aircraft. Barely in control, the pilot prepared to make an emergency landing. Just at touchdown, the bomb jarred loose and exploded, destroying the plane. But the crew did survive uninjured.

In the War of Independence any plane was anything that the Israelis needed it to be. The same can be said for the pilots and crewmen of these planes who found their way into the conflict. Leaving relatives, businesses, everything behind except courage, these men rushed off to take part in Israel's efforts. The story of one, a man named Sam Katz, was typical of many others who flew the freight for Israel. A World War II veteran and a businessman, this American tells it this way:

> In 1948 I got calls about going to Israel from three different places one day. The first call was from New York and they asked me if I was willing to go and I said that I would think about it. The second call was from Cleveland (the same day) and they said, "Would you go?" and I said, "Well, I think I would, but give me some time to think about it,"; then the third call came that afternoon . . . from Indianapolis and I said that I had decided that I would go. . . . "Leave this afternoon," they said—next day I was on a plane. "Go to the Lee Hotel . . . and register under the name of Don Alter. . . ."
>
> The desk clerk said, "Jesus Christ, you're the fourth Don Alter that has registered tonight." Later, some men, working for an organization called "Land and Labor for Israel," asked me for pertinent information about what kinds of planes I could fly. I had been a pilot of twin-engine aircraft—C-47s and AT-7s—in the American air force. So they took the info and paid back the money that I had spent and gave me money to live on . . . a few days later, "Go to the Edison Hotel." Make sure that I wasn't being tailed.
>
> So I went to the hotel. There was a man named Steve Schwartz who figured actively in the recruiting and expediting of air force personnel to Israel. He asked me what planes I could fly, if I could fly A-20s, and if I could fly them to Israel from the United States. I said fine ·. . . so Steve Schwartz handed me a roll of bills, including enough money for air fare. "Go to Miami." In Florida, I was to go to a certain hotel and register and Nat Kahn

would get in touch with me. Was down there for a couple of days and Nat Kahn got in touch with me and four guys were there. Three of them were not Jewish, they were hot rods; one of them was later killed in an airplane crash . . . don't remember their names. One was a redhead . . . another was an older fellow that had millions of hours, or some kind of deal like that.

Nat came to us after a couple of days and said, "We gotta get out of here," and we were on a plane to El Paso and then we took a train to Oklahoma City where we spent half a day and Nat came to us and said, "We gotta get out of here and you can go anywhere—just leave your addresses with me." It turns out—I got the story later—the FBI or somebody was a day behind us and it looked like trouble, so I went back to my brother's place in New York and waited. This was also the time of the B-17 deal and they had asked me sometime during this period if I would fly copilot on that plane, but they pulled me out for the A-20 deal.

After this El Paso deal, and Oklahoma, I waited in New York. . . . They gave me tickets to Geneva, Switzerland. Went to Geneva; same instructions, "Wait there." Finally, I contacted an Israeli who said, "Go to Rome." Airplane passage was given to us, plus a few dollars to go to some hotel and wait. Same thing happened in Rome and after about a week in Rome, I finally got the contact that a plane would pick us up at the Rome airport, a C-47 that was coming up from South Africa with a South African crew on board. Crew and aircrew to go to Israel.

So we got on the plane and on the plane I met two people who were to become my crew in Israel. One was named Dennis Goshen. These were both South Africans. Dennis was my wireless operator and he had a friend with whom he had grown up, evidently, and had known for years, a non-Jewish kid named Milton Bottger—he lives in England now.

After we were in Israel for a while, Milton Bottger took the name of Butch ben Yuch. Everybody was taking the name of somebody *ben* (son of) somebody and Butch took this name, "Butch, the son of a Gentile."

We decided that we were going to be a crew. Dennis was the navigator and Butch was the radio operator and we stuck together all the way through Israel. When we got to Israel, we landed in Tel Aviv. We stopped in Athens on the way over—our plane ran into trouble . . . some engine trouble, as I recall. We had to stay in Greece—Athens—overnight and we were under armed guard the whole time, kept under constant surveillance.

We got to Israel the next day and we were received at the Tel Aviv airport where we landed and were billeted in hotels around Tel Aviv. At that time, the headquarters of the Israel air force was in the—I think the name of the hotel was the Yarkon

Hotel—near the park in Tel Aviv. We stayed there for a couple of days and they asked me questions about what I could fly and about what I was willing to fly and they registered us in the army, although Americans never took the oath at that time. It was considered that we would lose our American citizenship if we did.

I am sure that you know that we had some problems getting passports. Where I went to register for a passport, if they found someone with a Jewish name—they made him sign a mimeographed excerpt along with the regular passport. The excerpt from the application was the part that says, "I will not fly for, or engage in—become a member of the armed forces of any foreign government," etc., etc.

Okay, so I hung around Tel Aviv for a few days and finally they sent me to Ramat Aviv in the Emek. At that time the 103 Transport Squadron was just being formed. It was really in the embryo stages and I think at that time there were damned few pilots. There was Claude Duval, who was in and out. I really don't know his history. He wound up getting killed, I understand, trying to do a slow roll in a C-47. He was a South African, one of these magnificent flying types who didn't look the part; he looked more like a souse but evidently he was a great pilot. Maybe Danny Rosen (first C.O. of 103 Squadron) was there. I don't know. The only other one that I remember was a non-Jewish fellow named Jimmy Blackwood from Detroit.

I was at Ramat Aviv a couple of days. I don't even remember if I got a checkout, but I got in on a mission. Jimmy Blackwood was the pilot and I was the copilot. It was one of the most interesting missions that I was involved in while I was in Israel.

It turns out that at this time—it must have been July or August of '48—there was a kind of (Israeli) salient coming in off the coastal region and going around Jerusalem. The Israeli intelligence found that the Arabs—both the Jordanians on the north from around Nablus or Tulkarm and the Egyptians from the south—were planning on pinching off this so that they could cut off supplies to Jerusalem.

Jimmy Blackwood, with me as copilot, took off one night with seventeen empty parachute container cans. They were about six feet high, maybe two or three feet across and supposedly loaded with supplies. Our job was to drop them on the outskirts of Nablus, enemy territory which was north of that salient. The idea was to suggest that the Israelis had troops behind enemy lines.

Well, the thing worked so well that two nights later we were back with eleven cans again; ten of them were completely empty. We dropped them outside of Nablus. The eleventh was loaded with supplies—food, ammunition, instructions to "Israeli commanders" behind the lines, quote, unquote. That one we dropped very close to Nablus—almost in town—with the idea that, well, it was too close for our troops to get.

Included in this container were several things of interest. Number one, the messages to the imaginary Jewish commanders were designed to create suspicion, jealousy, and hostility between the various Arab commanders. Also there were some little colored capsules in this can. They were kind of strange looking, I guess, to the Arabs, who complained to the United Nations representative in Haifa. The Arabs said the Israelis had dropped something to poison their water supplies and the Israelis were engaged in unfair practices, etc.

As it turns out, the person that they complained to in Haifa, the U.N. man—a captain—happened to be an American and he took one look at the capsule and he popped one in his mouth and ate it. It was a jelly bean. That worked quite well. Evidently the Arab pressure came off.

Then I got checked out and I started flying missions to the southern part of Israel, in the Negev. As you know, there were various kibbutzim down there and they were, for the most part, completely surrounded by Arabs. There was Dorot and Derchoma and Nevatim. I can't even remember the other places. We also went to Sodom on these flights. [We] were supplying the groups stationed down there on the kibbutzim.

One place—Dorot, as I recall—had an airfield that not only was too short, but in the middle it had a little hill. Right over the hill, it had a little curve so it was quite interesting landing. Besides that, the Arabs completely encircled the thing and, occasionally, on the final approach, we'd get small arms fire. Thank goodness, nothing hit us. We'd bring back people who were either wounded or were sick or were ready for leave or things like that.

Well, we kept flying missions for quite some time. Sodom was one of our stops, always a very interesting place to go into. The landing field was like 1,175 or 1,150 feet *below* sea level, which was only part of the problem. There was always a direct crosswind. The only way they could set up an airfield was along the base of the cliff which went *up* to sea level.

The airfield was very small, very short. One of the other little hazards with this place was that the ground, which was loaded with salt, kept absorbing the moisture in the air at night. If you wound up even halfway off the runway you'd get mired in sand and salt. It was very interesting. A couple of times I wound up staying there two or three days with various troubles with the engines. I don't remember how many months we kept flying this type of mission. We'd fly maybe two or three missions a night to these outposts and perhaps have the next day or the next two days off.

After the breach of truce I wound up flying combat missions. I had never flown combat before in the American air force. I had been with Training Command all the way through and when the first breach of truce took place, Danny Rosen, a South African who had been in World War II as a combat pilot, was the pilot and I was the copilot. I remember once when we took off our target was Gaza. We were in Ramat Aviv, outside of Haifa. We went out to sea, flew down the coast, and came in to Gaza and the people were really not expecting it. People down in the streets were waving to us and we dropped the bombs—which was not very nice.

Anyway, my favorite target was El Arish. I had Butch ben Yuch and Dennis Goshen as my crew and various other types as my copilot quite often. Butch and Dennis used to stand behind me and tell me how to take evasive action. I had never flown in combat before.

El Arish was probably the toughest target. They had radar. Ack-ack was tough. I remember, one time, when we were over there and they opened up on us, Butch and Dennis were standing behind me. Dennis was my navigator and he was trying to get me out to sea [after the mission]. We came over Rafa at about a thousand feet or less and it scared the hell out of us.

On one of these missions, I had L.M. as my copilot. He was one big goof-off. Robert St. John, in his book, *Shalom Means Peace* wrote about him, called him Red somebody or other.

L.M. was probably the lousiest pilot in Israel. He was probably lousier than the Israelis, who were just learning to fly. I took him to Sodom one night as my copilot and we were on the final approach. The flaps are really a matter of tremendous, cautious concern. I may have had [something] like 15% flaps and I may have told him to give me an extra 5° flaps—or some kind of a deal like that—and he did exactly the opposite. When I asked him for an extra 5°, 10° flaps, he pulled up the flaps and I almost went into the ground.

They put him into Training Command and he was teaching some Israeli kid how to fly a Cub and he turned around to talk to the Israeli kid. He turned to his right and he had his elbow out. His elbow hit the throttle and the plane revved up real loud. He sat there for about thirty seconds wondering what in hell was going on, because he didn't know. He was a character.

The C-47s had an olive drab camouflage. When we flew with them on bombing runs, we flew with the cargo doors off the planes and we had crude bomb racks under the wings. The pilot was also the bombardier and it was a rather crude bomb-by-sight deal. We had a switchboard up on the copilot's side with a master switch and toggle switches . . . about nine toggle switches. I think we carried about eighteen bombs and, when we got near the targets—what with the basic laws of physics on dropping things—we'd call off, "Master switch on!" and then, "Toggle switch one . . . toggle switch two . . . toggle switch three . . ." It is amazing that the results were as good as they were. On some of the missions to El Arish, we were even successful in knocking out planes with that very crude form of bombing.

On another of the missions to El Arish, we didn't have too many bombs. We dropped spikes. They were four-pronged spikes so that there was always one prong up and we dropped them on the runway so that their planes couldn't take off.

Sam Katz was *Mahal*, a foreign volunteer. He survived a lot of crazy and dangerous experiences in the War of Independence. Like the memories of any veteran of combat, his are selective and somewhat disjointed impressions of events, people, and places. But the essence of what Katz experienced is there in those memories. The war was sometimes amusing but it was rough. Often it was both at the same time. It was also a glorious adventure which was deadly serious.

Sam Katz found his way to Tel Aviv, the Negev, and to impossibly crude airstrips and battered aircraft to lay his life on the line for a dream of centuries. Though that dream might have come true without him, he chose to be there and help make sure that it did. An experienced pilot, he flew dangerous missions for the transport service just like a lot of others. And he would have thoroughly resented anyone who suggested it couldn't or shouldn't be done. He and the others knew it had to be done.

3
MOGEN DAVID FIGHTERS

AT TWILIGHT ON THE EVENING OF MAY 29, 1948, 500 Egyptian armored vehicles, an entire armored brigade, stood temporarily stalled before a ruined bridge two miles north of Ashdod. The delay was not expected to be a long one. Engineers would soon clear the way. Then the column would overwhelm the hard-pressed Israeli Givati Brigade facing it and sweep on to Tel Aviv, less than twenty miles away.

Suddenly, out of the gathering dusk, four sleek, ominous-looking single-engine fighters streaked low across the desert toward the column. At first they were thought to be friendly Spitfires, for the Israelis were supposed to possess no fighter planes. But if any Egyptian soldier did correctly identify the intruders he must have been thunderstruck, for the oncoming aircraft would have seemed to him sinister revenants from a dark past. Far from revealing the flowing lines of Spitfires, they assumed the menacing, shark-like shapes of Messerschmitt 109s, the most formidable fighter planes of Hitler's vanished Luftwaffe.

A moment later they were over the column, bathing it in a torrent of steel and fire—500-pound bombs, 13-mm machine gun bullets, and 20-mm cannon shells. Some of the Egyptians fled; others manned their weapons, sending up a miniature storm of counterfire. One of the Messerschmitts, trailing smoke, curved across the darkening sky and crashed onto the desert floor. Another seemed to stagger but kept station on its companions as they roared off toward the horizon; damaged, it would crash when it attempted to land on its home field. Israel's first fighter mission had cost it half its operational fighter strength. But even allowing for a 50% attrition, the mission was crowned with victory; the demoralized Egyptian column turned back, and the threat to Tel Aviv receded.

How the Jewish pilots came to be flying Nazi Germany's premier fighter plane painted with the Mogen David (six-pointed star) insignia of the *Chel Ha'Avir* is perhaps no stranger than most of the stories that came out of this strange time. Which is to say that it is a very curious story indeed.

Long before Israel's independence it had been clear that the new state would be virtually helpless to defend itself against Arab air raids unless it possessed some modern fighter planes. But of all types of aircraft, fighters were the hardest to come by. Unlike lightplanes, transports, or even demilitarized bombers, their ultimate purpose was impossible to disguise—fighters can be used for only one thing. Nor, despite the large numbers of fighters produced in World War II, were many being offered for sale in world markets. It was out of the question to try to smuggle fighters into Palestine while the British were still there; and even after independence, assuming that fighters could be found, it would be extremely difficult to ferry them into the country because most of them had such short ranges.

But moral necessity cannot accede to difficulty, and in the months before independence Jewish agents scoured the world looking for possible sources of supply. Improbably, the hunt ended in Czechoslovakia.

For most of the war years Germany had used the Avia aircraft works in Czechoslovakia to manufacture Arado Ar 96B trainers for the Luftwaffe. But toward the end of World War II, as the pressure of Allied bombings stretched Germany's aircraft industry to its limits, Avia was given a more important assignment: to produce the latest and deadliest version of the Messerschmitt single-engine fighter, the Messerschmitt Bf 109G-14. Just when Avia's production had begun, Germany surrendered to the Allies.

Since Avia was already tooled up, it seemed logical that Messerschmitt production should be continued for the benefit of the new postwar Czech air force. The plane was given a new designation, the S-99, and a two-seat trainer version, the CS-99, was also undertaken. But almost immediately a serious problem developed. After only twenty S-99's and two CS-99s had been produced, the warehouse where the Daimler-Benz powerplants originally intended for the Messerschmitts had been stored was destroyed by fire. No more Daimler-Benz engines could be obtained.

A search was made to find an alternative engine for the large number of airframes that were now beginning to accumulate at the

Avia works. The only engine readily available, however, was the 1,350-horsepower Junkers Jumo 211F which the Germans had stockpiled for use in their Heinkel He 111H medium bombers. This ponderous engine, together with its paddle-bladed propeller, made a grotesque marriage with the otherwise sleek Messerschmitt airframe. Nevertheless, the Czech air force decided to authorize production of the hybrid, designating it the S-199. Unhappy Czech pilots soon found other names for it, the mildest of which was *Mezec*, or "mule."

The transplanted Jumo not only robbed the Messerschmitt of most of its original virtues, but seriously exaggerated its vices. The new engine was both less powerful than the Daimler-Benz and much less reliable. At the same time, it was heavier, making the S-199 dangerously nose-heavy. This was bad enough for in-flight stability, but it made landings and take-offs positively treacherous.

Ground handling had always been one of the Messerschmitt's weakest points. The plane had been designed so that, unlike that of most other fighters, the retractable landing gear folded outward from the wing roots rather than inward from mid-wing attachments. This meant that when the gear was extended, the lateral distance between the wheels was much too narrow, giving rise to a distressing tendency for the Messerschmitt to ground loop at the slightest provocation. The original Messerschmitts had at least been well balanced and their pilots were specially trained; even so, the Luftwaffe had suffered something on the order of 1,300 landing and take-off accidents directly attributable to the instability of the narrow-track landing gear. But the landing and take-off characteristics of the S-199 would have appalled even the most proficient Luftwaffe pilot.

Under the circumstances, it is perhaps not surprising that the Czech government was quite willing to sell some of its S-199s to the Israelis. A contract for the purchase of ten Avias, with an option to buy fifteen more, was signed in Prague on April 23, 1948. The price was $190,000 per aircraft, including spare parts and ammunition. The Israelis were well aware that the Avias were wretched planes, but they came with one overriding recommendation: they were all that were available.

The Avias could not, of course, be brought into Palestine until after the British mandate had ended, but in the meantime their pilots had to be recruited and trained. Recruitment proved to be the least of the problem; once the word was out, volunteer pilots from England, the United States, Canada, and South Africa began to apply for *Mahal* (foreign volunteer) service in considerable numbers. They were sent first to a secret military flying school in Rome, code-named Alicia, for preliminary training and indoctrination, and those with fighter experience were then flown on to Czechoslovakia for a two-week course to familiarize them with the Avias.

Two weeks is hardly time enough to familiarize anyone with a "hot" airplane, let alone the beastly S-199. For those volunteers who had had experience only with wide-track fighters—Mustangs, Thunderbolts, Hurricanes, and the like—the first encounters with the Avias were memorable. Even pilots who had flown the relatively narrow-track Spitfires were dismayed. In addition, the fledgling *Mahal* volunteers discovered other unpleasant facts about the Avias, some of which we shall let one of the pilots describe in his own words in due course.

As soon as the mandate ended and the war commenced, the transfer of the Avias to Israel began. The first four were disassembled, loaded aboard DC-4 and C-46 transports, and flown to Tel Aviv in the third week of May. They were hastily put together at Tel Nof and slated for an initial ground-attack mission against the Egyptian air base at El Arish. But, as described earlier, an emergency situation was developing at Ashdod where a large Egyptian armored column was threatening to overwhelm the Israeli Givati Brigade and drive on to Tel Aviv. The commander of the Givanti Brigade appeared in person to plead for air support, and consequently it was the costly Ashdod mission which introduced the S-199 to combat.

As more Avias arrived, they were formed into a unit known as the 101 Squadron and moved to the newly opened airfield at Ekron. Rudy Auergarten, an American volunteer, recalls what operations in those days were like:

> Our commander was moaning about Messerschmitts with no manuals. The Me-109 had two 20-mm cannons, one in each wing, and two 13.2-mm machine guns in the fuselage cowling that had to be synchronized. Many times people shot props off. We never could get the cannons to work at the same time, which caused the plane to slip and skid. No one understood the hydraulic or electrical systems fully. These planes were inertia-started with a hand crank. You wound it up, pulled an engaging mechanism that gave the power to the propeller.
>
> During (my) first ten days, 50 percent of the take-offs or landings ended in accidents. There was always something major going wrong. We had a code for the Messerschmitts— TEMFRITZ. T for trim tab adjustment, F for flaps down 20 degrees. TMFRTS . . . stood for Trim, Mixture, Flaps, Release brakes, Throttle, Set tail wheel lock. You had to lock the tail

wheel, set your flaps down, set your mixture rich, set your trim tabs and such. I remember that vividly.

My first turn to fly came up with Modi Alon and Sid Anton. They had bombs on their planes. I didn't. They took off. I forgot the TMFRTS code and took off. You normally have to take your trim all the way back so when you run up your prop, it holds the tail down. I had trim set all the way back which had an effect like somebody pulling back on the stick. When I pulled full throttle, I went down the runway 150–200 yards and the plane started to come up but hadn't enough flying speed. One of the wings stalled, going to the left side. Then I realized what happened. I counteracted it by pushing down on the stick to keep the plane from climbing too fast.

I was fighting the stick. The plane was in a slow turn to the left. There was a tree 200–250 yards off the runway and they tell me my wing brushed through. But I got off.

From this point, the Avias continued to arrive in twos and threes from Czechoslovakia. Keeping them running was a problem and there were seldom more than a few Avias available at any one time. On May 30 the fortress of Iraq Suweidan was attacked and another Avia was lost.

On the afternoon of June 3, two Egyptian C-47 Dakotas, modified as bombers, attacked Tel Aviv. While they were still off the coast, they were attacked by a single Avia. It was piloted by Modi Alon, squadron leader of 101 Squadron. He shot up one of the Dakotas with machine gun fire and it crashed on a beach, killing its entire crew. Then he took on the second Dakota, scored hits, and it too crashed in Arab-held territory. These plane–vs–plane victories were Israel's first, and the raid also marked the last attempt by Egypt to bomb Tel Aviv with Dakotas. They knew now their planes no longer faced an air force of little moths which could not really fight back.

Still the number of Avias continued to dwindle. On July 8, 1948, after some technical difficulties, four aircraft were scrambled for an attack against Egyptian concentrations. One aircraft crashed on take-off and a second did not return from the mission. On July 18, three Avias attacked an Egyptian armored column near Bir Asluj. On the way back they encountered two Egyptian Spitfires and Modi Alon shot one of them down; it was his third victory. But on returning to their base, another Avia was damaged on landing. So common was it for the unstable Avias to flip over on landing that long sticks were kept on hand to open the canopies on the aircraft to release the pilots.

Canadian volunteer pilot Denny Wilson recalls these planes none too fondly: ". . . The Me-109s were made in Czechoslovakia at the Skoda Works. In the fall, all of them were out of commission. They had been flown in [to Israel] in the belly of C-46s. They were pieces of shit (dummy parts in the engine; the Czechs had sabotaged them). Dumps all over Europe were cannibalized for missing parts. . . ."

Rudy Auergarten echoes Wilson's comments: "Our Messerschmitts were terrible. We didn't have enough experience with them. They were made to land on grass and we used them on concrete runways. They were blowing tires. . . . Messerschmitts didn't have VHF [frequency radios]. They had medium frequency, and it never worked. You wouldn't even have contact with the fellow on the mission with you. . . ."

Despite his opinion of the Czech plane, Auergarten made do: "One day I was sent on a picture-taking mission and the Egyptians were expecting our B-17s and had a couple of Spitfires waiting. I ran into them and shot one down. . . ."

With all its faults, the Avia, as Israel's first fighter plane, was performing an invaluable service. But the *Chel Ha'Avir* had not relented in its search for alternative equipment. Sometimes this quest assumed aspects that were downright bizarre—as in the case of the Bristol Beaufighters.

A big twin-engine two- or three-seater, the RAF's Beaufighter had been designed just before World War II at a time when the idea of large, long-range escort fighters was much in vogue. By 1940, however, small single-engine fighters had become the cynosure of the world's air forces and the Beaufighters had been shunted aside to do such useful but unglamorous tasks as flying anti-shipping patrols for the RAF Coastal Command. Then, in 1941, Britain's requirements changed. RAF Fighter Command, which was now beginning to fly offensive sorties over France, was discovering that the Spitfires and Hurricanes that had performed so well in a defensive role in the Battle of Britain were relatively ineffectual as ground-attack aircraft. Moreover, they were completely useless as night fighters, for which, as the Blitz intensified, there was now a desperate need.

This was the moment when the half-forgotten Beaufighter came back into its own. Its long range, its massive firepower of four 20-mm cannon and six .30-caliber machine guns, and its capacity to carry a respectable number of rockets or small bombs under the wings made it a formidable ground attacker. Moreover, it was large enough to carry an airborne radar set, thus enabling it to become Britain's first effective night fighter. Soon Beaufighters were all the rage, heavily engaged in action in Europe, North Africa, and Asia, as well as over the Mediterranean, English Channel, and North Sea. Eventually, newer, more efficient planes replaced the Beaufighter in most of its combat roles, but by that time the big fighter had firmly established its reputation and won an enduring place in the RAF's hall of fame.

All of this persuaded English-based Emmanuel Zur in 1948 that it would be a good idea to make a movie about the exploits of some New Zealand pilots who had flown the legendary Beaufighter. Zur was not, in fact, a film-maker. He was a secret Israeli purchasing agent, and the proposed film was simply part of a baroque scheme to get war-surplus Beaufighters past authorities who were zealously enforcing the British arms embargo against Israel.

Although Zur was sternly warned that none of the five Beaufighters he had been allowed to purchase for the film would be permitted under any circumstances to leave the United Kingdom, officials were nevertheless basically enthusiastic about the projected cinematic Beaufighter epic. Thus, when the "script" called for it, Zur had little difficulty in obtaining permission to fly the planes to a remote part of Scotland which, he insisted, would make a perfect location for some of the New Zealand flying sequences.

When more than enough time had elapsed for the Beaufighters to have reached their destination in Scotland, the inconsolable Zur was obliged to report them all as unaccountably "missing." They were by that time well on their way to Ajaccio in Corsica, whence they would fly to join the *Chel Ha'Avir*.

But Zur's work was still not done. Without guns or spare parts the Beaufighters could not be used operationally. So Zur, whose relations with British officialdom were now beginning to decay somewhat, set about trying to obtain the required equipment. Against all odds he somehow contrived to procure spare parts for the Beaufighters, even including four spare engines. Through some friends in the British military, he even managed to acquire the necessary guns from an RAF depot to arm the Beaufighters. The problem of getting all of this equipment out of England, however, still remained.

Zur found a ship captain, who offered—for a price—to smuggle the equipment out, but he was arrested and imprisoned for smuggling cigarettes before he could help Zur. Then a British-born Israeli pilot, John Harvey, came up with a solution. He was able to charter a friend's war-surplus Halifax bomber in which the guns and parts could be ferried to Israel. This effort went smoothly until the Halifax attempted to land at the Israeli air base at Ekron. There were no lights, no one answered the pilot's increasingly frantic calls and, after one of the Halifax engines quit, the pilot flew on to Tel Aviv. There a second engine quit and he made a forced landing at the airfield north of Tel Aviv. The runway was too short for the converted four-engined bomber and it slid off the end, damaged beyond repair. But the cargo was safe.

The Beaufighters proved useful, but their accomplishments hardly matched Zur's efforts. The war-weary aircraft, normally based at Ramat David, required a great deal of maintenance. One had to be cannibalized to keep the others flying. Further, whereas four of the planes had radial engines, the fifth aircraft was a merlin-powered Mk. IIF, which complicated the spares problem.

The high point in Beaufighter operations came when a Beaufighter flown by Len Fichert, a Canadian Christian pilot, was attacked by an Iraqi Fury fighter. The Fury, a far newer single-seater, was about 100 mph faster and far more maneuverable than the lumbering, three-seat Beaufighter. Fechert, alone in his aircraft, threw the Beaufighter into a dive, the Fury on his tail. Just above the ground he pulled out, then turned sharply. The Fury tried to turn inside him. It spun out and crashed into the ground, killing the pilot.

On October 15, 1948, one Beaufighter was damaged by anti-aircraft fire during an attack on the Egyptian air base at El Arish in the Sinai Desert, but managed to make it home. Another time, a Beaufighter, one of two attacking the Egyptian-manned fortress at Iraq Suweidan, opposite Kibbutz Negba, was also struck by anti-aircraft fire and crash landed, the crew being captured and killed. The pilot was Len Fichert, who had come to Israel to help in the War of Independence. The copilot was Stanley Andrews, a Jewish volunteer from the United States, and the bombardier, Dov Sugarman, from England.

After brief careers the Beaufighters, then attached to 103 Squadron at Ramat David, were no longer operational. There were no replacements and no spare parts for them. The Beaufighters that were left were grounded in November 1948, for lack of spares.

The Avias and Beaufighters had made crucially important contributions to Israel's survival, but the *Chel Ha'Avir* still needed a fighter that could meet the Egyptian Spitfires and Iraqi Furies in air-to-air combat on close to equal terms. When the British evacuated Palestine, the Israelis had desperately scoured RAF scrap heaps in the hope of finding enough parts to assemble at least one flyable Spitfire. While this effort was proceeding, the Israelis had a small stroke of luck. On the first day of the war an Egyptian Spitfire was hit by ground fire over Tel Aviv and crash-landed in Israeli-held territory. With the use of the RAF spares and what was left of the Egyptian fighter, two rickety Spitfires were pieced together. Not much, but infinitely better than nothing.

The real break came in the summer, when the Czechs, still gloating over the Avia deal, offered to sell Israel fifty Mark 16 Spitfires recently acquired from Britain. This seemed almost too good to be true—virtually the solution to the *Chel Ha'Avir* air-to-air defense problem. Yet there was one formidable difficulty: how to ferry the short-range Mk. 16s the long distance to Israel.

An American aeronautical engineer Sam Pomerantz hit upon a solution. The Spitfires would be stripped of armor and armament—everything not essential to keeping them in the air. Then, auxiliary gas tanks would be installed in the aircraft. Even with these modifications, an intermediate stopover point had to be found. Israel, after much effort, managed to obtain landing permission from the Yugoslav government at the remote airfield at Podgorica, near the Albanian border. This meant the Spitfires had to fly 1,400 miles nonstop. The maximum range of the Spitfire 16 was 980 miles. Only Sam Pomerantz's modification could hope to bridge the difference.

On September 24, 1948, six Spitfires with extra tanks took off from Czechoslovakia. Two were flown by Sam Pomerantz and Boris Senior, a third by Modi Alon. The first leg from Kunovice to Podgorica was uneventful, but one plane jammed its landing gear and crashed on landing.

On September 27, the remaining five set out, with a DC-4 lead plane for navigation. Two Spitfires had to make emergency landings on the Greek Island of Rhodes. The Greek Government seized the planes and arrested the pilots. After interrogation, the pilots were released, but the Spitfires were impounded. Because of the notoriety, Yugoslavia refused further use of the field at Podgorica.

Undaunted, Sam Pomerantz had three extra fuel tanks added within the fuselage of each plane. This time, even the radios were stripped out. Even so, the loaded weight of the Spitfires was now 1,500 pounds more than design limit. Would the landing gear take this added load? Furthermore, at this great weight, the Spitfires would be unstable.

On December 18, six Spitfires led by a DC-4 took off. They soon ran into a severe winter storm. Four of the Spitfires were forced to return to base. The other two crashed, killing their pilots, one of whom was Sam Pomerantz.

On December 19, twelve Spitfires left in two flights, each led by a C-46; they headed for Yugoslavia, which had again granted landing rights. All arrived safely. There, the Yugoslav markings which had been painted on the aircraft (to meet Czech demands) were removed and Israeli markings substituted. On December 22, the twelve planes were to depart for Israel. One had mechanical difficulties and was left behind; a second was forced to turn back because of engine trouble. But ten Spitfires arrived safely in Israel to join the three that had made it earlier and the two patched-together planes. Other Spitfires would arrive later.

With the advent of the Spitfires, the initiative in the air at last began to pass from the Arabs to the Israelis. Although technically somewhat inferior to the Iraqi Furies and the Egyptian Spitfire Mk. 18s, the Israeli Mk. 16s were very much better piloted. In the hands of such veterans as Jack Doyle, a non-Jewish Canadian World War II ace, or Slick Goodlin, a famous American test pilot, the Mk. 16s could outfight anything the enemy could send against them. (The Israeli pilots, at this stage, preferred their Mk. 16s even to American Mustangs, four of which were acquired in October—although to be sure, the Mustang's special virtues came to be better appreciated at a later date.) Thus the sacrifices of the men who, like Sam Pomerantz, made it possible for the Spitfires to reach Israel were not made in vain. It was with the Spitfire that the *Chel Ha'Avir* first gained that aerial ascendency in the Middle East which it has never since relinquished.

4

MAHAL VICTRIX

THE FINAL PHASE OF THE WAR WAS NOW AT HAND: ISRAEL was preparing to go over to the offensive. The first objective would be to clear the Egyptian army out of the Negev, a project the Israeli planners code-named "Operation Ten Plagues." As usual, the build-up for this offensive would have to depend heavily on air supply. To that end a site in the Negev near Ruhama was selected; bulldozers created an airstrip capable of handling Constellations and C-46s, and roads were put in. On August 22, the airlift, code-named "Operation *Avak*," began. Before it was over, it would make 417 flights to Ruhama, delivering 2,000 tons of supplies and 1,900 personnel.

The second U.N.-sponsored truce collapsed on October 15, 1948. Repeated Arab violations of the cease-fire agreement and consistent Arab refusal to negotiate a final settlement had merely served to confirm the Israelis' long-standing conviction that peace could probably be obtained only through victory. Thus "Ten Plagues"—or, as it had been renamed for security reasons, "Operation *Yoav*"—was begun.

Air combat operations started on October 17 with a raid on Migdal by a B-17. On the same day Ashdod was attacked by Avias, two of which were damaged and crashed while attempting to land. Both pilots were killed. One was Morris Mann, an English volunteer; the other was Modi Alon.

October 20, Danny Rosen and Len Fichert, flying Beaufighters of the 103 Squadron, attacked the Iraq Suweidan police station with napalm bombs. Fichert was hit and crash-landed in Egyptian-held territory. He, his copilot, Stan Andrews, and the bombardier, Dov Sugarman, were captured and tortured to death.

49

By October 22, when Operation *Yoav* ended, the IDF/AF had flown 239 sorties, dropped 151 tons of bombs on 21 targets, and lost three aircraft (the third was a Dakota). The operation had been a complete success and, as a bonus, the airbase at El Arish had been put out of commission, thus temporarily knocking out the Egyptian air force.

On the eve of *Yoav* the *Chel Ha'Avir* had had a total of 100 aircraft, 22 of which were nonoperational. The disposition was as follows:

> *At Ramat David:*
>> 3 B-17s (69th Squadron, the "Hammers")
>> 5 Dakotas
>> 3 Beaufighters
>> 7 lightplanes
>> 1 Mosquito (not in operation)
>> 2 Hudsons (not in operation)
>> 2 Beaufighters (not in operation)
>
> *At Herzlia:*
>> 8 Messerschmitts (i.e., Avias, 101 Squadron)
>> 5 Spitfires (101 Squadron)
>> 7 Messerschmitts (not in operation)
>> 4 Mustangs (not in operation)
>
> *At Sde Dov:*
>> 28 light planes
>
> *At Ekron:*
>> 6 Curtiss C-46 Commandos
>> 5 Noorduyn Norsemen
>> 1 Noorduyn Norseman (not in operation)
>> 5 Messerschmitts (unassembled)
>
> *At Dorot:*
>> 5 light planes

There were, in addition, three Constellations used primarily for long-range transport duties on overseas resupply missions.

On the same date, October 15, the IDF/AF had approximately 150 pilots. Perhaps the most significant thing about this figure is that nearly two-thirds of these pilots were *Mahal*, foreign volunteers. It is clear that the *Chel Ha'Avir* could not have achieved ascendency without *Mahal*, and it is possible that the war itself could not have been won without them.

They were an extraordinary group. They came from the far corners of the earth. Some were Jewish, some were not. Many were idealists, some were mercenaries, a few were madmen. The only things they had in common were a taste for adventure and an exceptional degree of professional competence. When they departed the Middle East after the war's end, they left in Israel the nucleus of a great air force.

Wally Reiter, a notary public from Toronto, was Intelligence Officer at Qastina. He recalls "how it was" with some of the North American contingent of *Mahal*:

> The first air force headquarters was in the Yarkon Hotel in Tel Aviv. The first airmen were billeted in the Bristol and Yarden Hotels. This was a "waiting war" like the South Pacific, where the guys sat around playing gin rummy in the ops shack.
>
> Ralph Moster, from Vancouver, came over with Sonny Wosk and Ray Rudin. They were among the first gang of Canadians in the Israeli air war. Moster was later killed in a Widgeon in Lake Tiberius. They arrived in Israel before May 15 when the British left. Ralph got his wings in the RCAF before the end of the [Second World] war, but had never been in operations. He was a drifter around Vancouver. When the clarion call came from the *Haganah*, Ralph and his two buddies joined up immediately as general volunteers. This was in late April. He was smuggled into a secret camp and assigned to Palmach. Later, when the air force materialized, he went with it. Ralph finally hacked a place for himself in the air force flying Piper Cubs. He gave a good account of himself in the Palmach.
>
> Jack Doyle, a Canadian fighter pilot, participated in the Sicily landing. He had five or six German kills and a head full of metal. He was a sales manager of National Motors truck division. In 1956 he went back into the RCAF. He was stationed for a while at a NATO base at Grostenquin, France. He had a freak accident; fell in the mess. Pinched a nerve in his hand. Had to have the nerve removed.
>
> Lee Sinclair was an ex-RAF wing commander. Denny Wilson is now with Adam's Distillery, Montreal.
>
> These men were not screwball pilots. They were mature pilots and they could absorb it all in a five-minute briefing. It was the most frustrating experience the first time I had to brief these crews . . . these characters. Nobody seemed to be listening. Nobody seemed to care. Nobody seemed to be interested. Like talking in a dream to a big crowd and everybody's got their backs turned. But they were absorbing the information and you could brief this gang in about five minutes. Their specific assignments were handed out to them by Sid Cohen [a South African, 101

Squadron CO after the death of Modi Alon] or Rudy [Auergarten].

There was nothing in writing. They would empty their pockets before going out to their planes. They had proper Canadian or American or British Intelligence procedures and flying experience. There was to be no material on their person which could assist enemy Intelligence. This was the way that I found out that they were really listening to what I had to say. They had respect for Intelligence and Security procedures. Each man would automatically empty his pockets into a brown manila envelope. They would turn their pockets inside out. I never asked this of them, but they would turn their pockets inside out and I would seal the envelopes and put them in a safe. They'd then pick up their flying gear.

They wore the old American Army issue or surplus or what have you. A lot of the American boys had their old leather flying jackets. We had a practice of cutting up parachutes for silk scarves. They wore them when they were flying. They would very often be wearing the RAF gray-blue sweater . . . they'd be wearing that jacket over it . . . flight leather jacket . . . American Army Air Corps issue or Navy issue . . . Marine issue. We had them from everywhere.

They'd be driven out to the planes by jeep or Chrysler limousine. These were all stolen vehicles, basically. Whatever transportation we had on the field was stolen transportation. It was Sid Cohen's Used Car Lot. It was a very rare occasion when somebody didn't come back from town with a stolen car or vehicle or truck.

. . .They'd take off in their flights—two or three or four at the maximum. Kind of a la movie style. Then roughly 45 to 70 minutes would elapse from take-off to return. If the man just came in and landed then it was a matter of the ground people picking him up and bringing him in. If a man buzzed the tower, we got excited. And if a man did a barrel roll then we knew there was a kill.

The war the *Mahal* volunteers had to fight was singularly grim, but for the most part they faced their challenges with a kind of high-spirited insouciance that would have done justice to a remake of *The Dawn Patrol*. Rudy Auergarten, an American volunteer in 101 Squadron who ended his tour in Israel with three and a half kills, insists he actually enjoyed flying missions to El Arish because that's where the Egyptian Spitfires were. "That's always been the dream of every American boy," Auergarten said, "to shoot down fighter planes."

John McElroy, a Canadian who had won the DFC with bar for shooting down ten enemy planes (plus eight probables and four damaged) in World War II, was perhaps a bit more dour than Auergarten. (According to his friend, Denny Wilson, when McElroy first landed at Haifa and was asked what he was doing in Israel, he said simply, "I came to fly your fucking airplanes.") But evidently he was not without a strain of black humor. When he joined 101 Squadron the unit had already acquired its four Mustangs and thus was operating three different fighter types simultaneously. McElroy found this "the funniest thing I ever seen anywhere in flying." As he described a typical mission:

> . . .in October . . . the fighter escort [for the B-17 bombers] from 101 Squadron took off and they had two Spitfires and two P-51s [Mustangs] and two Messerschmitts. This represented three air forces. The enemy never touched the fighter airplanes— it was the entire strength of 101 Squadron at the time—and the funniest part was, I was listening in on the briefing, and they decided because the Messerschmitt was the most dangerous airplane to fly and the Spit was the most valuable, they'd get the two Spitfires off first and then they'd send off the two P-51s and let the '109s get off the ground last. And it was the same when they got back. The landing was the same procedures. The Spitfires landed first, and then the Mustangs [and then the Messerschmitts]. I thought that was quite humorous.

Joseph John "Jack" Doyle was another Canadian veteran of World War II. He arrived at 101 Squadron on October 18 and was checked out by Rudy Auergarten. Within 25 minutes of their take-off Doyle had performed so many hair-raising World War II-style maneuvers ("You come in with a quick screaming turn, drop her in, and get the hell out of there") that Auergarten simply said, "To hell with him; let him go solo." Doyle was operational.

On his first mission, flying a Spitfire in company with Auergarten, Doyle had his first fight near El Arish:

> It was a lovely day and we saw these (four unidentified) aircraft and I figured it couldn't be anything else but Spitfires. I knew they couldn't be ours because we were the only two in the air because that's how few aircraft we had. So Rudy and I went straight into them. We had a nice hassle with them. Once we started firing in anger, they realized we were Israeli and took off. But, well, I shot down one and damaged a couple. They roared straight

home. . . . They were not about to run off if they had been
Luftwaffe. Luftwaffe fought back. But these jokers just turned tail
and went like a bomb.

Doyle was to prove himself as formidable on many subsequent missions. On January 7, 1949, for example, he and another pilot were in Mustangs escorting some Harvards on a dive-bombing mission to Deir-El-Ballah. Suddenly, on the desert floor below, Doyle spotted the shadows of several aircraft flying above him.

I called for Boris. I called him. I could count that there were
eight of them—so I called him and I said there are enemy aircraft. . . . The other boys were sitting on waiting list on the back
of the drome so I hollered like hell right away to scramble off the
boys that were on the ground to come up.

Well, there would be about a ten-minute flight even though
they were damn good at getting up in the air. I went down and I
am sorry to say this chap Boris didn't follow me all the way down.
I don't know where he got to. I got in behind these eight aircraft
and I recognized them from aircraft recognition and the fact they
had been used in Italy as Fiat G-50s [they were actually Fiat
G-55s], so I got in behind one of them. . . . So I destroyed
one . . . and then I hacked another one. I only claimed him as
damaged because I was going so goddamned fast I went whistl-
ing straight by them. And got off to the side. I bumped off to the
side to pick off another guy.

Just how important to Israel's fledgling air force the *Mahal* pilots were is suggested by a single statistic. In the two campaigns against the Egyptians during the last quarter of 1948, one-third of all the Arab planes shot down were accounted for by just three *Mahal* pilots: Denny Wilson, Jack Doyle, and John McElroy. By the war's end, 101 Squadron had 35 kills. It had lost only one plane in direct air combat.

Operation *Yoav* was followed in December by Operation *Chorev*, which was intended to reduce and, if possible, eliminate the Egyptian grip on the coastline near Gaza. From just before Christmas until early January 1949, air fighting was heavy. Although the Egyptians had supplemented their fighter force with Italian Fiat G-55s and Macchi MC-205s, as well as with a number of Iraqi Furies, the *Chel Ha'Avir*'s mastery in the skies continued to grow. But on January 7 there occurred a dangerous incident that might easily have changed the course of the war.

On this date, while Israeli troops were rapidly driving the Egyptians back into Sinai, British Spitfire Mk. 18s of the RAF's No. 208 Squadron flew to the front on what the British later claimed to be a peaceful reconnaissance mission. Even if the British claim had been true, the manifest folly of sending RAF Spitfires into such a battle zone would have been inexplicable. But, in fact, the Spitfires were engaged in bombing and strafing Israeli vehicles on the ground, an activity which immediately provoked a confrontation with 101 Squadron. McElroy describes the scene:

> On January 7, we had done a couple of patrols and we had been told that there was going to be a truce effective at 4:00 P.M. I was sitting in the dispersal hut down on the field at Qastina with Slick Goodlin and Lee Sinclair. It was late in the afternoon; I think it was probably around 2:15 or 2:30. And I said to Slick: "I got a funny feeling there's a patrol in the area now down around the El Arish–Auja area. Let's see if we can get a couple of airplanes and take off down there for one more patrol." Well, Slick said he'd go along and Lee said he wanted to go, so I went to the Engineering Officer and asked if he had any serviceable airplanes and he said he had two Spitfires ready to go and he said there's maybe a P-51. I said: "Fine. Slick and I will fly the Spitfires and Lee will take the P-51 and act as sort of a top cover for us and we'll go down and see what we can find."
>
> Slick, though an American, didn't take the P-51 because during that period he had indicated a preference for the Spit for combat work. He thought it was easier to handle and more maneuverable. Slick liked the 20-mm cannon which we had in our Spits; more effective firepower. The Spitfire had two 20-mm cannon and two .50-inch machine guns, the standard American weapon. . . .
>
> I showed the boys the area on the map where we'd go and what area we'd look for. The Engineering Officer came in and said that the P-51 was not serviceable. He had thought it was, but it wasn't. So Lee Sinclair couldn't go. Slick and I went by ourselves. The two of us went down there, down the coast. We were flying at 16,000–18,000 feet. We didn't say much. We were trying to observe radio silence. I didn't know what effect it would have but we didn't want too many people to know we were coming. And it was pretty uneventful for the first 20 to 25 minutes of flight. And then, all of a sudden, I said to Slick—he was on my left wing—I said, "Look at that smoke over here to the left, on the ground." It seemed to be about eight or ten miles away.
>
> We were a good 40 to 50 miles south of Faluja. It was right on the front line. And there was three columns of smoke—pretty heavy black smoke—going up about 1,000 feet. So I said, "Come on. We'll turn and have a look at this." And as we got closer, I

said," My God. It's a. . ." We could see trucks burning. We could
see a couple of light armored vehicles and a number of jeeps. We
saw no airplanes at that time. And then I saw four Spitfires going
in. They were strafing. They had three vehicles on fire. . . .

There were no markings on the Spitfires. Two of them were
heading in an easterly direction. And there were two that had
gotten out of sight in a dive. They were diving and we lost them.
So I warned Slick to watch out and we got over the convoy.

Slick was right beside my wing. He'd crossed over on the
starboard side and I pulled another turn and turned south to see
if we could pick up the other airplanes. Slick moved over to my
left. And just as he did, I yelled, "There's an enemy aircraft at
twelve o'clock, right in front of us." They were about 3,000 feet
lower than us. So we stuck our noses down and Slick moved off
to the left and started firing. We were right on top of them. They
pulled up right in front of us and I blasted one, I guess from about
200 yards, and I saw many explosions all around. Engine.
Cockpit. I knocked quite a few pieces off his wings.

They'd just pulled out of this dive. They didn't see us at all.
They didn't know we were even in the area. I broke off, looked at
Slick. He had disappeared from view, but I saw an airplane going
down off to my left. It was on fire and smoking, in a fairly steep
dive around to the left.

I took a quick look around, behind and above. Nothing
behind me at all and I looked over and saw another airplane off
about two o'clock to me—just off to my right and slightly below. I
took one look and saw it wasn't one of ours by the markings.
Ours had the tails painted with big red and white stripes. I looked
for the red and white tail markings of our airplanes. They were all
marked the same and they showed up many miles away.

It wasn't one of ours, so I just dropped my sights on
him—it was about 400 yards—and I let fly. I got strikes all over
him. Right down the fuselage and the engine. And I didn't wait
around. I just broke off. I got a good burst in, probably about
three to four seconds, which is a fairly long burst, and well clob-
bered with cannon shells and the 50 caliber. I broke off, looked
around and couldn't [see Slick].

I told him where I was [on the radio]. I said I'd orbit over the
convoy. It was on fire, this burning convoy down there, this
armored convoy . . . They were still burning and you could see
them for 15 to 20 miles. So I orbited over there. Slick picked me
up and we went home.

"It was Slick, when we got back home, on the ground, it
was Slick that told me. He said those were British Spitfires. And I
said, "Oh, no. You're crazy. The British wouldn't be down there.
That's behind our line." Now where this convoy was on

fire . . . where the strafing around was going, was behind the Israeli lines—I would say, roughly, three to four miles behind the Israeli front lines. And that's the first thing I knew. Slick said that the British fighters were in the area. That's the first I knew they were even down that way. I never noticed any markings on them. I knew they weren't ours and that's all I needed.

. . .We certainly regretted it. We didn't want to get mixed up with the British. However, as I've explained to many people, we were flying and fighting for the Israelis. There were aircraft— at the time it didn't matter whose they were to me—attacking Israeli vehicles and Israeli personnel. It was our job and our duty to stop it and that was the only way we could stop it. It was too bad, as I say, but we had no indication that the British were in that area.

In all, the British lost five Spitfires, one to ground fire and four to the guns of McElroy and Goodlin.

Later that same day an RAF patrol consisting of one Mosquito with an escort of Hawker Tempests conducted a reconnaissance sweep of the Ismailia-Beersheba road looking for the missing Spitfires. They, too, tangled with 101 Squadron. The red-nosed Israeli aircraft made a single pass at the intruders, shooting down one of the Tempests. The remainder of the British flight withdrew.

For a few tense days it looked as if the incensed British might attack Israel. As official charges and countercharges flew back and forth, RAF Canberra jet bombers were being massed on Cypress. But eventually cooler heads prevailed. Former Prime Minister Winston Churchill was able to persuade Foreign Secretary Ernest Bevin that a British military intervention on the side of the Arabs would amount to a diplomatic disaster. The British chose not to act.

In February and March 1949, Israel signed a series of armistice agreements with her Arab neighbors. The War of Independence was over. One by one the members of *Mahal* left, some in 1949, others in 1950 and 1951. Many of them, before leaving, helped train their Israeli replacements. But never again would Israel have to rely on outsiders to come to her rescue. Now she was on her own.

THE
CHEL HA'AVIR
COMES
OF AGE
1949–1967

5
SUEZ

THE END OF THE WAR BROUGHT NO PEACE TO ISRAEL. THE armistice agreements Israel signed with her neighbors were not peace treaties, and although all the agreements contained pious words about facilitating "the transition from the present truce to permanent peace in Palestine," no one had any illusions on that score. Without exception, the Arab states refused to recognize Israel's existence, and Arab political rhetoric continued to demand the extermination of the Jewish state.

The old pattern of terrorism was quickly reestablished. Syria and Egypt set up schools to train armed Arab commando teams and soon *fedayeen* were raiding Israel in force from bases in Syria, Egypt, and Jordan. Most *fedayeen* attacks were directed against civilian targets—buses, schools, and the like. Whenever Israeli troops chased the raiders back to the borders, Syrian or Jordanian troops were usually on hand to open fire on the pursuers.

It was inevitable that these raids would eventually provoke the Israelis into making reprisal raids. Indeed, it is probable that that was one of the purposes, for the reprisals often led to direct clashes between Arab and Israeli troops, thus hastening the coming of a new war.

Arab provocations were by no means limited to semi-clandestine activity. In 1951 Egypt (in contravention of the Treaty of Constantinople), closed the Suez Canal to Israeli shipping on the grounds that the two countries were still at war. Although other states, including the United States, have called upon Egypt to reverse the decision, it remains in effect to this day. Next, Israeli ships were excluded from the Gulf of Aqaba (an international waterway), an economic boycott was instituted, and foreign airline flights to or from Israel were forbidden to overfly or make stops in Arab countries. Meanwhile, Arab diplomats in the U.N. routinely subjected Israel to vitriolic denunciations.

None of this escalating provocation came as much of a surprise to the Israelis. The Arabs had made it plain enough that another war was inevitable and, that indeed, as far as they were concerned, the last one had never truly ended. Of more immediate concern to the Israelis was whether they would have the military strength to win the coming battle.

The opposing military forces had been fairly evenly balanced immediately after the first Arab-Israeli war, which only meant that both sides would have to indulge in a furious arms race in order to be ready for the next one. By 1955 it appeared that the Arabs were winning this race. Egypt had already obtained from England 41 Centurion tanks, 200 tanks destroyers, two "Z" class destroyers, and some 70 de Havilland Vampire and Gloster Meteor jet fighters to supplement their 20-plane bomber force. And later in the year 30 more Vampires were received from Syria.

But what really tipped the scales in the Arabs' favor was a massive arms deal concluded between Egypt and Czechoslovakia in October 1955, to be followed by a similar Czecho-Syrian deal in 1956. Under the terms of the initial arrangement Czechoslovakia (i.e., the USSR) was to send the Egyptians 50 huge Stalin III tanks, 150 T-34 medium tanks, 200 armored troop carriers, 100 self-propelled guns, 2 destroyers, 2 submarines, 15 mine sweepers, and masses of artillery and small arms. Syria subsequently received 100 T-34s, and, again, very large quantities of artillery and small arms.

The aerial component of the two deals was equally overwhelming. Egypt received 120 MiG-15 swept-wing jet fighters, 50 Ilyushin Il-28 twin-jet bombers, and 20 Ilyushin Il-14 transports. Syria got an additional 100 MiG-15s. The only jet fighters that the Israelis had then to defend themselves against this looming threat were a handful of Meteors.

This vast infusion of Soviet military equipment meant that the outbreak of war could not be long delayed. In fact, it was destined to begin on October 29, 1956. And surprisingly, it would be the Israelis who would strike first.

In order to understand how the *Chel Ha'Avir* brought itself to a condition whereby it could fight and win such a war, we must go back and take a look at what had been happening to the Israeli air force in the years between 1949 and October 1956.

From the start, Aharon Remez, the first "peacetime" Commander of the IDF/AF, had an uphill battle to improve the *Chel Ha'Avir*. *Mahal*, composed of volunteers and a sprinkling of mercenaries, had been largely undisciplined. As a result, the air force had a devil-may-care, soldier-of-fortune attitude. Then too, by no stretch of the imagination could the bulk of the IDF/AF aircraft in 1949 be considered military. Desperation had required that Austers, Bonanzas, Dragon Rapides, and Norsemen be used for roles never intended by their designers. And even the true combat planes were war-weary. But, with most of the experienced pilots gone, the training of Israeli pilots had to come first. This placed a high priority on training planes.

The three Avro Ansons originally intended for use as light bombers, but impounded on Rhodes during the War of Independence, were released by Greek authorities after the war. But there was no need for makeshift bombers. And so, together with some Airspeed Consuls, the Ansons were used to train Israeli pilots in navigation and to give them experience on multi-engine craft. Then, as Dakotas and Commandos were acquired, trainees went on to these and other multi-engine aircraft.

The Consul was essentially a postwar conversion of the wartime Oxford trainer to a light transport. Shortly after the War of Independence, the IDF/AF acquired a number of Consuls to supplement the Avro Ansons which were already in inventory and performing similar functions. The Consuls were popular in the training role and, together with the Ansons, continued to function as trainer and light transport for almost ten years, finally being retired when IDF/AF revamped the training curriculum for pilot and navigational trainees for multi-engine aircraft.

Faced with the task of training pilots from the ground up, the *Chel Ha'Avir* purchased a number of PT-17 biplanes. During the Second World War, these had been used by the United States Army Air Corps and by the United States Navy as primary trainers. They were cheap, reliable, and available in large numbers. For about ten years Israel continued to use them as trainers and as do-anything aircraft. With the introduction of other, more modern, trainers and a change in pilot training techniques, these sturdy little craft, like the Consuls and Ansons, were phased out. Some of those still intact were sold to private firms where they were re-engined and used for agricultural spraying.

Another aircraft acquired in small numbers was the Chipmunk primary trainer. The aircraft were manufactured in both Canada and the United Kingdom, and some 60 were made in Portugal under license. Canada built a total of 1,014, while the United Kingdom constructed 214. For operations in the hot Israeli climate, the Chipmunk was vastly underpowered and required considerable field length to operate for an airplane of its size. This wasn't exactly appreciated in a country which has placed great emphasis on short field performance. The Chipmunks lacked flexibility but were still used.

In the early Fifties, Temco (Texas Engineering & Manufacturing Company, Inc.) produced an all-metal primary trainer, the TE-1A Buckaroo. This aircraft, which utilized approximately 80 percent of the tooling of Temco Swift, a civilian aircraft, was a low-wing aircraft with retractable landing, having exceptional performance for an aircraft of its power. Saudi Arabia was furnished a number of Buckaroos and Israel acquired a small number.

Israel was also concerned about collecting transport aircraft for her still-minuscule air force. Never mind quality; it was quantity that mattered. As important as numbers of aircraft was price. Therefore, shortly after the War of Independence ended in 1949, Israel snapped up an offer from South Africa of two Miles M-57 Aerovan aircraft. These were light twin-engined freight or passenger aircraft, slab-sided and of all-wood construction. They were simple aircraft to operate, however, with fixed landing gear and medium-pressure tires which allowed them to operate anywhere in Israel. But, the boxy freighters had little else to recommend them. With two 150-horsepower air-cooled engines, they were capable of cruising at a mere 110 mph. The Dakotas, which had now become plentiful, completely overshadowed the Aerovans, although, to be fair, the Douglas transport was a larger design, with far more powerful engines. The Aerovans' only advantage was that they could use some fields too small for Dakotas.

But acquisitions of light trainers and transport planes during the first year or two after the War of Independence hardly solved the main problem. All was not well with the *Chel Ha'Avir*. In other areas it was going downhill.

Major General Remez was now being forced to view the slow disintegration of the air force which had been so painfully built during the war. True, new trainers had been added to the inventory, but, to counterbalance them, the RWD-13s, old and tired, had to be scrapped. The Messerschmitt fighters had suffered an appalling accident rate due to their poor landing and take-off characteristics, and by 1950 only a handful of the original 25 remained. The Spitfires, good as they were, were by contemporary world standards now thoroughly obsolete.

Remez badly wanted to update the IDF/AF equipment, especially in fighters. But he had the prime minister, David Ben-Gurion, to contend with. "The old man" couldn't see the need for a strong air arm. Ben-Gurion believed in the Kibbutz system, where each settlement was a fortress. He felt that any money spent should be spent on bolstering ground forces. After all, he argued, wasn't it ground forces which had blunted the Arab attacks and driven their armies out of the Jewish homeland?

When, after two years of pleading, it became plain that he could not alter the prime minister's views and would therefore have to lead a dangerously weak air arm, Aharon Remez, Israel's first "peacetime" commander of the *Chel Ha'Avir*, resigned in 1950. In so doing, Remez made it clear to David Ben-Gurion and also to Yigal Yadin, overall commander of Israel's armed forces, that he could not function with the limited budget and limited autonomy available to him. It was Remez's view that the air force role had to go beyond just providing support to the army.

Remez's successor was Shlomo Shamir. Shamir had been a naval commander. Nothing in his background really fitted him for the job he was now called upon to do. Nor could he rise to meet the challenge. During his tenure as commander of IDF/AF, the air arm continued to deteriorate, and within a year he resigned.

The next commander of the *Chel Ha'Avir* was Chaim Laskov. A former infantry officer, he was later destined to serve with distinction as the commander of Israel's military forces. Laskov was quick to realize the problems that he faced as head of the air force, for like Aharon Remez, he lacked much autonomy for direction of the air force and the improvement of its equipment.

Laskov's budget battles were a little more successful than those of Remez, but not much. Still, in 1951 the IDF/AF was allowed to purchase 25 Mustang fighters from Sweden. This was a small first step, but at that time most of the world's major air forces had re-equipped with jets. Israel's new first-line fighter was about 200 mph slower than the MiGs and Sabres now dueling over Korea and 100 to 150 mph slower than service machines in Europe.

In a like manner, Israel also purchased about 60 de Havilland Mosquitos from France. These were worn-out Mk. IV bombers, Mk. VI fighter-bombers, and Mk. 36 night fighters. Some were bought as scrap from the French government for about $200 apiece and were then refurbished; others were bought from England and ferried to Israel.

Because of extensive cannibalization necessary to keep the obsolete Mosquitos flying, distinctions between the various models soon became blurred. Bombers flew with the armored windscreens of fighter-bomber models, and night fighters, stripped of their radar, were used as bombers.

During the early to mid-Fifties, the Mosquitos were the mainstay of the IDF/AF bomber force, but luckily the situation changed prior to the 1956 Suez Campaign. Early models of this plywood aircraft had been put together using cassein glue as the bonding agent. It was found, however, that in tropical countries, the glue failed, and terrible things happened to the molded plywood and wood structure. Formaldehyde glue was substituted and this seemed to do the job somewhat better, but not even that is certain. Whether the wrong glue had been used when repairing the war-weary Mosquitos or whether they simply had reached the end of their life, Israeli Mosquitos experienced a number of crashes, some of them resulting in fatalities. "I was flying my Mosquito at a demonstration," one pilot recalled, "and I was supposed to loop it. I started to and the next thing I remember I was hanging by my parachute straps. My crewman died when the Mossie just disintegrated."

In 1954 Egypt acquired MiG-15s, and this spelled the end of the Mosquitos in Israeli service. During the Second World War, Mosquitos had used their speed to escape interception, but there was no way a Mosquito could outrun or elude these jet fighters. The combination of vulnerability to interception, structural failures, and the acquisition of new jet equipment spelled the end for the Mosquito in IDF/AF service. A few trainers remained, but soon they too were retired. Only a single squadron—about fifteen aircraft—were on hand at the start of the 1956 Suez War.

Dan Tolkovski became head of the Israeli air force in 1953. His was a fateful appointment. Perhaps more than any other single individual, Tolkovski, a veteran of the Second World War, molded the Israeli Defence Force/Air Force into the crack fighting army it is today. He had very strong opinions about the direction and structure of Israel's air arm, and unlike his predecessors, Tolkovski was able to battle Ben-Gurion and win. He had the courage and the foresight to step on toes for the good of the air force—and the country.

The organization that Tolkovski inherited from his predecessors was in poor shape. When the War of Independence ended, most of the foreigners had left, taking their expertise with them. The leadership of the *Chel Ha'Avir* had passed into the hands of Israeli officers whose distinguished war records were not always matched by their administrative abilities. Many, whose inadequacies were all too obvious, were retained in senior positions largely for reasons of sentiment. "When we needed someone to help us," one Israeli explained, "these men came forth. We had no one else. Now that the crisis is over, how, in good conscience, can we discard these men?"

But sentiment is hardly the best foundation on which to build a modern air force, and in the five years since the War of Independence, the Chel Ha'Avir had paid a considerable price for its faltering leadership. Even allowing for the objective difficulties that beset the Chel Ha'Avir—Ben-Gurion's indifference, the special pleading of army generals, financial limitations, the stringencies imposed by the Middle East arms embargo—it must be said that the air force had not been very well run.

Procurement policy—or lack of it—provides a striking illustration. The catch-as-catch-can methods of acquiring new aircraft that had been necessary during the War of Independence had been thoughtlessly maintained in the immediate postwar years. The result was that the Chel Ha'Avir was equipped with a hodgepodge of too many different types, too few of which were first-line. Standardization was virtually unknown, and the IDF/AF's maintenance record was rapidly descending from wretched to appalling.

With the advent of Tolkovski, all this was to change radically. Tolkovski started a revolution within the IDF/AF. There was to be standardization of equipment. Old and nonstandard equipment was retired. Uniforms, drills, practice, became the order of the day. With the advent of Tolkovski, the Israel Air Force/Defence Force gradually began to assume the efficiency which was later to be its hallmark.

Tolkovski, a South African who had served in the RAF during the Second World War, recognized that, since Israel could never hope to match its neighbors in the quantity of aircraft in service, it was imperative that the aircraft of the Chel Ha'Avir must be superior and that its pilots must excel in everything. Ground crews, too, were drilled. Turnaround time was shortened, with aircraft refueled, guns reloaded, and bombs or rockets installed in ever shorter periods.

Tolkovski was not popular with the political leaders of Israel. Ben-Gurion, particularly, stressed the role of the ground soldiers, the products of kibbutzim. To him the air force was secondary, its function only to support the troops on the ground. And since its function was simply that of support, why bother to buy new and expensive aircraft? The air force could make due with the toys it had. But Tolkovski and his theories prevailed and it was in his image that the Chel Ha'Avir was shaped. His ideas were basic enough:

1.   Israel could not afford a multitude of specialized aircraft in
      military roles. What the country needed were as many of the

best multi-purpose aircraft obtainable. Bombers were out. Interceptors were unacceptable; their functions must be performed by all-purpose fighters capable of battling with other fighters as well as functioning as fighter-bombers. For example, Tolkovski later resisted pressure to purchase Mystère IIC interceptors which were immediately available. Instead, he chose to wait for the Mystère IV, which had a multi-mission capability.

2.   Tolkovski believed that the first objective in any future war was to destroy the enemy's air force. Then and only then, was the air force to turn its attention to strike and reconnaissance missions in support of ground forces.

3.   What counted, in Tolkovski's opinion, was the number of serviceable aircraft rather than the total inventory of an air force. Maintenance received the highest priority. Turnaround time was stressed. By the 1967 Six Day War (and again in 1973), from the time a fighter landed after a mission to the time it was ready to take off again with a full fuel and bomb load only seven to ten minutes had elapsed—this at a time when the United States prided itself on a turnaround time of twenty minutes. The Egyptians, on the other hand, had a turnaround time of between three and four hours.

4.   According to Tolkovski, a country with limited resources must have a qualitative edge. He therefore instituted pilot standards which were probably the stiffest in the world. The washout rate of pilot candidates was astronomical. But what Tolkovski was left with was the cream of the cream. Many who didn't qualify for the *Chel Ha'Avir* would have passed courses sponsored by other air forces with flying colors.

5.   Pilots were honed to a razor edge through constant training. Tolkovski developed an elite flying corps which was the equal of the German Luftwaffe's best in the Second World War. The comparison becomes even more valid when it is realized that Tolkovski's introduction of the two-plane fighting element was based on the Luftwaffe pattern. Such formations, though small, avoided the unwieldy formations of eight or more aircraft such as were flown by the Egyptians. A pilot could attack an enemy, confident that he was covered from the rear by his wing man. A two-plane formation could also maneuver more readily without danger of collision.

The slapdash air force disappeared. Tolkovski would settle for nothing less than complete professionalism, and this is what was achieved. When he retired in 1958, his successor, Ezer Weizman, added some refinements but basically followed in Tolkovski's trail.

And when Motti Hod succeeded Weizman, it was still Tolkovski's air force in spirit.

In 1953, before Tolkovski became head of the *Chel Ha'Avir*, Britain lifted her embargo on sales of arms to the nations of the Near and Middle East. The scramble was on. Israel acquired Gloster Meteor F.8 fighters and T.7 trainers. They were one of the final contributions Laskov made to the air force, the first jet aircraft to join the *Chel Ha'Avir*. But in order to maintain some semblance of "neutrality," England matched the eleven F.8 aircraft to Israel, with fifteen sold to Egypt and twelve to Syria. (In 1953 the United States, in a political about-face, also granted an export license to Israel for three World War II vintage PBY-5 Catalina seaplanes. Two of these amphibians were purchased. Hardly warplanes—they lacked guns—they were based at Haifa and were intended for air/sea rescue duties as well as maritime reconnaissance. The U.S. embargo, if not lifted, was at least developing leaks.)

The Israeli F.8 and T.7 aircraft were fitted with pylons for American HVAR 5-inch rocket projectiles for ground support as well as Martin Baker M2E ejection seats. The 20-mm cannon armament was fitted to the aircraft by Israel. Shortly after the delivery of these aircraft, the *Chel Ha'Avir* ordered nine Meteor FR.9 reconnaissance fighters.

During the 1956 Suez Campaign, Meteors were used to provide top cover for Ouragon and Mustang fighter-bombers. The Gloster fighter was victorious in combat against Egyptian Vampires during the brief campaign. But it was soon recognized that the day of the Meteor was passing. It had been outfought several years earlier by Soviet MiG-15s during the Korean War. And, with increasing Russian involvement in the Middle East, more of the swept-wing Russian jets were to be seen in the skies of the Arab countries.

Between 1955 and 1956 Great Britain sold and delivered to Egypt, Syria, and Israel six each of the Meteor NF.13 night fighter. This aircraft, designed for use in tropical countries, was built by Armstrong-Whitworth. The NF.13 featured an elongated nose to house the large radar dish, air-conditioning for crew comfort in warm climates, and larger nacelle intakes than previous Marks to accommodate powerplants with higher thrust ratings.

The Meteor NF.13 was a useful addition to the *Chel Ha'Avir*, providing Israel with that nation's only all-weather defensive capability until the arrival of the McDonnell F-4E Phantom II many years later. With the arrival of Phantoms, the all-weather Meteors were phased out.

Welcome as these acquisitions were, by 1955—especially after the announcement of the big Arab-Czech arms deal—they were perceived as woefully inadequate. The *Chel Ha'Avir* badly needed a new transport to supplement the aging Dakotas, Commandos, and Aerovans; and, above all, it needed a contemporary jet fighter to replace its few old Meteors and prop-driven Mustangs and Mosquitos. All these needs were to be met by planes designed in pre-Gaullist France.

The new transport was the big twin-engine Nord 2501 Noratlas. In 1955 Israel acquired twelve of these aircraft, the first few from France directly and the remainder from West Germany. Although the Noratlas's troop-carrying capacity was slightly less than that of the Commando (45 versus 50), it was superior in all other respects. Unlike the Commando, the Noratlas had no difficulty operating on a single engine. Moreover, its take-off performance in the high-temperature environment of Israel's desert climate was good, which was hardly true of the C-46. But most important, thanks to its bulky fuselage and twin-boom design, the Noratlas was an ideal plane for making paradrops. Troops, cargo, and even medium-sized vehicles could be ejected from the rear of the fuselage through the gaping exit created when the great clamshell doors were opened.

The Noratlas was to prove its worth many times over when the war finally erupted in October 1956. When it was employed in dropping supplies to the rapidly advancing Israeli ground forces in the Sinai Peninsula, its performance exceeded the most sanguine expectations.

Much more crucial to Israel's survival were her new fighter planes, two French types that the *Chel Ha'Avir* would shortly make world-famous in combat. The first was the Dassault Ouragon, destined to have the longest operational career of any aircraft to serve with the IDF/AF. In a sense, the Ouragon was to Israel what the Republic F-84 Thunderjet was to the United States. Both were unswept annular-flow jets that were called upon to do battle with the much faster swept-wing MiG-15, the Thunderjet over Korea and the Ouragon in the cloudless skies above the Sinai.

The physical resemblance between the two aircraft is more than coincidental. In 1947, when Marcel Dassault, né Bloch, embarked upon design studies to produce a first-generation jet fighter for France, there were few directions to which he could turn for inspiration. The Germans had produced the Messerschmitt Me 262 and the Heinkel He 162 during the war, the British had the de Havilland Vampire and the Gloster Meteor in production, while the United States was then manufacturing the Lockheed F-80 Shooting Star and the Republic F-84 Thunderjet. Russia was, at that time, an enigma.

So Dassault borrowed features from the F-80 and the F-84 for the Ouragon. The Ouragon employed the nose inlet of the Thunderjet and the low wing of the F-80. Unfortunately, by the time the prototype flew, in 1949, the Ouragon had been rendered obsolete by the second generation of subsonic jet fighters, which incorporated swept wings. It was clearly outclassed by the American F-86 and the Soviet MiG-15 when it entered service with France's Armée de l'Air in 1952.

The Ouragon design had no sooner been fixed than the Dassault Works began work on a swept-wing version. This, with refinements, would become the Mystère. The Mystère IV did, in fact, begin to supplant the Ouragon in French air force service in 1955—a mere three years after the Ouragon had first seen service with that air arm. But before the admittedly unspectacular Ouragon could pass into the limbo of little-known aircraft destined never to fire their guns in anger, political events altered its career.

The IDF/AF had at first placed an order with Dassault for 24 Mystère IIC fighters. These were little more than swept-wing Ouragons. In addition, Israel attempted to buy from Canada 24 Canadian-built CL-13B Sabre 6 fighters. The United States at that time maintained a strict arms embargo to the nations of the Middle East, and Russia by then had moved to the Arab side. Because of the threat of renewed warfare in the Middle East, Canada canceled the Israeli order for Sabres as part of a general arms embargo to the area. Realizing that lacking quantity, it would have to rely on aircraft quality, Israel canceled its order for the Mystère IIC and opted instead for the more advanced Mystère IVA. But this meant further delays, since the later model was not yet available. Israel knew that a paper order was no deterrent. As a stopgap, Israel ordered the Ouragon.

France could scarcely have been more pleased. It isn't every day that a nation can sell its obsolete, and surplus, air force fighters for profit instead of scrapping them. In 1955 Israel took delivery of some 75 Ouragons, at least 42 of them refurbished Armeé de l'Air machines.

In 1956 the first trickle of Dassault Mystères began to arrive in Israel. But, as the Arab threat grew, the Ouragons remained as the backbone of the IDF/AF. *Fedayeen* terror raids were staged across the borders of Israel with increasing regularity. Trained in Egypt, the terrorists had staging bases in both Jordan and Egypt. Threats to Israel were broadcast daily on Egyptian radio. Egyptian aerial reconnaissance began in earnest.

On April 12, 1956, an Egyptian Vampire, one of a pair on reconnaissance patrol over Israel's Negev Desert, was shot down by an Ouragon. This was the first kill by the French fighter.

In spite of this, the IDF/AF was not overly optimistic about the Ouragon's chances in combat. Its performance was not significantly better than that of the older Meteors. What's more, time was running out and it became apparent that there would not be sufficient Mystères available for combat operations. And only Mystères, it was believed, could survive against the MiGs.

In October 1956, Israel began the Suez War with an attack. For weeks it had been apparent that an Arab invasion was imminent. The *fedayeen* attacks had intensified, Egypt had reinforced her main forward air base at El Arish in Sinai and had established a joint command with Jordan, and Iraq had moved large bodies of troops through Jordan and poised them on the Israeli border.

Israel struck into Egypt on October 29. England, angered by Egypt's closing of the Suez Canal, did not this time give moral support to the Egyptians, but instead, along with France, attacked Egypt on October 31. Under such pressure, the Arab war effort was foredoomed. In seven days the war was over.

Brief though the fighting was, Israeli air power was destined to play a relatively large part in it. Israeli Dakotas opened the campaign by dropping paratroops at the Mitla Pass. Mustangs raced through the Sinai Peninsula, cutting telephone lines—with wings and propellers! Meteors, Mustangs, and Ouragons were used for ground attack, Mystères for top cover. In the entire campaign Israel lost only one aircraft in air combat, a Piper Super Cub downed by a MiG-15, but losses from ground fire were considerably more severe.

On the second day of the war, two Ouragons shot down four Egyptian Vampires. Under difficult combat conditions, the Ouragons proved to be rugged and stable shooting platforms. Rarely had an aircraft been so underestimated.

It was inevitable that the Ouragons, which were fast becoming the scourge of Egyptian armor, should meet the vaunted MiG-15 in combat. Twice, the French-built fighter met the MiG-15 and on both occasions came through with flying colors. On the first occasion, two Ouragons, while attacking an armored column, were jumped by eight MiGs. Four MiGs remained as top cover during the battle. The Israeli fighters, maneuvering frantically to survive, were able to hold on until two Mystères came to their rescue. The two Mystères shot down one of the MiGs and the others ran. One Ouragon had been hit by 37-mm cannon shells, but survived. The other Ouragon ran out of fuel and force-landed with only slight damage. The following day both aircraft were back in combat.

In the other engagement, between two Ouragons and two MiG-15s, one of the Soviet-made aircraft was downed without loss to the Israelis. But there was more to the saga of the Ouragon in the 1956 war.

On October 31 two Ouragons, armed with sixteen armor-piercing rockets, crippled the *Ibrahim-el-Awal*, a British Hunt-class destroyer escort that had been sold to Egypt. The punishing attacks by the fighters contributed to the surrender of the fighting ship to Israeli Naval units, although it would be difficult to apportion credit for the victory between sea and air units.

Although the Ouragon must be credited with most of the Egyptian armored vehicles destroyed from the air during the Suez War, it was technically much inferior to the MiG in the fighter-versus-fighter role. That Ouragons were so successful in their encounters with MiGs has to be ascribed to the relative excellence of the Israeli pilots and, doubtless, to a certain amount of luck. For dogfighting with MiGs, the planes the Israelis really had to rely on were its handful of Mystère IVAs.

Unlike the Mystère IIC, the IVA was a completely new design, with more sharply swept wings and a higher top speed. It was on this aircraft that Israel rested her hopes for parity with the more numerous MiGs of her Arab neighbors. In late 1955 and early 1956, 60 of these latest Dassault aircraft were supplied to Israel, although not all had been integrated into squadron service by the time the 1956 war erupted in October.

Used as top cover for the slower Ouragons and Meteors, the Dassault Mystère IVA proved to be more than a match for the opposing MiGs. Israeli tactics called for them to be used in pairs and they frequently joined in combat with the formations of six to twelve aircraft utilized by the Egyptians. In the course of the 1956 fighting, at least three MiGs were downed by Mystères without loss to the Israelis. On another occasion, two Mystères blasted four Egyptian Vampires without even dropping their drag-producing external fuel tanks.

During the fighting, Israeli pilots found they had transonic capability in the sturdy Dassault fighter, whereas the MiGs did not. Moreover, the MiGs were not stable gun platforms at high speed. Although the MiGs had a higher climb rate, this feature was nullified by the higher speed and initial zoom capability of the Mystère.

During the course of the 1956 war, only one Mystère was lost and that was to ground fire. It was replaced by the French after the fighting. Two Ouragons had been lost, both to ground fire.

In keeping with the ideas and operational theories of Dan Tolkovski, high-performance, multi-purpose aircraft played the major roles for Israel during the Suez War. These constituted the striking edge of the *Chel Ha'Avir* and they and others continued to dominate subsequent conflicts. But even Tolkovski, the ultimate leader and airman, had to concede that on occasion there was a place for and a use for lesser, older, and more specialized breeds.

There was the old Mustang, for example, the aircraft that had first demonstrated to the Israelis that the odds for victory in modern air combat favored the fastest, most powerful plane over more maneuverable ones with less speed, altitude, and power. Mustangs were the first aircraft of the *Chel Ha'Avir* to go into action during the 1956 Suez Campaign. Though outclassed by then, they did some good work. They roved the length of the Sinai, attacking tanks and other vehicles. Still, no fewer than ten Mustangs were brought down, some by ground fire and a few through wing damage incurred in ripping down the telephone lines. Yet, of the ten, five were repaired within 24 hours.

But when the war ended, the IDF/AF analyzed their Mustang losses. More Mustangs had been brought down than any other type. Their engine was liquid-cooled and the Mustang was vulnerable to hits in the cooling system (during World War II, on ground-attack missions Mustangs had three times the loss rate of the Thunderbolt, which was powered by an air-cooled engine). Mustangs were gradually phased out of first-line operations.

The 1956 Suez Campaign was the swan song for another specialized battler. Vulnerable to ground fire and to MiGs, the old B-17s were used for the last time in this campaign. They were retired in 1958.

6

"GIRD UP NOW THY LOINS"

THE OLD BEN-GURION DEFENSIVE DOCTRINE OF SELF-contained kibbutz island-fortresses in an Arab sea was one of the first casualties of the Suez Campaign. Indeed, long before the fighting began, Israeli military thinking had been moving steadily toward the idea of defending Israel at its frontiers, erratic and inconvenient though these borderlines often were. And now, added to the border defense concept, was the possibility of a new and more aggressive strategy: the preemptive strike.

The long-term benefits to be gained from preemptive attack were difficult to assess on the basis of the Suez fighting. The campaign had been very short and the decisive factor had been the Anglo-French intervention. But those successes apparently attributable to the initial Israeli attack were sufficiently impressive to persuade Israeli planners that Israel ought to try to maintain a first-strike capability. This implied a heightened emphasis on armor and ultra-mobile infantry and artillery units on the ground. It also resulted in a sudden burst of official encouragement for developing capabilities for air-army cooperation, ground-attack and air-to-air combat beyond anything the IDF/AF had ever enjoyed. Israel's air force, once a feeble poor relation of the army, was now coming to be thought of as potentially the nation's premier military service.

Nearly eleven years would pass between the end of the Suez Campaign and the time when the *Chel Ha'Avir* would be called upon to demonstrate what it had learned about delivering preemptive strikes. During this period the IDF/AF's warplane inventory would change enormously. The world would learn the significance of those changes in June 1967, in the spectacular campaign known as the Six Day War.

The Suez Campaign had ended on November 6, 1956. For the Egyptians, the losses in material proved only a temporary setback. Immediately after the fighting stopped, Russia set about reequipping the Egyptians, often with newer and better equipment than before. The MiG-15s, for example, were now being replaced with the MiG-17, a fighter technically superior to the Mystère.

Thus the arms race which, in qualitative terms, Israel had won just long enough to win the war, now resumed in all its fury. Another war was bound to come, and once again the *Chel Ha'Avir* returned to the exhausting task of searching for the new equipment on which its survival would depend.

The 1956 Suez War had hardly ended before the *Chel Ha'Avir* began a critical examination of itself and its equipment. Despite the victory, the Israelis were not complacent.

The Mustangs had proven to be vulnerable to small arms fire in their ground-attack role. Nor were they fast enough to escape an encounter with the jet fighters which equipped the Arab air forces. The three B-17 bombers were too slow, too vulnerable, and too few in number. The Ouragons, which had been the workhorse in the ground-attack role during the campaign, were really just fighter aircraft. Now outmoded in air-to-air combat operations, their payload was insufficient. They were, at best, fighter-bombers. What were needed were larger, more powerful attack bombers.

During World War II, Bristol Beaufighters, Douglas A-20s, and Mosquito FB VIs had fulfilled this function for the Allies. They had an armaments punch in the ground-attack role which few fighters could hope to match. And because of their speed, they had little to fear then from interceptors at the low altitudes at which they operated. During the post-World War II period, the Douglas B-26 and Bristol Brigand served as attack bombers. But these were prop planes.

By the mid-Fifties the jet era had arrived. There were only three jet attack bombers which were designed to fulfill the traditional role of the earlier piston-engine aircraft. These were the English Electric Canberra, the Soviet Ilyushin IL-28, and the French Vautour.

The Canberra, originally a high-altitude bomber, was the least suitable for ground-attack work. Its huge wing was designed for its original job at high altitude. The IL-28 had been furnished to Egypt and Soviet-bloc countries. Obtaining them was out of the question. That left only the Vautour.

The Vautour, the prototype of which first flew on October 16, 1952, was designed to meet a 1951 requirement by the French Air Staff for a single design capable of being adapted to the roles of light bomber, reconnaissance, night, and all-weather fighter. The result was the SO.4050, with twin underslung wing-mounted engines and bicycle landing gear.

The first machine, 4050-001, was configured as a two-seat night fighter. As such, it was the prototype for the IIN night fighter, its solid nose filled with SCR.720 radar supplied by the United States. On December 4, 1953, the second prototype, the single-seat forerunner of the IIA ground-attack bomber, took to the air. The following year the prototype of the light bomber flew. This third aircraft, numbered 4050-003, had a transparent nose for bombing with optical bombsights. This last machine, used for development work for the IIB bomber, unlike the other variants, was not intended to carry a gun armament. The reconnaissance version was never built.

The largest production order placed by the French Air Staff was for the Sud-Aviation Vautour IIA single-seat attack bomber. Three hundred were ordered, but only 30 were built or near completion when the order was cancelled in 1957. Of these aircraft, 25 were sold to Israel and delivered in 1960. The IIA attack bomber had a solid nose and, like the IIN night fighter version, carried four 30-mm DEFA cannon. The IIA also had the internal bomb bay of the IIB, a feature which was deleted in the IIN.

France also placed an order with Sud for 70 IIN two-seat night fighters, several of which were later sold to Israel. At least one IIB appears to have also been sold to Israel.

Although few in numbers, the Vautour served Israel well. During the 1967 war, the Vautour would spearhead the first attack on air bases and installations deep within Egypt, facilities which were beyond the range of the smaller fighters. Later in that campaign, Vautours raked Egyptian armor in the Sinai with their formidable cannon armament.

Even before the 1967 campaign, Vautours proved themselves to be versatile machines. A number of aircraft were fitted with special pods containing photo-reconnaissance equipment. These were used to monitor military movements by hostile forces. And even much later, in the 1970 War of Attrition on the Suez Canal, some surviving Vautours were fitted with ECM equipment to confound Egyptian SAMs. There were even a few still available during the 1973 Yom Kippur War.

The Vautours will not soon be forgotten by those who saw them returning from missions. Their landing approach was spectacular, consisting of a high-speed pass over the runway, then a steeply banked turn to bleed off speed, followed by a touchdown on the highly unusual bicycle landing gear and stalky little outrigger wheels.

The mauling received by Israeli Mustangs from ground fire during the 1956 Suez Campaign convinced Israeli planners of the need for an all-jet air force. Negotiations were begun with the French Fouga company (which was to become part of the Potez group until Magister production was undertaken by Sud-Aviation, which in turn became Aerospatiale) to allow construction of Magisters in Israel under license.

Production in Israel began in 1960, with a single French aircraft, fully assembled, and parts for twelve more being supplied by Fouga. Legend has it that, from the thirteenth aircraft onward, the Magisters were made entirely of parts manufactured in Israel. This just isn't so. Production of wings lagged, so entire wing assemblies were purchased from Heinkel, the German firm which was manufacturing the Magister under license for the Luftwaffe.

Israeli Magisters differed from the French aircraft in having larger, unpowered ailerons. (The Fouga-built machines had power ailerons.) And, with the introduction of the Magisters, the *Chel Ha'Avir* changed pilot training procedures. After primary training on Piper Super Cubs, pilot cadets were shifted directly to Magisters.

On the eve of the 1967 Six Day War, the IDF/AF had about 96 Magisters. They were equipped with two 7.62-mm machine guns in the nose and with racks holding anti-tank rockets beneath the wings. The little two-seaters roved over the Sinai landscape to harass the Egyptian armored columns. While the Mustang had first and foremost been a fighter, the Magister began as a trainer. Still the latter was effective as a tank-killer, though the price was high. Nineteen Magisters were shot down by ground fire during the course of the 1967 conflict. This was the last time that the unarmored trainer served in the ground-attack role. Pilots of the Magisters during the Six Day War were, in many cases, highly experienced ex-fighter pilots who were considered too old by IDF/AF to pilot fighters. These were highly experienced men; they had to be to take the Magisters out on near-suicidal missions.

After the war, the number of Magisters in service continued to grow. By the end of 1971 there were 120, and a year later the number had increased to 150.

The Magisters in Israel have changed considerably from the original French machines, but changes, for the most part, are beneath the surface. A great many components that were originally of metal are now made of fiber glass. Areas where fiber glass has replaced metal include parts of the upper decking behind the canopy and portions of the air intake.

Experience gained in the construction of the Magister—the first aircraft actually built (though not designed) in Israel—has enabled Israel Aircraft Industries to build Westwinds, Aravas, and *Kfirs*.

The Ouragons still remained in service, though in steadily dwindling numbers. Two squadrons—about 40 aircraft—would remain on hand to participate in the Six Day War in 1967, attacking airfields, radar installations, and enemy armor. Indeed, *eighteen years after their initial delivery*, about 30 Ouragons were still available for use in the 1973 war. But soon after Suez it was clear to the *Chel Ha'Avir* planners that the Ouragon was neither the ideal ground-attack vehicle nor in any way capable of holding its own in air combat with the new Soviet fighters.

The Mystère IVA was also rapidly becoming obsolete. Sixty were on hand for the Six Day War, and they acquitted themselves well, mostly in the role of ground attackers. And, like the Ouragons, a few survived to fight again in 1973 (when, it is said, attrition among the remaining Mystères was very high). But even in 1956 it was already apparent that the days of the Mystère as an air superiority fighter were numbered.

In 1958 the deliveries of the supersonic MiG-19 to its hostile Arab neighbors created fresh problems for Israel. Although the IDF/AF had been outnumbered all along, its force of highly trained pilots and the marginal superiority of its Dassault Mystère IVA fighters had made up for an obvious numerical inferiority. Now this was changed. To redress the situation, Israel sought to obtain a fighter with a supersonic performance comparable to the then first-line Mach 1.4 MiG-19. Israel's options were severely limited.

The United States, which possessed several potent aircraft in its supersonic fighter arsenal, would not sell any to the Middle East nations. Great Britain had no supersonic fighters: they had cancelled the thin-wing Hunter, and the English Electric (now BAC) Lightning had not yet flown. Only France among the nations of West Europe had an aircraft with the performance needed by the *Chel Ha'Avir*.

The Dassault Super-Mystère was the first supersonic fighter of West Europe. The first prototype, designated the Super-Mystère B.1, flew on March 2, 1955, powered by a Rolls-Royce Avon RA.7R. It was followed by five Atar-powered B.2 models, the first of these flying on May 15, 1956. A production order was placed by the French air force for 200, but this was cut back to 180 because of the imminent Mirage with Mach 2.0 performance.

In late 1958, Israel ordered 24 Super-Mystère B.2 aircraft, which were delivered in short order. Equipping one squadron of the *Chel Ha'Avir*, the Super-Mystère made its public debut in a fly-past on Israel's Independence Day in May 1959.

Until the debut of the Mirage, the Super-Mystère was used in the role of interceptor, with some aircraft always on standby alert to climb after the MiGs which, from time to time, undertook reconnaissance missions over Israeli territory. In April 1967, Super-Mystères downed six Syrian MiG-21s, inflicting these losses on the superior-performing aircraft without loss to themselves.

In the 1967 Six Day War, the Super-Mystères were used in the initial attacks against Egyptian air bases and installations. In the course of that brief war, three aircraft were lost, including one which fell in combat with a MiG-21.

In common with other aircraft with supersonic capability, Super-Mystères suffered considerably from metal fatigue—a common affliction of aircraft equipped with afterburners. With the French embargo of military equipment to Israel after the Six Day War, serviceability of the Super-Mystère became a problem, mainly because of lack of parts for the SNECMA Atar 101G powerplant.

With the subsequent influx of A-4 Skyhawks and Pratt & Whitney J-52-P-8A engines (which powered them) a solution presented itself, one which required considerable rework of the French fighter. But during the 1969 War of Attrition the IDF/AF felt that whatever changes were necessary were warranted in order to keep the Super-Mystères in the air.

The French engine produced 7,500 pounds of static thrust and, with its afterburner operating, 9,900 pounds of thrust. By comparison, the Pratt & Whitney engine, which lacked an afterburner, produced 9,300 pounds of static thrust. As a result, although there was a slight loss in maximum power, fuel consumption of the American engine was much better.

With afterburner operating, the SNECMA engine "drank" fuel at the rate of 2.2 pounds per hour for every pound of thrust produced. With afterburner off, this consumption dropped to 1.07 to 1.1 pounds per hour for each pound of thrust. The Pratt & Whitney engine consumed only .86 pounds of fuel per pound of thrust per hour.

Since the American engine was about 22 percent lighter than the Atar 101G, the aft fuselage of the Super-Mystère had to be lengthened and the engine moved rearward to maintain the same center of gravity. The airplane was beefed up and the French avionics were replaced by more advanced American equipment.

Although the changes gave the Super-Mystère a new lease on life, steady attrition continued to eat into their numbers. At the outbreak of the 1973 Yom Kippur War, only 9 of the original 24 remained, and 3 of these were lost during the fighting. The survivors were refurbished and, early in 1977, were sold to Honduras. For nineteen years they had served Israel well.

But for the headlong pace of the Middle Eastern arms race, the Super-Mystère might today still be remembered as the best Israeli fighter plane of the Six Day War. That honor, however, must go to another plane, far superior to the Super-Mystère and destined, in Israeli hands, to become one of the most famous fighters in aviation history.

In 1958 the Israelis had acquired Super-Mystères to counter the threat posed by the MiG-19. By the beginning of the 1960s, however, a potential new threat was looming. The standard day-superiority fighter of the Soviet Bloc nations was rapidly becoming the deadly new MiG-21, and it seemed inevitable that this Mach 2 class warplane would soon be exported to Egypt and Syria. Since the Super-Mystère could not hope to compete with the new MiG, Israel now had to find a means of acquiring a plane that could. The cast-offs of other air forces would no longer do. What was needed was nothing less than the best machine the Western world could produce.

Once again Israel turned to France. Just then entering French service was a new delta-wing fighter known as the Dassault Mirage III. After much haggling and political maneuvering, the French somewhat reluctantly agreed to sell Israel 72 examples of this promising but as-yet-untried aircraft. The Mirage entered the *Chel Ha'Avir* service in May 1963, and that same month it was first shown publicly in an Independence Day fly-by over Jerusalem, Tel Aviv, and Haifa.

From the first the Mirage seemed an exciting machine. Its SNECMA Atar turbojet could, with afterburning, produce better than 13,000 pounds of static thrust, enough to drive the trim little fighter to a maximum speed of nearly 1,400 miles per hour. And despite its somewhat unconventional pure delta configuration (i.e., unlike the partial delta-form MiG, it had no horizontal tailplane), it proved to be remarkably maneuverable. Since the MiG-21 was still an unknown quantity, there was no way to be sure that the Mirage could compete with the Russian fighter, but the *Chel Ha'Avir* was encouraged to hope so.

At the time Israel purchased the Mirage, Dassault was offering several equipment options. One was an additional 3,372-pound thrust SEPR rocket motor that would not only assist the plane in making quick take-offs, but would give it brief extra bursts of sprint speed at high altitudes. Welcome as this augmentation of performance might have been, the Israelis decided against it. For one thing, the rocket motor controls would further crowd the already-cramped cockpit. More important, the fuel pack for the motor would displace ammunition for Israel's choice for the fighter's main offensive armament, two DEFA 30-mm cannon.

The Israeli decision to elect the option of cannon armament for their Mirages was regarded at the time as somewhat idiosyncratic. Most major air forces were then arming their latest jet fighters with air-to-air homing missiles. Conventional wisdom had decreed that cannon were outmoded, particularly if their retention meant reducing aircraft performance. But the Israelis were unfashionable enough to be suspicious of the current vogue for missiles. They were by no means sure that, as pundits were claiming, the day of the aerial dogfight was past. And if it were not, the Israelis wanted guns, not weapons intended for a style of warfare that still lay in the future. Subsequent events would fully endorse this decision.

Because the *Chel Ha'Avir* was always maintained on a semi-war footing, the Israelis soon logged more flying time on Mirages than the French Armée de l'Air itself. Thus most of the early technical improvements made in the machines derived from Israeli, rather than French, experience. It was found, for example that the landing gear struts had a tendency to develop fatigue cracks and that the afterburner seals allowed leakage of hot gases. Information and suggestions on these and a host of other "bugs" were relayed to France, whence Dassault engineers replied with a stream of modifying prescriptions. Not only the *Chel Ha'Avir* and the Armée de l'Air, but numerous future foreign customers for the Mirage reaped the benefits of this exchange.

Before the Israeli Mirages had a chance to fire their guns in anger, they were involved in a curious incident which has never been fully reported, but which, at the time, occasioned a certain amount of diplomatic tension. In July 1963 a United States Air Force RB-57A took off from its base in Saudi Arabia, its mission to overfly Israel and, with the "black boxes" in what would normally have been its bomb bay, electronically map Israel's radar defenses. The big American reconnaissance bomber headed west, climbing steadily until it was over the Red Sea, and then turning north. It continued to climb until it reached 50,000 feet.

The spy plane headed north over the Red Sea—Egypt to its left, Saudi Arabia to its right—continuing on course up the Gulf of Aqaba, the Sinai Peninsula beneath its port wing, until it crossed into Israeli air space near the port of Eilat. It remained at 50,000 feet, its pilot confident of avoiding interception by Israel's Super-Mystères. Then there were white contrails approaching fast. The twin-engined bomber banked, preparing to turn south. Too late!

Two delta-wing fighters flashed past. The bomber's pilot applied full throttle and continued south. One of the fighters, sporting a blue "Star of David" in a white roundel, posted itself menacingly behind the bomber. The other fighter fired its two 30-mm DEFA cannon at the spy plane. Tracers streaked across the RB-57A's nose. The plane dropped its landing gear, a sign of surrender. It had been caught. With one of the fighters buzzing by perilously close in a series of passes and the other behind the bomber in position to shoot it down if it attempted to escape, the American aircraft was led to Lod Airport. During the flight, the American pilot photographed the Mirages with a Polaroid Land camera and, upon landing, presented his captors with the photos.

The incident was an embarrassing one for the United States. It had been caught, red-handed, spying on a pro-West nation, a country which was the only democracy in the Middle East. Quickly, a cover story was concocted. The bomber, it was conceded, had flown over Israeli air space and had come from Saudi Arabia, but had suffered "engine trouble." What remained unanswered was how an airplane could maintain itself at 50,000 feet on a single engine! Israeli air force men, examining the plane, noted the special electronics gear in the belly of the reconnaissance bomber.

The Americans were lying. The Israelis *knew* the Americans were lying. The Americans *knew* the Israelis *knew* the Americans were lying. But, in the interests of American-Israeli harmony, the Israeli government accepted the story at face value. Its censors went to work and no mention of the incursion ever appeared in the press. It was as though the incident never took place. A few days later the RB-57A departed.

It was understandable that the United States underestimated Israel's defensive capabilities. The first two Mirages had been delivered in May, a scant two months earlier.

On another occasion, Israel had been overflown at very high altitude by a U-2 spy plane and Israel had lodged a formal complaint. The United States, at a loss as to how they had been spotted at so high an altitude, apologized. When an Israeli official was later asked how Israel knew the offending aircraft was American, he responded: "It was simple. Our radar picked it up. We went to *Jane's All the World's Aircraft* to find out what could fly at that speed and altitude."

It was plain that, with the advent of the Dassault Mirage into the IDF/AF inventory, nothing less than a U-2 could hope to venture over Israel with impunity.

In 1962, when Israel ordered the Dassault Mirage, preliminary Arab intelligence reports indicated that the order was for 40 aircraft.

The Soviet Union, in response to this, delivered 40 MiG-21F day interceptors to Egypt in the summer of 1962. When it was learned that the preliminary reports were short of the mark, additional MiG-21s were delivered until, on the eve of the 1967 war, Egypt had on hand 163 MiG-21s and 55 Sukhoi Su-7s as part of its force of 369 fighters.

How would the MiG-21 compare with the Mirage? Both were Mach 2 fighters, but little more was then known for certain, except that numbers were heavily on the side of Egypt. Then in August 1966, the mystery surrounding the MiG-21 was cleared up in a startling and unexpected manner when an Iraqi pilot defected to Israel in a late-model MiG-21F-13 (Fishbed-C), for which he received a considerable bounty.

Israeli pilots test-flew the MiG, entering into mock combat with their own Mirage delta-wing fighters. The weak points of the Soviet fighter were uncovered, the myths exposed. It was found to be un-derpowered, though fairly maneuverable, in both the subsonic and supersonic regimes, at high altitude. Although it possessed excellent acceleration—attained through its small size and aerodynamic re-finement rather than through a high-thrust engine—the MiG-21F was found to be very limited in range.

Armed with full knowledge of their major adversary, the Israeli pilots entered the 1967 Six Day War with considerable confidence. The source of this information was treated in accordance with its value. In addition to its Israeli markings, it was given a coat of bright red trim and, whimsically, the code number "007" after James Bond, the fictional British spy.

At the time that Israel purchased 72 Mirage III CJ single-seat fighters, in 1962, an additional three two-seat Mirage III B trainers were ordered. Lacking only the cannon armament of its single-seat sisters, the Mirage III B was capable of carrying the same complement of external stores and armaments with the same performance poten-tial. The Mirage III B was approximately two feet longer to accommo-date the additional crewman.

The Mirage III BJ trainers served the same squadrons as the single-seat aircraft rather than being held back for the purely trainer role. The "J" suffix, incidentally, indicates to the French the aircraft's purchaser, the "J" standing for "juif," or Jew (the Mirage III EP indi-cates that the aircraft is a Mirage III E purchased by Pakistan, the Mirage III EL is for Lebanon, the III S for Switzerland, etc.).

In 1967 the Israeli Mirage III Bs were part of the strike force. They were again in operation in the 1973 war. It is believed that at least one, and possibly two, are still in service.

The war ended with 66 Mirages still on hand. But there would be no replacements. French foreign policy, which had begun to swing toward the Arab side when Charles deGaulle came to power, had become firm on a pro-Arab stance, a position which has become stronger with the passage of time.

An Israeli order for 50 Mirage 5 fighters was embargoed, with France refusing delivery of the completed aircraft for which they had received payment in full. Eventually, the money was refunded to Israel and the aircraft retained by the Armée de L'Air. One hundred ten Mirages, however, were sold to Libya. Of these, 36 were later transferred to Egypt and served against Israel in the 1973 war.

High performance warplanes were not Israel's only need, however. The 1956 Suez Campaign convinced Israeli planners that a need existed for a large troop-carrying helicopter to supplement the Dakotas and Noratlas transports which were used for paratroop operations. Six Sikorsky S-55s were therefore obtained and evaluated by the IDF/AF. One weakness quickly developed: Although the S-55 was rugged enough for troop operations, when it was deployed operationally in Israel's scorching Negev Desert, the air-cooled 700 horsepower was insufficiently powerful. Having discovered this, the IDF obtained seven Sikorsky S-58 helicopters directly from the United States in 1959. An additional 24 were diverted from Germany to Israel in 1960. Only slightly larger than the S-55, the Sikorsky S-58 was able to carry much larger loads, due to the installation of a 1,525-horsepower engine. With the arrival of S-58s, the S-55s were used for air-sea rescue work and for operations in the north and central parts of Israel, where the heat wasn't normally as severe as in the desert.

The S-55, S-58, Bell 47G and, later the Sud Super Frelon were formed into a helicopter group. Sikorsky S-58 helicopters were used for close support duties, commando strike operations, and casualty evacuation duties. American helicopter tactics in Vietnam were studied and applied to anti-terrorist operations. In addition, the S-58s were used to transport cargo both internally and with the use of external slings. In the latter method, damaged war equipment, such as jeeps, were hoisted and flown back for repair during the 1967 Six Day War.

During the 1967 war, S-58 helicopters flew paratroopers in battalion strength against fortified Syrian bunkers and artillery positions on the Golan Heights. Whenever a pilot was down, all other duties were dropped in order to affect a rescue by helicopter. On the Egyptian front, an S-58 that was evacuating wounded during the Six Day War was attacked by two MiG-21s. The pilot took evasive action but, because of the wounded that he was carrying, these were of necessity restricted. Finally, to avoid his attackers, the pilot landed in a palm grove. This tactic was not particularly surprising, since Israeli helicopter pilots are given courses in fighter avoidance tactics.

Typical cargoes for S-58s on logistic support missions included a ton of fuel in jerry cans for armored vehicles, or small arms and tank ammunition, jeeps, mortars, and so forth. One-ton cargoes were normally carried, using external slings. For medical evacuation work, the S-58s were fitted with folding litters for eight wounded and space for a doctor and an aide.

The French Super Frelon was a helicopter type that was to prove valuable to the *Chel Ha'Avir*. The Israelis had had an earlier, relatively unsuccessful experience with French helicopters. Shortly after the Suez Campaign they had ordered five Sud-Aviation Alouette II helicopters and 15 Alouette III rotorcraft for evaluation, but neither aircraft proved up to operating in desert conditions, and both were, in any event, too small to be very useful. In fact, prior to the advent of the S-58s and Frelons, the *Chel Ha'Avir* had been obliged to train its cadres of future helicopter pilots in hardy little three-seater Bell Model 47Gs imported from the United States.

The Super Frelon helicopter, an outgrowth of the lower-power Frelon, first flew in 1964—the largest helicopter to be developed in France. Initially, it was available in the SA 321G amphibious model for anti-submarine duty and the non-amphibious SA 321K transport model. This version can carry 27 to 30 fully equipped troops or up to 9,920 pounds of cargo.

Israel opted for the SA 321K, and the twelve Super Frelons ordered were delivered in 1966, in time for operations during the Six Day War. Super Frelons made a major contribution by hoisting artillery and troops to the rear of Syrian positions on the Golan Heights, in effect setting up two fronts against the strategically located fortifications. Without the Super Frelons, Israeli casualties would have been far higher in their successful conquest of the Golan.

In addition to heavy cargo carrying work, Super Frelons have been used to carry commandos. An example of such use by the IDF/AF was the commando assault on the island of Shadwan during the 1969 War of Attrition. Israeli commandos, flown in by Super Frelons, held the island for 36 hours, while Soviet-supplied radar gear was flown back to Israel.

Super Frelons also played a key role in the 1973 Yom Kippur War, when Israel was attacked on two fronts. The large rotorcraft were vital in shuttling material to the Egyptian front after the Syrian drive against the Israeli Golan Heights positions had been blunted.

Of the twelve Super Frelons originally purchased, nine remain in use. French hostility toward Israel, coupled with the influx of the larger Sikorsky S-65 helicopters, make it unlikely that additional Super Frelons will be ordered.

In the early sixties, the *Chel Ha'Avir* also began to modernize its other utility aircraft. What was needed, planners recognized, was a rugged aircraft, not unlike the Piper Super Cubs in IDF/AF inventory, but larger and faster, with better all-round performance. The aircraft ordered was the Cessna Model 185 Skywagon, which the USAF had ordered for itself as the U-17.

The Model 185 had fixed landing gear and tail wheel. Following introduction of this type, which was used for liaison and light transport duties, the IDF/AF ordered the Model 205. Aside from minor design differences such as swept vertical tail, the Model 205 differed from the 185 by utilizing fixed tricycle gear. Although this reduced top speed by a couple of miles per hour, it made the aircraft better suited to medical evacuation work, since a litter would remain level in the ground attitude. Both models mount a fiber glass cargo pack beneath the belly. The Cessnas are in widespread use in the IDF/AF, supplemented by other types primarily where certain operational requirements (such as STOL performance) must be met.

The Swiss Pilatus Turbo-Porter, which flew for the first time on May 2, 1961, as a turboprop development of the piston-engined Porter, was brought to Israel in July 1963. In the scorching midsummer heat, the Turbo-Porter demonstrated corkscrew climbs and maneuvers which were not dimmed by the elevated temperatures that sap the power of conventional piston-engine aircraft. The Ministry of Defence was sufficiently impressed with the single-engined seven-passenger utility transport to buy the aircraft (c/n 529, with Swiss registration HB-FBB) on the spot and place a follow-on order for additional aircraft. Turbo-Porters have remained in service since then. With seats removed, the Turbo-Porter can carry almost a ton of cargo and can also be used to evacuate wounded.

In the early 1960s it was painfully apparent that a need existed within the IDF/AF for a long-range strategic transport. A glance at a map made it clear that, if hostilities with surrounding Arab countries again broke out, Israel's enemies, which possessed powerful Russian-supplied naval vessels and long-range bombers, could conceivably interdict surface shipping to Israel. In that event, military supplies could be brought in only by air. Other requirements existed for air-to-air refueling, heavy cargo drops, and so on, which could not be fulfilled by the transports in the Israeli inventory.

The medium-sized Dakotas and Noratlases were still being used to the best of their abilities. The Noratlases, particularly, were used for shuttle flights between Europe and Israel, and during the Six Day War they continued to perform valuable paradrop operations. (One such Noratlas, used in commando operations against terrorist bases in Syria, bore a special nonstandard camouflage scheme* of medium gray/dark gray upper surfaces.) In fact, the Noratlases are *still* in use today, but by the end of the Suez Campaign it was already plain that an altogether larger transport type would also be needed.

The ideal aircraft to fulfill the projected role was the Lockheed C-130 transport. The Ministry of Defence therefore approached the United States with a view to obtaining these aircraft, but were rebuffed at that time. Clearly, a substitute was required. And this substitute proved to be the Stratocruiser.

While the United States government would not furnish Boeing C-97 aircraft to Israel, there was a way around this embargo. In order to understand what came next, it is necessary to know something about the background of the Stratocruiser.

The Stratocruiser had its origins with the Boeing B-29 Superfortress of World War II fame. In 1942, a year after development work had begun on the B-29, design work began on a transport version, incorporating the engines, wing, and empennage of the bomber. In order to increase the fuselage volume without going to a completely new design, Boeing engineers designed a "double bubble" fuselage, where the lower—smaller diameter—section was the basic B-29 fuselage of circular cross-section.

On January 9, 1945, the first XC-97 flew across the United States, a distance of 2,323 miles, with a 20,000-pound payload. Ten more aircraft were ordered by the air force, the first six as YC-97 aircraft, followed by C97s up to full production standards. Full production standards, in this instance, meant the use of B-50 engines, wing and tail surfaces. The B-29 had been found to be underpowered, so its Wright R-3350 engines were replaced by the more powerful Pratt & Whitney R-4360. This in turn necessitated the beefing up of the wing structure, including addition of hard points on the wing, and larger tail surfaces to accommodate the additional power.

After the close of the Second World War, Boeing engineers adapted the C-97 to civilian use, with 55 aircraft built and delivered to Pan American World Airways, Northwest Airlines, and BOAC between January 1949 and March 1950. The commercial Stratocruisers differed from their military counterparts. The heavy-duty cargo floors

---

*See Appendix V.

were removed and replaced with a lighter structure for lower density cargo—in this case, passengers. Passenger seats were installed and the cargo loading doors beneath the tail were deleted. Cargo doors on the fuselage side were omitted and more windows were cut into the fuselage to increase passenger comfort.

Since Israel was unable to purchase the military C-97 Stratocruiser, the Ministry of Defence decided to purchase the civilian aircraft and modify it to military standards. As a result, ten aircraft were purchased from Pan American which, having shifted to Boeing 707 jetliners, had no need for the piston-engined airliners.

The changes to the Stratocruiser that were envisioned included adding the deleted clamshell cargo doors beneath the tail, installing a heavy-duty cargo floor, and installing a "swing tail" for large cargo on some aircraft, this last inspired by the Canadair CL-44D-4, a cargo version of the Bristol Brittania. To reduce the amount of actual work required, entire C-97 aft fuselages, together with empennage, were purchased.

Before the Stratocruisers were actually delivered, the Ministry of Defence decided to undertake a feasibility study and obtained one of the original YC-97 "small tail" Stratocruisers which, in itself, had a most interesting history.

When the Belgian Congo received its independence, the mineral-rich province of Katanga attempted to break away from the rest of the Congo. This effort was led by Moise Tshombe. A company in Luxembourg, using the YC-97, flew military equipment in to the breakaway province to be used by mercenaries fighting with the Katangese. The YC-97 suceeded in flying considerable amounts of weaponry into Katanga, including two CM-70 Fouga Magister jets armed with machine guns. The Stratocruiser was finally impounded by the United Nations, dropping from sight until it reappeared one day in Israel, to be used as the guinea pig for the feasibility tests. After tests were successfully completed by Israel Aircraft Industries personnel, the aircraft was scrapped, its component parts being strewn about the IAI scrap heap at the airport in Lod.

The Stratocruisers, capable of carrying 96 combat troops, added a new dimension to the capabilities of Israel's air force. They were used for in-flight refueling during the 1967 operation. Some paradropped heavy cargo to Israeli armored units during the six-day operation. During the War of Attrition in 1969 and 1970, some were adopted for ECM duties and, in this role, one aircraft was destroyed by a SAM missile some twelve miles from the Suez Canal. Additional C-97s, surplus to USAF needs, have augmented the number of commercial Stratocruisers.

While the Stratocruisers have been overshadowed in recent years by the Lockheed C-130 transports which Israel finally obtained from the United States, the old Stratocruisers continue to function and will no doubt remain in service for a number of years.

Israel also got some Arab Aircraft during this period. These usually fell into Israeli hands intact. Most came when Arab pilots defected from their own air forces and sought asylum in Israel. The aircraft which Israel received in this way ranged from small training craft to the latest fighter aircraft in the Arab arsenal. In the latter case, evaluation of the flying characteristics proved invaluable and the lessons learned became part of the training of the combat pilots of the *Chel Ha'Avir*.

There was the Bucker Bestmann, for example. First produced in 1939, it was used by the Luftwaffe as a primary trainer throughout World War II. After the War it was manufactured in Czechoslovakia as the Zlin Z-281 and Z-381. Egypt decided to adopt it as a primary trainer and production was undertaken at the aircraft facility at Heliopolis. Two versions were produced, the first equipped with a Walter Minor engine and designated the Gomhouria Mk. 1, the second built with a Continental C 145 engine as the Mk. 2. In the mid-Sixties an Egyptian pilot defected to Israel in a Gomhouria, landing at an Israeli base in the Negev. For a short while this curiosity was operated by the IDF/AF as an all-purpose ship.

In 1965 Pilot Officer Chilmey of the Egyptian air force defected to Israel in a Yak-11 basic trainer. The aircraft was forced down by Israeli fighters at a military air base in the Negev Desert. After inspection and evaluation, the trainer was used as a "hack" ship until lack of spares grounded it permanently. For some unknown reason, when Israel announced the defection, Chilmey's aircraft was incorrectly referred to as a "Yak-18."

What of Chilmey? Like other defecting pilots, he was paid a bounty by the Israelis, provided with a new identity, and allowed to leave Israel. Chilmey went to Buenos Aires and settled there in his new identity. However, he was unable to refrain from boasting and, in doing so, he revealed his true identity. As a result, he was murdered in Buenos Aires by persons believed to be Egyptian agents.

It is the wish of every air force to be in a position to test-fly combat aircraft that is in service with the enemy, to probe for hidden weaknesses in design and performance that could be exploited if they were known. Not often can such a wish be fulfilled. In 1956 a MiG-17 was discovered in the Great Bitter Lake, a victim of aerial combat during the Suez Campaign. A salvage operation was mounted and the aircraft recovered. Immersion in the salt water had made the aircraft unflyable, however. Almost a decade passed before the IDF/AF had the opportunity to evaluate a MiG-17 in the air.

In 1965 a Syrian pilot defected to Israel aboard a MiG-17. Several months later Israeli interceptors forced seven Syrian MiG-17s to land at a military airfield in the north after they had penetrated Israeli air space; subsequently, the Syrian pilots and five of the MiGs were returned to Syria in exchange for Israelis held in Syrian prisons. The remaining three MiG-17s, in Israeli camouflage and markings and broad identification striping, were incorporated into a special unit. During the 1967 Six Day War, the three MiGs were used against targets in Syria. After the war, lack of spare parts for the Soviet-built aircraft finally resulted in their grounding and they are no longer in service with Israel.

As has been mentioned earlier, Israel had already gotten hold of a MiG-21 prior to the 1967 war. But during the war, another plum, in the form of a flight of six MiG-21s, fell into Israel's lap when their Algerian pilots landed at El Arish in the Sinai Desert. They had believed radio reports of Israeli defeats at the hands of Egyptian armed forces and were surprised to find themselves prisoners of the advancing Israeli troops.

After the war, four of the MiG-21s were turned over to the United States and were flown to America in C-130s for extensive testing at Wright-Patterson Air Force Base. Because of the secrets that it yielded, the MiG-21 was more valuable to Israel than many aircraft which actually were in Israeli service.

7

THE
SIX DAY
WHIRLWIND

THE SIX DAY WAR ITSELF WAS EVERYTHING THAT DAN
Tolkovski had predicted future conflicts would and should be for the
Chel Ha'Avir. His creation was ready, and it did its job with such
dispatch and efficiency that even experienced observers of military
aviation were stunned by the quick results the Israelis achieved. Tolkovski himself, however, was not in command.

In 1958 Dan Tolkovski had retired and was replaced as C-in-C
by Ezer Weizman. Weizman, an ex-RAF pilot, had been one of the
first fighter pilots of 101 Squadron, later becoming its squadron
leader. He continued the policies of Tolkovski, emphasizing, as did
his predecessor, training to the point of perfection. Also, it was during Weizman's tenure that Israel, with the Mirage, achieved qualitative parity with the fighter planes owned by her enemies. In 1965 Ezer
Weizman stepped down as C-in-C of the IDF/AF, to be replaced by
Mordechai Hod. Weizman became head of operations and, in that
capacity, was responsible for planning the tactics which were to be
employed in the 1967 Six Day War.

One of the immediate causes of the 1967 Six Day War dates back
to 1953, when President Eisenhower sent Eric Johnston as a special
envoy to the Middle East. Johnston devised a means of dividing the
waters of the Jordan River for irrigation purposes, alloting percen-
tages to Israel and the Arab countries bordering the river and its
arteries. Jordan began a project to divert waters from the Yarmuk
River, which fed the Sea of Galilee, the source of the Jordan River.
Israel, too, began plans to divert her share of the water in order to
irrigate the arid Negev Desert.

In June 1961 the Arab Defence Council stated that Israel's diversion of the waters would be cause for a united military action against the Jewish state. Rather than attack Israel directly, the Council decided to divert all the water from feeders entering the Sea of Galilee, to establish a joint command to defend the diversion projects, and to foment agitation through the creation of an organization which they named the Palestine Liberation Organization. Early in 1965, *fedayeen* of the PLO, under the sponsorship of Syria, undertook sabotage activities in Israel. For their part, the Syrians began construction on the project to divert the Jordan River waters. In retaliation, Israel struck at the project with fighter-bombers of the IDF/AF and with artillery. Syria attempted to defend the project with its own air force.

On April 7, 1967, there was a large-scale dogfight over the Sea of Galilee in which seven MiGs were shot down without loss to *Chel Ha'Avir*'s Mirages. The air battle increased tensions. Infiltration and terror raids by *fedayeen* were stepped up.

The final straw was a false intelligence report supplied to Egypt's Nasser by the Soviet Union. According to the report, Israel was planning an attack against Syria. The report also claimed that Israel had already massed troops on the Syrian frontier and was poised to attack. Radio Moscow also broadcast in Arabic that the United States had been involved in the aerial engagement against Syria on April 7 and that a fighter manned by an American had been shot down, with its pilot taken prisoner by the Syrians. The Soviets also claimed that Israel, with the help of West German experts, was planning to launch a poison gas attack against Syria. Abdul Gamal Nasser accepted—or professed to accept—these Russian claims as fact. Egypt had dropped poison gas canisters from aircraft during the civil war in Yemen so, to Nasser, there appeared to be a ring of logic in the claim.

Israel invited U.N. Secretary-General U Thant to the Israeli-Syrian border and a statement was made by the Secretary-General to the effect that there were no Israeli troop concentrations. The Israeli Premier, Levi Eshkol, gave his assurances that no military moves were planned by Israel. Nasser, however, took this as a sign of weakness on the part of Israel and prepared an escalation of tension. On May 14, 1967, the Egyptian army was mobilized. The Soviet ambassador to Egypt, Dimitri Zhubakhin, a KGB officer, assured Nasser that Israel was weak and would be unable to respond to Egyptian pressure.

On May 15, Egyptian troops began to move in force into the Sinai Peninsula toward the border with Israel. In response, Israel mobilized an armored reserve brigade. The move toward the confrontation that neither side wanted had begun.

The act which made war almost inevitable came on May 16 when Nasser ousted U.N. troops in the Sinai, which since 1956 had acted as a buffer. Simultaneously, Syria and Jordan mobilized their forces. Jordanian Patton tanks, which had been supplied by the United States to Jordan with the stipulation that they be kept away from the border with Israel, were ordered to the front. In the Gaza strip, the U.N. flag was lowered, to be replaced by the flag of the PLO. Then, on May 20, the Egyptians dropped an airborne battalion at Sharm el Sheikh and Nasser announced that the Straits of Tiran were closed to ships bound for Israel. This blockade was the first direct act of war. By May 22, 70,000 Egyptian troops, supported by tanks and artillery, were at their stations in Sinai. MiG fighter squadrons at El Arish were reinforced.

Nasser, in announcing the naval blockade, had said: "Israel does not today have Britain and France as she did in 1956. We stand face to face with Israel. The Jews threaten war and we say to them, 'Welcome! Come forth!' " There has been much subsequent speculation about Nasser's motives. Did he really want war or was he bluffing? Did he expect Israel to do nothing in the face of the blockade? Whatever the truth may be, it is certain that by leaving Israel no options he made war unavoidable.

On May 26, 1967, Nasser's close friend, the editor of the semi-official newspaper *Al Ahram*, wrote: "There is no alternative to armed clash between the United Arab Republic and the Israeli enemy. . . . In Israel's defense philosophy the blocking of the Straits is the Achilles' Heel on which Israel's existence depends."

At this hour of crisis, Israel stood alone. England and France refused to stand behind the 1956 guarantees of peace in the Middle East. West Germany and the United States would take no stand on the blockade. On June 3 France declared that an arms embargo was in effect for Middle Eastern countries. Since Egypt and Syria were supplied with arms from the Soviet Union and only Israel was the recipient of French arms, Israel was the only nation to be affected by the French action.

By now, there were 100,000 Egyptian troops in the Sinai, supported by 1,000 tanks. Algeria, Sudan, and Kuwait sent small contingents of troops to fight beside the Egyptians. The situation had snowballed and Nasser, carried along by the tide of events, could no longer bluff.

Egyptian commandos were flown to Jordan, while Iraqi troops moved into Jordan, poised for attack against Israel. Iraqi fighter aircraft flew to air bases in Jordan. Israel could wait no longer. There would be no help from the rest of the world and the Arab invasion forces were growing stronger and more confident with each passing day. In the air alone, the Arabs had an overwhelming superiority in numbers, the combined forces of Egypt, Jordan, Syria, Iraq, and Lebanon being 969 aircraft, some 650 of which were fighters.Israel's total was 354, of which only 196 were fighters. Table 1 gives a breakdown of air strengths as of June 1, 1967.

TABLE 1: AIR FORCE STRENGTHS

Type	On hand June 1, 1967	Losses	On hand June 30, 1967 (includes Russian replacement of Arab losses)
Israel			
Dassault Ouragon (2 squadrons)	40	3	37
Dassault Mystère IV (3 squadrons)	60	8	52
Dassault Super-Mystère (1 squadron)	24	3	21
Dassault Mirage III CJ (3 squadrons)	72	6	66
Sud Vautour II (1 squadron)	25	5	20
Fouga Magister (2 squadrons)	76	6	70
Nord Noratlas	20	1	19
Boeing Stratocruiser	5	—	5
Douglas C-47	10	—	10
Super Frelon	6	—	6
Sikorsky S-55	2	—	2
Sikorsky S-58	12	—	12
Alouette II	2	—	2
Total	354	32	322
Total fighters	196	20	176
Egypt			
MiG-15/17 (5 squadrons)	150	75	75
MiG-19 (4 squadrons)	80	20	120
MiG-21 (6 squadrons)	120	90	120
Sukhoi Su-7M (1 squadron)	30	12	18
Ilyushin Il-28 (3 squadrons)	40	27	13
Tupolev Tu-16 (2 squadrons)	30	30	24
Antonov An-12 (1 squadron)	20	6	14
Ilyushin Il-14 (2 squadrons)	70	19	51
Douglas C-47 (1 squadron)	8	—	8
Mi-4	10	1	9
Mi-6	12	6	6
Mi-8	10	—	10
Total	580	286	468
Total fighters	380	197	333

Jordan

De Havilland Vampire F.B.5	8	2	6
(1 squadron)			
Hawker Hunter F.6	21	21	—
(1 squadron)			
Lockheed F-104A	5	—	5
De Havilland Dove	6	4	2
Scout	3	—	3
Whirlwind	4	—	4
Alouette III	3	1	2
Miscellaneous	6	—	6
Total	56	28	28
Total fighters	34	23	11

Syria

MiG-15/17 (4 squadrons)	100	20	80
MiG-21 (2 squadrons)	36	30	6
Ilyushin Il-28 (1 squadron)	6	2	4
Ilyushin Il-14	10	2	8
Douglas C-47	6	—	6
Mi-1	4	—	4
Mi-4	10	—	10
Total	172	54	118
Total fighters	136	50	86

Iraq

MiG-17	20	—	20
MiG-19	15	—	15
MiG-21	20	12	8
Hawker Hunter Mk. 59	33	5	28
Il-28	10	3	7
Tu-16	12	1	11
An-12	10	—	10
Il-14	10	—	10
Mi-1	4	—	4
Mi-4	9	—	9
Westland Wessex	6	—	6
Total	149	21	128
Total fighters	88	17	71

Lebanon

Hawker Hunter F.6 (1 squadron)	12	1	11
TOTAL ARAB AIRCRAFT	969	390	753
TOTAL ARAB			
FIGHTER AIRCRAFT	650	288	512

It was in view of this overwhelming disproportion that Israel elected to pursue the strategy of the preemptive strike in order to win mastery of the skies. There was no prior guarantee that it would be carried out effectively or, even if it could be, that it would bring Israel ultimate victory. But every other alternative promised certain defeat.

On the morning of June 5, 1967, the air force of Israel made history. In one day it won the most decisive aerial victory ever recorded for such a brief period. In a lightning strike against the Egyptian airfields, Israel shattered her enemy's air force. Wave after wave of planes attacked. Turnaround time back at base was an unbelievable seven minutes—seven minutes to refuel the aircraft, reload guns, and place rockets or bombs on the racks! As a wave of aircraft approached its targets, a second wave was on its way back and a third wave was on the ground and about to take off again. It is no wonder that Nasser, knowing the approximate size of Israel's air force, was convinced that the *Chel Ha'Avir* had received massive reinforcements from another country.

Israeli aircraft flew as many as eight sorties a day. Egypt was capable of no more than two sorties per day per aircraft. The Jordanian and Syrian air forces were quickly smashed. By the end of the first day of combat, over 350 Arab aircraft were ruined. Egypt alone suffered almost 300 aircraft lost at seventeen airfields. Dummy aircraft scattered at different points were left untouched. By the end of the Six Day War, the Arab countries had lost 390 aircraft of all types.

Virtually every front-line type of Israeli combat plane was used in the strike on the enemy airfields—Vautours, Mystères, Super-Mystères, Ouragons, and Mirages. So sudden and devastating was the initial attack that relatively little air-to-air combat had a chance to develop during the first day, but in one brief dogfight that took place over Abu Sueir sixteen Mirages made short work of a force of about twenty Egyptian MiG-21s which quickly disengaged after losing four of their aircraft. In the days that followed the Israeli Mirage was repeatedly to demonstrate its decisive superiority over Arab-piloted MiG-21s and Sukhoi Su-7 fighter/ground-attack aircraft. One IDF/AF Mirage pilot is credited with having downed five enemy fighters in just two days. In all, only six Mirages were lost during the war, five of them to ground fire. The sole Mirage to fall in air combat was downed in an unequal contest against eight Egyptian MiGs. The international reputation of the suave little French fighter soared; soon Dassault would be flooded with foreign orders.

The war against Egypt was won in two hours and fifty minutes. Another hour was all that was necessary to smash five airfields in Syria, two in Jordan, and one in Iraq.

Delayed action bombs kept the enemy airfields out of action. Only El Arish's runways were spared. Before long, they would be host to the IDF/AF. With the Arab forces demolished, the *Chel Ha'Avir* turned its attention to the enemy armored forces. In the clear, cloud-less skies over Syria and Jordan and the Sinai, Israeli aircraft swooped down to deal with Arab strong points. Jordan's Arab Legion at-tempted to withstand the thrust of Israeli tanks, only to have napalm, phosphorus, and high-explosive bombs, rockets, and fragmentation bombs slaughter men and armor.

This had been a gigantic gamble, a move unprecedented in avia-tion history. Israel risked its future as a nation on a single toss of the dice. Almost every available combat aircraft in the nation was launched in attacks on the enemy. Only eight fighter aircraft were retained for the defense of the nation. Had the aerial armada met with disaster, Israel's enemies—already prepared for war—would cer-tainly have triumphed.

Why did Israel take such a dangerous chance? Part of the reason was the belief then that there was no other way to survive. No words can now convey the desperate feelings and passions of that time. Daily, Israelis had heard Radio Cairo threaten them. And they knew these threats were not just bluffs. The Arabs had giant armies liberally supplied with armor and under a unified command.

Egypt alone had 1,200 armored vehicles, including 450 modern T-54 main battle tanks, 350 T-34s, 60 Stalin JS-3 heavy tanks, 150 SU-100 tank destroyers, and 30 Centurions. There were 150,000 troops available, backed by 120,000 reservists. An additional 40,000 were mired in the bloody civil war in Yemen. Syria had 300 T-55 tanks and 82,000 troops; Iraq's 80,000-man army had 320 tanks, both British and Russian, while Jordan's highly trained army had 125 tanks (85 M-47 Pattons and 40 Centurions). Total Arab manpower on the ground amounted to half a million men and almost 2,000 armored vehicles. Against these, Israel's ground troops number only 50,000 plus 200,000 reservists supported by 850 armored vehicles (250 mod-ern Centurions and 200 M-48 tanks, and 200 Sherman tanks of World War II vintage plus about 100 self-propelled artillery vehicles). On top of this, the Arabs had more than three times as many supersonic fighters as Israel. In addition they had numbers of heavy jet bombers; Israel had none.

The great gamble paid off. On the very first day of the Six Day War the IDF/AF destroyed some 350 Arab aircraft, 300 of which were Egyptian. Some 79 of these were shot down; the rest, which included all Egyptian Tupolev Tu-16 heavy bombers, were smashed as they sat at their airfields preparing to take off to destroy Israel's planes and soldiers.

For this victory Israel paid a price. She lost 50 aircraft, mostly to ground fire, and 20 of her superbly trained pilots. But the Arabs never recovered and their ground forces were smashed by slashing attacks of the Israeli army supported by the *Chel Ha'Avir* which ruled the skies.

When it was over, Israel was jubilant, and her air force basked in a glow of euphoria. No air force in history had ever achieved such a victory in a single day. Surely, now, peace would come, for a foe so beaten would never dare challenge Israel again.

But, again, the total defeat of the Arab armies failed to secure ultimate peace. The Soviet Union saw to that by immediately resupplying the Arab countries, more than making up for losses. The remaining MiG-17s and MiG-19s were replaced with MiG-21s and Sukhoi Su-7s, while T-54 and T-55 tanks replaced T-34 tanks. There was no need for the Arab countries to negotiate a permanent peace for the Middle East and no desire to do so. The agony would go on.

CLAWS OF
THE LION
1967–1978

8

COSTLY VICTORIES

AN ISRAELI PILOT WAS JUST PREPARING TO PUT HIS MIRAGE into a dive and a strafing run when a gaggle of MiGs appeared in the blue skies over the Sinai. It was a clear day, bright and sunny, and the Israeli could make out the markings on the MiGs. Not that he needed to. Such planes were sure to be Egyptian.

The nose of the Mirage lifted, its 30-mm cannon ready to send a burst of shells into any MiG that crossed their muzzles. Other Mirages were doing the same. The Israelis were confident. They, after all, were still the better pilots.

The Israeli tossed his little plane around, finally getting on the tail of one MiG. But the Egyptian pilot was disconcertingly good. The Israeli cursed as he tried to hang onto the Egyptian plane, firing brief bursts of his cannon, but missing each time. This kind of thing had been happening more and more often of late: the Israeli pilots were having to work harder to knock enemy planes out of the sky.

The Israeli pilot gritted his teeth in frustration as another burst from his cannon missed. He took a deep breath and tried to settle himself down. This one was going to take more doing than most he had faced. With his free hand he reached over to the radio panel and flipped a selector switch to the Egyptian air-to-air frequency. Then, in flawless Arabic, he shouted into his headset microphone, "Break left! Break left!"

Obediently the MiG skidded into a violent left turn—just in time to collide with the lethal cluster of 30-mm cannon shells that the Israeli pilot had thoughtfully placed in its way. The Israeli had won the victory, but it had been a near thing.

Dogfights like this one were symptomatic of the changed military conditions that followed the Six Day War. Israel had won a great victory, not only in the air but on the ground. She had more territory under her control than she could possibly manage with her small army, but some of it was very valuable in both a strategic and tactical sense. Further, some of it was land which many Israelis had long considered a historic part of the ancient Jewish state, and thus a rightful part of the modern Jewish state.

In the north, Syrian troops had been driven from the Golan Heights, mountains which overlooked the plains of Israel and from which the Syrians had constantly shelled and harassed Jewish farms and settlements. In the central part of the country, Israeli troops had taken possession of a large, rectangular section on the west bank of the Jordan river and now stood guard on the river's banks. This meant that the entire holy city of Jerusalem was now in Jewish hands and that the country's midsection was no longer a narrow strip of land between the sea and Arab armies.

But it was in the south that Israel had overrun truly vast amounts of territory. The entire Sinai was in her grasp, and her troops now stood on the banks of the Suez Canal, a blocked waterway now choked with the rusting hulks of vessels between which others were trapped. And across that narrow canal were the Egyptians, angry, bitter, licking their terrible wounds and vowing vengeance. It was another ironic situation. Having won all this territory with numerically inferior but hard-hitting mobile forces supported by aircraft, Israel hardly had the means to hang onto it.

Israel's army and air force had never been designed for anything but a war of rapid movement, slashing thrusts and quick victories. That she had won such victories in the past was in itself a miracle of training, organization, and determination. But now she was faced with a stalemate, a front line separated from the enemy by a narrow ditch, and an enemy beyond it who had suffered defeat but had not surrendered. Further, behind Israel's front line lay vast miles of territory and Israel could occupy only key segments of it, such as vital passes and some oil fields.

Thus, paradoxically, Israel's stunning victory in the Six Day War had left her with a new set of liabilities. Her military establishment was not well-suited to defend the territory she had won; and it was doubtful that she could rely on the strategy of preemption to work for her again in a future conflict, for the Arabs, having been twice burned, were not likely to be caught napping a third time.

To complicate matters further, France, on whom Israel had in the past depended so heavily for new weapons, now made a diplomatic *volte-face* toward the Arabs, laying down an embargo on shipments of military equipment of all sorts to Israel. The immediate effect of this policy was the cancellation by France of an Israeli order for 50 new Mirage 5 jets, as well as for spare parts for the Mirage III, some Super Frelon helicopters, and some missile gunboats.

No one understood the new difficulties confronting Israel better than the Arabs, and they set about confecting a strategy that would exploit these difficulties to the fullest. In 1969 Egypt's Abdul Gamal Nasser invoked what he called a "War of Attrition" against Israeli forces lodged on the east bank of the Suez Canal. More than 1,000 pieces of Egyptian artillery were brought up to the Canal and began a methodical shelling of Israeli positions. To protect the artillery replacements against Israeli air attack, the Egyptians deployed a new and deadly anti-aircraft weapon: the Soviet-supplied SA-2 (SAM-2) ground-to-air missile.

Israel, unable to match Egypt's vast arsenal of Soviet-supplied artillery, sought to use her aircraft as flying artillery, but the SAMs on the west bank of the Suez made that an expensive proposition. It was plain that, if the artillery was to be silenced, the SAMs had to be dealt with first. The duel between SAMs and aircraft was bitter, with losses to both sides. But there was a difference. Egypt, with Russian backing, had an almost unlimited supply of missiles, whereas, because of the French embargo, each aircraft lost to the deadly SAMs, or *Tillim* (telephone poles) in Israeli parlance, was irreplaceable. Unless an alternate source of aircraft was found, such a conflict could have but one conclusion.

Besides France, there were only three Western countries—Sweden, England, and the United States—which produced aircraft which could be used. Sweden, which was strictly neutral, would not supply any of her Draken fighters. England's Hawker Hunter fighter was subsonic and could easily be intercepted by the Mach 2 MiG-21s in Egyptian service, and the newer British BAC Lightning was not considered suitable because of range and armaments limitations. This left only the United States.

At this critical juncture, the United States changed her policies and came to the aid of Israel with supplies of F-4E Phantom II and A-4 Skyhawk aircraft. In addition, C-130 transports and S-65 helicopters were furnished to Israel. About 120 IDF/AF personnel were sent to the United States for training.

Numerically, the A-4 in its many variants was to become the most important aircraft in the inventory of the *Chel Ha'Avir*. The Israelis found, to their great delight, that this simple, straightforward aircraft was rugged, reliable, highly maneuverable and, though small, capable of carrying a far greater payload than the Mirage III C.

Although the IDF/AF would have preferred a fighter aircraft, the F-4 Phantom was denied to them at first, so in 1967 Israel took delivery of 48 single-seat F-4H and two tandem-seat TA-4H aircraft. The A-4H differed from the USN's A-4F in that the two American 20-mm Mk.12 cannon were replaced by a pair of larger 30-mm DEFA cannon, preferred by Israel for its punch. In addition, the Israeli aircraft had an enlarged square-tipped vertical tail fitted with a drogue chute at its base. The dorsal avionics package on the A-4F was also omitted, although it was later retro-fitted to those models not having it.

In 1969 a further batch of 25 ex-USN A-4E Skyhawks were delivered to the IDF/AF. By the end of 1971 the *Chel Ha'Avir* had a total of 120 Skyhawks and, a year later, 180. By the mid-1970s there were well over 250 A-4E/A-4H/A-4N Skyhawks in six squadrons.

The Skyhawks would become the workhorse aircraft of the 1969 War of Attrition and the 1973 Yom Kippur War and this is reflected in their losses. A total of 53 Skyhawks were lost during the October War, with losses being made good from United States stocks. Both American and Israeli ships to Israel carried, as deck cargo, the little modified-delta attack bombers.

Although too slow to be used as fighters, Skyhawks on a number of occasions were called upon to slug it out with Arab fighters. If any MiG was so rash as to attempt to turn with a Skyhawk, the maneuverable little aircraft stood a good chance of shooting it out of the sky. For defensive purposes, Skyhawks were often fitted with Sidewinders.

In the summer of 1970 a Skyhawk bagged a Syrian MiG-19 with a 2.5-inch air-to-ground rocket, while a Syrian MiG-17 was brought down with hits from the Skyhawk's DEFA cannon. During the 1973 Yom Kippur War, a Skyhawk pilot got into a maneuvering dogfight with three MiG-21s, shooting two of them down. He was on the tail of the third, but was incensed to have a Mirage move in and shoot it down. With the possible exception of the Northrop F-5, the Skyhawk is the most maneuverable combat aircraft in the Middle East.

The IDF/AF was delighted with the ruggedness of the Skyhawk. In the 1973 war many of them suffered hits from the SA-7 Strella but returned to base. On one assembly line there was a whole row of Skyhawks with Strella-induced tail damage. In June 1970 a Skyhawk had its wing punctured by an Atoll AAM which failed to go off. This aircraft also returned to base. Although Skyhawks were mauled in the 1973 war, losses would have been far higher with almost any other aircraft. What is more, on a loss per mission basis, the IDF/AF points to the outstandingly low figure of .6 percent—far lower than the 1967 Six Day War. Even today (1978) no replacement of the Skyhawk by the IDF/AF has been planned. "What will replace it?" one Israeli air force officer asked." What can do the job better?"

Along with the Skyhawks, the U.S. sent Israel a number of big Sikorsky S-65 helicopters. One of the first major uses to which the U.S.-supplied S-65 was put was in the extraordinary attack on Ras Ghareb, 115 miles from Suez, by helicopter-borne commandos, in the summer of 1970. A Soviet-built P-12 Barlock mobile radar unit, used to detect low-flying aircraft, was, in a matter of minutes, captured, disassembled, and loaded aboard two S-65s to be carried back to Israel. American technicians were allowed to examine this latest of Soviet radars in order to develop effective ECM equipment and to allow the United States to assess the state-of-the-art of Soviet electronics.

Altogether, some twenty S-65 C-3 helicopters were sold to Israel, including a number flown in by the United States at the height of the 1973 Yom Kippur War. Some of these were retro-fitted with the in-flight refueling probes found on the later CH-53D. Germany received a large number of CH-53G helicopters (CH-53G was the designation of the CH-53D intended for Germany; in contrast to the earlier S-65, they mounted an uprated engine and could carry up to 64 troops), and eighteen of these were transferred to Israel. Both S-65 C-3 and CH-53G helicopters were used for the transport of heavy cargo and for assault troop operations. They proved invaluable in the course of the two-front war in 1973.

In September 1969, United States air force and marine pilots also began ferrying in the first of Israel's big new fighter plane, the McDonnel Douglas Phantom II. The initial order was for fifty F-4E fighters and six unarmed RF-4E reconnaissance aircraft. At first some Israeli senior personnel had expressed reservations about the Phantom. In comparison to the trim little Mirage, the two-place American fighter seemed something of a monster. About a third larger than the Mirage in all dimensions and more than twice as heavy, the Phantom was so expensive (about $4.5 million each for the fighter version and more than $6 million for the RF-4E) that some officers wondered if Israel could afford to commit the plane to anything less than all-out war.

On the other hand, the Phantom was a truly formidable plane. Not only was it faster than the Mirage or the MiG, it had a much greater range. In addition to its standard 20-mm cannon armament it could carry a variety of air-to-air missiles and, for ground attack, up to 16,000 pounds of bombs or rockets on under-wing pylons (nearly twice as much as the Skyhawk and four times as much as the principal Egyptian fighter-bomber, the Sukhoi-7). It was considerably more sophisticated than the Mirage, yet it was both simpler to pilot and maintain and more resistant to damage. All things considered, at the time of its introduction to Israel the Phantom was easily the best fighter in the Middle East; and despite early reservations about its cost, it was soon put to work, for Nasser's War of Attrition was beginning to prove painfully effective.

The War of Attrition was different from any Israel had fought before. No territory changed hands. There were no tank thrusts or flanking movements. In fact, there were no large-scale troop movements at all. Instead, there were only repeated artillery bombardments and small probing actions. But as the Egyptian artillery assault along the Suez Canal began to erode Israeli defenses and as casualties mounted, it seemed that Israeli strength might soon be sufficiently weakened so that an Egyptian attack across the canal would be feasible.

The Egyptians had foreseen that the Israelis would try to silence their artillery with air attacks, and Egyptian SAM-2s and prowling MiG fighters were ready for the *Chel Ha'Avir*. In air-to-air combat the Israelis were giving as good an account of themselves as ever: throughout the entire period of the War of Attrition, from June 1969 to August 1970, the IDF/AF claimed a total of 113 Egyptian and Syrian aircraft shot down. But the Israelis were losing planes too, and these would not easily be replaced. Even though the Arab aircraft losses were higher, the Arabs could afford their losses and the Israelis could not.

This was the situation into which, in January 1970, the Phantoms were introduced. The Skyhawks had been successful in destroying numerous artillery batteries and SAM-2 batteries along the canal, but at considerable cost and only to see those batteries eventually replaced. A new tactic was needed, and the Phantoms provided the key.

With their great range and speed and their impressive load-carrying capacity, the Phantoms now made it possible for the Israelis to mount a campaign of deep penetration attacks against Egypt herself. The killing ground along the canal would be bypassed; henceforth the *Chel Ha'Avir*'s targets would be far inside the enemy borders, even including Cairo. At last the Israelis had found a means of returning to their favorite military posture, the offensive. The question now would be whether Nasser could take the pressure.

The pressure proved to be considerable. Neither the MiGs nor hastily erected SAM-2 batteries proved effective against the marauding Phantoms. In response to Nasser's pleas, the USSR sent the Egyptians a quantity of the new mobile SAM-3 missiles and ZSU-23 radar-guided anti-aircraft guns. There was no time to train the Egyptians in the use of these weapons, so they were manned by Soviet "technical advisors," one of whom, a high-ranking general, was soon killed in a Phantom flak-suppression strike.

Russian involvement now began to escalate dangerously. The Soviets sent Egypt five squadrons of MiG-21MF interceptors and 150 "volunteer" Russian pilots to fly them. Israel, well aware of what was going on, announced that she was fully prepared to confront the Russians if they intervened on the Egyptian side; but in the hope of relieving the tension somewhat, the Israelis began to abate their deep penetration raids. The Soviet-Egyptian response was to move the SAM-3s and new anti-aircraft guns up to the canal and to mount more aggressive fighter patrols. It seemed that the feared Russo-Israeli confrontation was becoming inevitable.

In June 1970, Russian-piloted MiGs intercepted some A-4 Skyhawks escorted by Mirages. The Israeli aircraft were driven back, one Skyhawk damaged by a Russian Atoll air-to-air missile. About two weeks later Egyptian radar spotted another attack by Skyhawks and about twenty Russian-piloted MiG-21MF interceptors were scrambled. They were jumped by a mixed force of Mirages and Phantoms. Five of the Russians were shot out of the sky, two by Sidewinder air-to-air missiles fired by Phantoms, one by a Mirage Sidewinder, and a fourth by Mirage cannon fire. Only two Russians managed to bail out and one of them later died of his wounds. Realizing that opposition was likely to stiffen, Israel had her last six Phantoms of the original order of fifty fitted with electronics for air-to-air combat.

Fortunately, at this dangerous juncture all sides decided to back off from a situation that now threatened to spin out of control. Both Moscow and Washington put pressure on Cairo to call at least a temporary halt to the fighting; and the Egyptians themselves, dismayed by the effectiveness of the deep-penetration Phantom strikes, and perhaps also alarmed by the dangers implicit in the growing Russian involvement, decided they had had enough. On August 8, 1970, a cease-fire was signed.

So the War of Attrition ended with nothing solved. The deadly, frustrating stalemate persisted. The Egyptians and Syrians once again set about building up their ground and air forces and planning for the next war. Israel, for her part, received replacements from the United States for all Phantoms and Skyhawks lost in the fighting. In addition, Israel placed orders for more Phantoms and Skyhawks and for new helicopters and transports. But even as the Israelis re-armed, an important psychological dimension seemed to be lacking in their preparations.

The Israelis had learned something from the War of Attrition, but not enough. Still bemused by their lightning victory in the Six Day War, the Israeli armed services—and perhaps especially the *Chel Ha'Avir*—remained complacent. They had had a foretaste of the changes that guided missiles were bringing to warfare, but they remained largely blind to the tactical implications of this new technology. If "pride goeth before destruction, and a haughty spirit before a fall," the Israelis were asking for trouble. On Yom Kippur, 1973, they were to get it in full measure.

9

YOM KIPPUR PRELUDE

THE AUGUST 1970 CEASE-FIRE WHICH BROUGHT AN END TO the War of Attrition included an Israeli agreement to cease bombing the Egyptian artillery positions and SAM sites. It was the round-the-clock bombing which had prevented the SAM missiles' being moved to the banks of the Suez Canal to dominate the skies over the east bank held by the Israelis. The Egyptians, in turn, pledged not to move their SAMs up during the cease-fire. No sooner had the Israelis stopped the bombing than the Egyptians immediately violated the agreement by rushing SAMs to emplacements adjacent to the canal. What they had been unable to do by force of arms they now did by deceit. Israel immediately protested to the United States (the architect of the agreement) but the United States—who was monitoring the new armistice through the use of SR-71 observation aircraft overflights—claimed that there was no positive proof that the agreement had been violated. Israel then produced photographs taken immediately before the cease-fire, along with others—taken 24 hours after the cease-fire went into effect—that clearly showed SAMs in place at the forward positions where they had not been before. Despite being presented with such proof, the United States chose to remain silent.

Israel should have been more concerned about this development. In fact, Israeli officials privately expressed the belief that the Arabs had neither the desire nor the competence to initiate another round of fighting in the immediate future.

In the spring of 1973 Israel was placed on alert when intelligence detected the mobilization of the Syrian and Egyptian armies. But, after a few weeks, the alert was called off. There was much criticism of the Israeli government for placing the country on an alert which had proven unnecessary.

On September 13, 1973, there was an air battle over the Mediterranean between Syrian MiG-21s and Mirages and Phantoms of the *Chel Ha'Avir*. Shortly after noon, an Israeli patrol off the Syrian seacoast was attacked by MiGs. Additional Israeli and Syrian aircraft joined the battle. Eventually, twelve Israeli and between twelve and sixteen Syrian fighters were joined in a swirling dogfight which saw nine MiGs and one Israeli aircraft downed.

The Israeli pilot parachuted safely into the sea and a rescue helicopter was dispatched to pick up the pilot. Overhead, Israeli aircraft patrolled the sky in order to protect the chopper. As the rescue helicopter approached the downed Israeli pilot, who had shot down a MiG just before his Mirage was hit, more MiG-21s appeared on the scene and engaged the Israeli top cover. In a short, sharp battle, four more MiG-21s were destroyed. These losses brought the Syrian total of aircraft lost since the 1967 Six Day War to 60 aircraft, compared with 4 *Chel Ha'Avir* aircraft lost to the Syrians. This latest victory further lulled the Israelis into a feeling that the Arabs would not have the nerve to attack.

When, in the autumn of 1973, Israeli intelligence detected the mobilization of the armies of Syria and Egypt, there were no feelings of apprehension. After all, everyone knew that the Arabs didn't have the guts to start a war—everyone except the Arabs, who counted on Israeli complacency.

Intelligence reports in September indicated that families of Russian military advisors in both Syria and Egypt were departing. This could be taken as a sign of an impending attack by the Arab countries on Israel's border or it could be interpreted as a rift between the Soviet Union and her Arab clients. The Israeli government chose to believe the latter. In the face of the Arab buildup on the borders of Israel, some hardliners in and out of government called for a preemptive strike against the massed forces, much in the manner of the 1967 war.

This solution was rejected by Prime Minister Golda Meir, for several reasons. It remains for history to judge whether those reasons were valid. The primary one expressed by Mrs. Meir was that world opinion would be sharply against Israel if she struck first. Events were to prove that, despite the fact that the Arabs struck first, most African nations condemned Israel and broke off diplomatic relations with her anyway. Nor would Europe be much more sympathetic.

In terms of weaponry the *Chel Ha'Avir* was not ill-prepared for

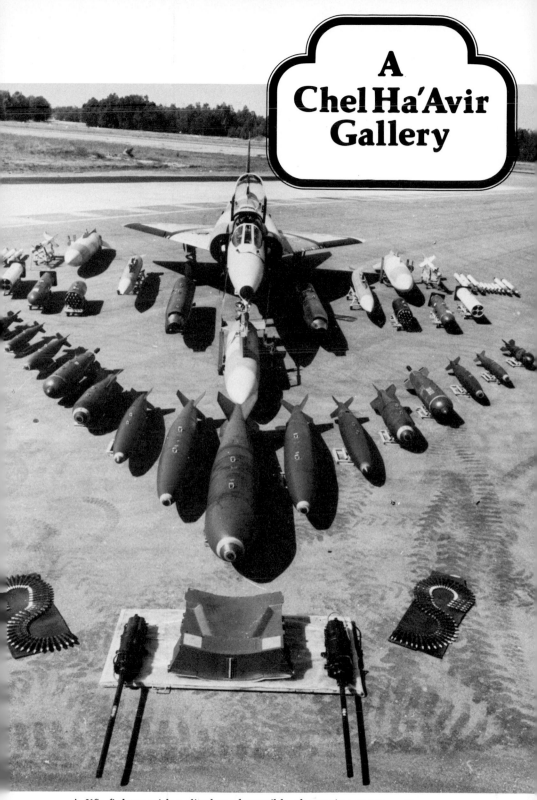

A Chel Ha'Avir Gallery

A *Kfir* fighter with a display of possible alternative armaments.

In the dangerous days before her independence, Israel's covert air force (the *Sherut Avir*) relied heavily on two lightplane types, the Taylorcraft Model C (top) and Polish RWD-13 (below), requisitioned from the Civilian Flying Club.

During the opening days of the 1948 war, Israel was obliged to use lightplanes for combat roles. One of the most useful types was the Auster A.O.P.-5 (top); one of the least was the frail little de Havilland Tiger Moth (below), this example being one of those purchased from Canada.

Some other unlikely warplanes used early in the War of Independence:
the de Havilland Dragon Rapide (top) and the Piper Super Cub (below).

The Beechcraft Model 35 Bonanza (top), along with the Dragon Rapide and a Fairchild, made a bombing attack on an Egyptian naval flotilla on June 4, 1948. Modi Alon, C.O. of 101 (Fighter) Squadron, stands beside a Republic RC-3 Seabee (below) used for liaison.

During the 1948 war, Israel operated an old Avro Anson twin-engine trainer (top) as a light bomber. Both of the *Chel Ha'Avir*'s Grumman G.44 Widgeons (below)—used for reconnaissance and liaison—were destroyed in accidents.

The world-famous Douglas C-47 Dakota (top) was a vitally important part of the infant *Chel Ha'Avir*'s 1948 inventory. Technically inferior to the Dakota, but important "because it was there," was the Curtiss C-46 Commando (below), shown here making a paradrop.

One of the *Chel Ha'Avir*'s most colorful aircraft was the lone Douglas DC-5, known to history as the "Bagel Lancer" (right and below).

Israel's first (and worst) fighter during the 1948 war was the Avia (Messerschmitt) S-199. The bottom picture illustrates the Avia's distressing tendency to ground-loop.

The famous Supermarine Spitfire, Mk. 16 (top), was the first Israeli fighter able to compete equally with Arab fighters in 1948. Subsequently Israel received North American P-51 Mustangs (below) from Sweden.

Pilots of 101 Squadron, Israel's first fighter unit, in 1948
(top). War-weary Bristol Beaufighters (below)
accomplished relatively little in the War of Independence.

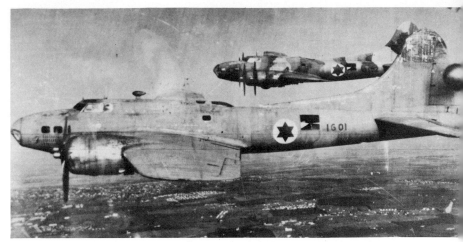

Three worn-out Boeing B-17G Flying Fortresses (above and below) were Israel's first heavy bombers. The wild saga of how they arrived in time to participate in the 1948 war (recounted in Chapter 2) is typical of the period.

The Douglas C-54 Skymaster (top) played an important wartime role as the IDF/AF's first long-range transport. North American AT-6 Harvard trainers (below) were used as light bombers in the War of Independence.

Acquired during the 1948 war was the hardy Noorduyn Norseman transport (top). The much larger Nord 2501 Noratlas transport was acquired in 1955 and performed valuable service in the Suez War of 1956.

Israel's first jet fighter, the Gloster Meteor (top), saw action in the Suez War. The Dassault M.D. 450 Ouragon fighter (below), acquired in 1955, is still carried in the *Chel Ha'Avir*'s inventory.

The Dassault Mystère IVA (top) was technically the best Israeli fighter during the Suez War. The improved Super-Mystère B.2 (below) was received after the war ended.

The Dassault Mirage III C, primarily because of its spectacular role in the Six Day War of 1967, became one of the most famous warplanes of the decade of the 1960s.

The Sud-Aviation SO. 4050 Vautour (top, nearest camera) was Israel's
first jet bomber. The Fouga CM 170 Magister (below), the first warplane
to be manufactured under license in Israel, was an effective tank-buster
in the Six Day War.

Israel's first cadres of helicopter pilots trained in the little Bell 47G (top).
The Sikorsky S-58 (below) was the *Chel Ha'Avir*'s largest helicopter at
the time of the Six Day War.

Two Israeli transport aircraft of the 1960s were the highly maneuverable
Pilatus Turbo-Porter (top) and the hardy Dornier Do 27 STOL aircraft (below).

The Boeing Stratocruiser (top), Israel's largest transport during the Six
Day War, has since been supplemented with the Lockheed Hercules. A
recently acquired light transport is the Cessna Model 205 Super Skywagon (below).

The McDonnell Douglas A-4 Skyhawk attack bomber (above and opposite) was one of the two leading Israeli combat planes during the bloody Yom Kippur War of 1973. Of 102 Israeli aircraft lost in the war, 53 were Skyhawks.

At the time of the Yom Kippur War, the McDonnell Douglas F-4E Phantom II was undoubtedly the best fighter plane in the Middle East. Attrition of Phantoms was so high and rapid that the United States had to supply replacements directly from its own service inventories.

A MiG-21 captured by the Israelis (top) was decorated with bright red paint and given James Bond's famous number. The SAM-6 rocket (below) was one of the IDF/AF's most dangerous enemies in 1973.

Credit: Tass from Sovfoto

A much-modified Mirage airframe plus an American J-79 engine is the basis of Israel's first indigenous fighter, the IAI *Kfir*-C2. Below, a *Kfir* assembly line.

The Lockheed C-130 Hercules, now Israel's most versatile transport, made international headlines for its part in the daring commando raid at Entebbe Airport on the night of July 3, 1976.

Among the larger helicopters recently acquired to
replace the aging S-58 are the Sikorsky CH-53 (left)
and the Bell 205A (above).

The indigenous IAI Arava 201 transport (top) features blister housings for forward-firing machine guns to be used against terrorists. A limited number of Bell 206A Jet Ranger helicopters (below) have recently been acquired to replace older Bell 47G's and Sud-Aviation Alouettes.

Two potential enemies of the IDF/AF: The MiG-23 (top, Libyan markings) is already in service with at least three Arab air forces. The Soviet air force's MiG-25, world's fastest fighter, could be exported to the Middle East at any time.

Israel's newest and most powerful fighter is the McDonnell Douglas F-15A Eagle. Said to be the only photo yet released of the Israeli machine is the unrevealing picture shown above. Below, a U.S. Air Force F-15.

It is believed that Israel will soon acquire the General Dynamics F-16A lightweight fighter (top) for the IDF/AF. Rejected in favor of the F-15 and F-16 was the big Grumman F-14A Tomcat fighter (below).

A *Chel Ha'Avir* ace whose victory markings adorn the fuselage of his Mirage. The world's highest-ranking jet ace is an Israeli, though his name is a carefully guarded secret.

the attack the Arabs were about to unleash. After the 1967 Six Day War the IDF/AF, seeking a replacement for the aging Sikorsky S-58, had decided upon the Bell Model 205A. An initial batch of thirty license-built Augusta-Bell 205 rotorcraft were purchased from Italy and were available during the 1973 war, at which time they functioned effectively in the casualty-evacuation role. It is believed that approximately five Model 205A helicopters fell prey to the deadly SA-7 Strella portable heat-seeking missile during the course of the war. After the war, the Augusta-Bell 205As were supplemented by the Bell-built UH-1D Iroquois.

The Model 205A can carry fourteen troops or six litters so that, in addition to casualty evacuation (CASEVAC) duty, it has also been used by Israeli ground forces to transport quick-reaction troops involved in anti-terrorist operations.*

In the early Seventies Israel took delivery of a number of Bell 206A Jet Rangers. These helicopters have been used primarily for liaison and communications duties, supplanting the inferior Bell 47G, Alouette II, and Alouette III. At least one of these fell prey, during the 1973 Yom Kippur War, to a Strella missile. It is believed that additional Jet Rangers were delivered to Israel since the October War, some of which may be the later Model 206B Jet Ranger II. In addition, the Bell Model 212, with improved performance and load-carrying capabilities, were added to the IDF/AF inventory following the 1973 war.

From the mid-Fifties on, the *Chel Ha'Avir's* first-line combat aircraft were as modern as could be obtained. However, the Ministry of Defence always did skimp in the area of noncombat aircraft, the standard military transport being the Dakota and Pipers acting as liaison aircraft. This attitude was no doubt a carry-over from Tolkovski's approach to how the *Chel Ha'Avir* should function. The Dakotas, through the years, have dwindled in numbers. Today, only about ten remain in service with the *Chel Ha'Avir*. The realization that new planes were needed was a long time coming. Finally, it was recognized that smaller, more efficient aircraft could handle jobs which had been in the province of the Dakotas. It had been less than efficient to use a Dakota simply because the Pipers and Austers were too small for a job. A false start was made in the late Sixties when a few

---

*Although Israel has operated Bell Model 205 helicopters with TOW anti-tank missiles and Alouette II & III rotorcraft with SS.11 wire-guided anti-tank missiles, there has never been a helicopter gunship in the *Chel Ha'Avir's* inventory. IDF/AF planners have been aware that such gunships are effective anti-infiltrator weapons and so, negotiations were undertaken between the governments of Israel and the United States to obtain Hueycobras.

SOCATA Rallyes were purchased from France. Although delightful to fly, the little four-seater was merely evaluated by the IDF/AF and that was as far as it went.

With the success of the earlier Cessna Model 185 and 205 in IDF/AF service, follow-on orders were placed in the late Sixties for the Cessna 206C and the 207. The Model 206C was essentially similar to the Model 205, but mounted a larger, more powerful engine. The Model 207 was nothing more than a "Stretched" Model 206C. Intended for the same light transport duties as the earlier models, the added power of the Model 206C and 207 improved performance at the elevated temperatures and altitudes found in the Israeli-occupied Sinai. Reliability of these models was as high as in earlier models.

Surrounded as she is by hostile neighbors, Israel is well aware that she must be ever vigilant. Terrorist raids are a constant threat. Military units must be in constant contact in order to effect coordinated action. For these reasons, Israel has begun to pay more attention to aircraft optimized for liaison duties, light transport, and casualty evacuation. Among the aircraft purchased for this purpose have been the single-engined five-seat Dornier Do 27 (whose seats may be removed for the roles mentioned) and its derivative, the fifteen-seat twin-engined Do 28D Skyservant. Both aircraft have STOL capabilities. Ten aircraft of each model have been acquired and are presently in service.

Israel maintains a relatively small standing army, but virtually the entire nation is in the reserve. Because of the hostility of her neighbors, it is imperative that she maintain the ability to mobilize totally within 72 hours. In the mid-Sixties Israel began to acquire Beech Model 80 Queen Air light transport aircraft which, in the event of mobilization orders, are used to shuttle key army and air force personnel to their predetermined staging points. Once mobilization is complete, the Queen Airs serve as light utility transports to supplement the larger, but dwindling, Dakota transports. Functionally, the twenty Queen Air aircraft are utilized in much the same way as the larger but slower Britten-Norman Islanders and Dornier Do 28 transports.

While the Queen Airs do not have the STOL capabilities of their stablemates, they do serve in the advanced training role. Pilot trainees who will go on to such aircraft as the Hercules or Noratlas or Stratocruiser transports gain multi-engine experience with this relatively high performance light twin.

Among the IDF/AF's more recent acquisitions is about a dozen Britten-Norman BN-2A Islander light utility transports. These aircraft, which can seat ten passengers in addition to a crew of two or the equivalent in cargo, are intended to fill in for the dwindling number of archaic Dakotas, some of which still remain in Israeli service. At one time, the workhorse Dakotas were called upon to carry cargoes too large for the smaller utility craft in the *Chel Ha'Avir*'s inventory. But, as it becomes increasingly difficult to keep the Dakotas airborne (many of them are into their fourth decade), a larger type of utility aircraft, represented by the Islander and the Do 28, will be utilized. For cargoes beyond the capabilities of these aircraft, Noratlas or Hercules transports will be used.

The Islander (and the Do 28) are also used for transporting patrols on anti-terrorist duties. A military version of the Islander also can carry under-wing rocket or gun pods.

Up to the 1973 Yom Kippur War, the *Chel Ha'Avir* had no orders for the indigenous Arava 201, the military variant of the Arava 101 commerical utility transport. The October War, however, changed that. There are now about half a dozen Aravas serving with the IDF/AF, with more on order. Foreign orders for the Arava 201 have been placed by Mexico, El Salvador, Ecuador, Bolivia, and Nicaragua.

Preliminary design studies for a simple STOL light utility transport were begun in 1965, with the first prototype, Arava 02, making its first flight on November 27, 1969. A year later, on November 19, 1970, the Arava was making its final certification flights when it crashed, killing the test pilot, Avraham Hacohen, and two of the crew. The problem was traced to a faulty wing strut (the Arava wing is externally braced to lighten the structure and simplify the design), and design changes eliminated the flaw.

In 1970, design work began on the Arava 201 light military transport. The *Chel Ha'Avir* was cool to the Arava, however, until an Arava 101 was requisitioned at the time of the Arab onslaught in the October War. The civil Arava carried out evacuation duties, while two military models sold to another country were pressed into use right from the production line for the duration of the war. Surprised by the versatility of the Arava under actual combat conditions, the IDF/AF placed orders.

As an assault transport, the Arava can carry 24 fully armed troops or a jeep mounting a 106-mm recoilless rifle together with its crew of four. Seventeen paratroopers can be carried. The jump exit for paratroops is through a side door while two one-ton pallets can be dropped through the rear exit. For casualty evacuation duties, the Arava can handle twelve litters, together with two attendants. Other proposed uses include such roles as navigational trainer and aerial tanker (for UH-1 helicopters). For limited anti-terrorist activities, the Arava carries two fixed, forward-firing .50-inch machine guns, with provisions for a third rearward-firing .50-inch machine gun mounted on a pintle at the rear of the fuselage. The blister-mounted fixed guns can be reloaded from within the fuselage. Eight thousand rounds may be carried in the aircraft. Hard points on the fuselage side permit 600 pounds to be carried on each side. Typical stores with this weight boundary include a pod of seven 68-mm rockets or two six-round pods of 82-mm rockets which were developed in Israel.

Beginning in the latter part of 1971, Israel began to take delivery of the huge four-engine Lockheed C-130E transport, the plane that was later to be used in the Entebbe raid. The original order for twelve was completed in 1972, but after the outbreak of the 1973 Yom Kippur War, additional refurbished ex-USAF machines were delivered. Israel received a total of twelve C-130E and twelve C-130H aircraft.

"If we could have gotten C-130s when we first asked the United States for them, we would never have purchased the Stratocruisers," one senior *Chel Ha'Avir* officer commented. Indeed, the C-130, in Israeli inventory, has been used for a wide variety of purposes, both before and after the 1973 October War. They have been employed as aerial tankers, assault transports, logistics resupply aircraft, and for parachuting men and heavy equipment.

The *Chel Ha'Avir*'s impressive build-up of helicopters, trans-ports, and other second-line aircraft prior to the October War was fully matched by its deployment of first-line combat planes. The Skyhawk inventory had swollen to about 180 and the complement of Phantoms had jumped from the original 50 to 132. In addition, a surprising number of old Ouragons, Mystères, and Super-Mystères were still available.

And then there were the Mirages. During the 1973 war there was a single recurrent question: Where did Israel's Mirages come from? Many answers were forthcoming—none of them correct. It was common knowledge that Israel had acquired 72 single-seat Mirage III C jets from France, beginning in 1963. But there had been losses in combat during and after the 1967 Six Day War. With the French embargo on planes and parts after 1967, it was expected that the Mirages, increasingly, would have become unserviceable for lack of spares, particularly engines. Some outsiders predicted that Mirages would soon be phased out in favor of U.S.-supplied Phantoms. And yet, with the onset of the 1973 Yom Kippur War, Mirages were on hand with the *Chel Ha'Avir* in considerable quantity. Obviously the numbers didn't add up.

Some thought that the South African government lent some of their Mirages to Israel. Others, far more charitable, thought that the French government had relented and had supplied Israel with more Mirages secretly so as not to affect their relations with the Arab countries whom they were courting. Another theory held that as Atar engines became worn out they were replaced by the J-79 powerplants normally found in the Phantoms. While there was, in fact, a germ of truth in this, the theory was far from accurate. Overlooked completely was the possibility that fighter aircraft—essentially Mirage derivatives—were actually being built in Israel.

It was as a measure of desperation that Israel began the manufacture of her own fighter aircraft. The move was not made hastily, but was a progression based on a political fact (Israel's relationship with France) and a military reality (the need to prevent crippling from a future embargo by any nation supplying armaments to Israel). Israel's arrival at the point of being a full-fledged manufacturer of a world-caliber fighter of at least partly original design was many years in the making.

When the Dassault Mirage III CJ entered service with Israel early in 1963, the interceptor was scrutinized carefully. Before long, the IDF/AF developed a list of things they would have liked in an "ideal" aircraft. Simplified avionics and greater ground-attack capability were two areas of potential improvement. The resultant dialogue with the parent firm of Dassault, reinforced by combat experience of the Mirage III CJ gained in the 1967 Six Day War, culminated in the evolution of the Mirage 5, for which Israel placed a 50-plane order.

But in the mid-Sixties, French foreign policy drifted toward an openly pro-Arab stance. With the war in Algeria ended, it was no longer necessary for the French to play Israel off against the Arabs. Therefore, in May 1967, when Egypt announced a blockade of the Straits of Tiran, Franch was deaf to Israeli pleas for support on the issue of free passage through that international waterway. When Israel launched a preemptive strike the following month against menacing Arab forces on her border, France declared an embargo on weapons to Israel. This embargo included the 50 Mirage 5s.

With the arrival of Phantom II fighter-bombers from the United States, a crisis due to growing unserviceability of the Mirages was avoided. The availability of J-79 engines, which powered the American-supplied Phantoms, led to studies centered on the substitution of the American powerplant for the Mirage's Atar. The J-79 was dimensionally similar and much more powerful. In 1969 the IAI (Israel Aircraft Industries) initiated development on this project under the code name "Black Curtain": a Mirage III CJ had its worn-out Atar 9 replaced by the J-79. The experiment was successful and a decision was made to re-engine all the Atar-powered Mirage III CJs then in service. Such refitted aircraft were called "Salvo."

But at about the time the Black Curtain program began, Israeli secret agents obtained plans of the Atar 9C from a Swiss engineer named Alfred Fraunknecht who was employed at the Sulzer plant in Winterthur. This factory built Atar 9C engines under license for Swiss Mirage III CS fighters. In addition, certain Frenchmen sympathetic to Israel covertly furnished plans for the Mirage III and Mirage 5 aircraft.

Armed with detailed plans for both engine and airframe, Israel now secretly began to build the Mirage in Israel, code-naming these Atar-powered aircraft *Nesher* ("Eagle"). *Neshers*, which first flew in 1971, were used in the 1973 Yom Kippur War.

Welcome as the *Neshers* were, the Israelis were even more interested in the possibility of constructing Mirages fitted with the powerful American J-79s. As preliminary work on the "Salvos" had indicated, this was far from simple. A comparison of the basic statistics relating to the Atar and the J-79 may suggest some of the reasons why:

	Snecma Atar 9C	General Electric J 79-GE-17
Length:	233.9 inches	208.7 inches
Diameter:	40.2 inches	39.0 inches
Weight:	3,498 pounds	3,835 pounds
Engine airflow:	154 pounds/second	170 pounds/second
Thrust, s.t., dry:	9,370 pounds	11,870 pounds
Thrust, s.t., with A/B:	13,225 pounds	17,900 pounds

Obviously the dimensions were different, and so were all the engine support locations. The American engine had a higher tailpipe temperature, and this required bringing cooling air aft via a number of ram air scoops, including one dorsal scoop filleted into the base of the tail. Also, the J-79 required a higher overall airflow than the Atar, so the aircraft's jet intakes had to be enlarged. And there were many other lesser modifications needed, such as shortening the tailpipe shroud, and so on.

The Israeli-built J-79–powered Mirage was called the *Barak* ("Lightning"), and by the fall of 1973 the *Chel Ha'Avir* had five completed. They were to see extensive action during the October War, when they used their improved performance and Israeli-designed *Shafrir* air-to-air missiles to very good advantage. Their first public appearance caused no little confusion in foreign intelligence circles.

The *Baraks* were based on the old Mirage-III airframe, but thanks to the work of the Israeli undercover agents in France, there was now the possibility that Israel could build an even better fighter based on a marriage of the new Mirage 5 airframe and the J-79. Work in this synthesis began in late 1971, the result being dubbed *Kfir* ("Lion Cub"). But far more extensive modifications (about which more later) had to be made on the *Kfir* than on the *Barak* and none of the planes was ready for use in the October War. In another sense, however, the very extent of the redesign work done on the *Kfir* made it a landmark. For all practical purposes it may be regarded as Israel's first indigenous warplane.

Thus, by the fall of 1973 the *Chel Ha'Avir* appeared to have reason to feel more secure than ever before. Its warplane inventory was both relatively large and fully up-to-date. Its pilots and ground crews were among the most skilled and experienced in the world. Even the old bugbear of resupply seemed on the verge of being banished, at least in part, by the incipient creation of a native aircraft industry capable of producing modern jet fighters. Yet reality was about to deal a rude blow to appearances.

10

WAR OF ATONEMENT

LATE ON SATURDAY, OCTOBER 6, 1973—YOM KIPPUR IN
Israel and the tenth day of Ramadan in the Muslim nations—Radio
Cairo informed the world that "at 1330 today the enemy attacked our
forces in the area of Za'faranah and Sukhnah." The report was a
fabrication, but it would have been irrelevant even if it had been true.
For at 2:00 that afternoon the Arabs had put their long-considered
and carefully planned "Operation *Badr*" into effect. Operation *Badr*
was the invasion of Israel by the armies of Egypt and Syria, supported
by troops and weapons contributed by Jordan, Saudi Arabia, Iraq,
Algeria, Sudan, Kuwait, Libya, Pakistan, North Vietnam, and North
Korea.

It was now the turn of the Arabs to strike first and of the Israelis
to be surprised. One might suppose that in view of the Meir government's decision to renounce the strategy of preemption, the Israelis
would have been doubly on guard against unpleasant surprises. They
were not. To be sure, on the previous day, October 5, the Israelis
seemed to have sensed that something might be afoot, for they had
placed their armed services in a condition of high alert. But such
action had often been taken before; more to the point, no effort was
made to call up the reserves—something that was undertaken only
scant hours before the invasion began.

The Arab commanders deserve credit for more than having
achieved the advantage of surprise. They had planned in great and
imaginative detail how the war would be fought and they were able to
confront the Israelis with a whole new set of problems that the Israelis
were barely able to solve. Even though the Israelis eventually won the
Yom Kippur War, the price of victory was very high. The fighting

dragged on for eighteen days, during which the small Israeli army lost 2,521 soldiers it could ill afford, and the *Chel Ha'Avir* lost a fifth of its aircraft, most of them first-line combat types. One of the most important casualties of the war was that mystique of Israeli invincibility which in the past had conferred such important morale advantages to Israel relative to her enemies.

But there is no escaping the fact that the Israelis bore a heavy responsibility for the difficulties in which they found themselves. The *Chel Ha'Avir*, for its part, had been guilty of that familiar sin of successful military organizations: preparing for the wrong war—i.e., the last one. The IDF/AF planners somehow imagined that the conditions they would have to face in the future would be the same as those they had mastered during the War of Attrition.

During the so-called "electronic summer" of 1970 the Phantoms and Skyhawks had perfected tactics which, combined with electronic countermeasures, had effectively dealt with the threat posed by SAM-2 and SAM-3 missiles. So confident was the Israeli Ministry of Defence that the problem of SAMs had been solved, that in 1970 it had rejected an American offer of an RPV (remotely piloted vehicle) weapons system that would have exposed inexpensive robots, rather than manned aircraft, to the Soviet missiles. "We consider the small losses in aircraft we would take in dealing with the SAMs to be acceptable," a complacent Ministry spokesman explained.

The flaw in this thinking was that it assumed that the Arab air defense would continue to be based on the old SAM-2/SAM-3 combination. The SAM-2 is a relatively long-range, high-altitude missile which requires permanent emplacements. It was the SAM-2 which shot down Gary Francis Powers, in a U-2, high over the Soviet Union. Another high-flying U-2 was brought down by a SAM-2 over Cuba. To knock out or evade a SAM-2, a pilot simply has to fly below the minimum effective altitude of this missile. Because of the SAM-2 and, later, the improved SAM-2, emphasis was placed by the Western powers on low-altitude penetration. Then the SAM-3 came along.

The SAM-3 cannot zoom as high as a SAM-2 and its range is less. But it is mobile and its minimum effective altitude is much lower. Yet the IDF/AF soon had the answer to the SAM-3 as well. Part of the answer was in effective ECM (electronic countermeasures) to jam the frequency used by the SAM-3's radar. The other part of the reply was to fly lower still.

But the Arabs and their Soviet mentors were at least as well aware of the weaknesses of the SAM-2/SAM-3 defense system as the Israelis, and not unexpectedly they tried to do something about it.

Accordingly, they introduced three new weapons into the equation. Foremost among them was the SAM-6, a highly mobile missile triple-mounted on a special tracked vehicle. Initially guided to its target by radar, the SAM-6 closes for the kill via an infrared homing device. Although it is effective up to about 50,000 feet, it is extremely dangerous at middle and low altitudes as well. During the War of Attrition Israeli pilots had sometimes found it possible to out-maneuver approaching SAM-2s, provided they were sighted in time; this was very much harder to do with a SAM-6. But perhaps the most deadly fact about the SAM-6 during the Yom Kippur War was that the Israelis had not yet discovered—as with the SAM-3s—how to jam its radar guidance system.

The general effect of the SAM-6 was to force Israeli aircraft to operate at low altitudes. The two other new Arab weapons were designed to capitalize on this. One was the radar-controlled rapid-fire ZSU-23 anti-aircraft gun. The Israelis had encountered this murder-ous, self-propelled four-barrel 23-mm weapon during the War of Attri-tion, but it had not been deployed in great numbers, and, in any case, Israeli pilots had not then been forced to fly at the low altitudes where the gun is most effective. And, as in the case of the SAM-6, the Israelis had not yet figured out how to jam the ZSU's radar.

The third new Arab weapon was the SAM-7 *Strella*. This is a small, relatively simple missile, either singly launched from a shoul-der tube or launched in salvos from multiple tubes carried on special vehicles. Optically sighted on launching, it homes on its target with a heat-seeking guidance system. Like the ZSU it is also at its most effective at very low altitudes.

By combining all these weapons—the SAM-2, -3, -6 and -7s and the ZSUs—the Arabs were able to construct zones of anti-aircraft defense that were denser, more sophisticated, and more nearly im-penetrable than any ever before encountered in combat, Vietnam included. The two most heavily concentrated zones were located along the Syrian front (based around 34 large-missile batteries) and along Suez (based around 62 batteries). For Israeli pilots facing such weapons arrays, all options would be unappetizing. No altitude would be safe, but the lower altitudes, at which the all-important air support and flak suppression missions had to be flown, would be nightmarish.

This massive buildup of anti-aircraft defenses was simply part of the larger Arab strategy, which was, in essence, to escalate attrition to levels that would be unbearable to the Israelis. Israel, with its small population of 3 million and its fatal dependence on external supply, was unable to bear the burden of a protracted war. The whole Israeli military establishment had been organized with an eye toward winning quick victories. Tank force had been built up, infantry neglected. The *Chel Ha'Avir* had been increasingly—or perhaps disproportionately—relied upon to administer war-winning early air strikes. The Arabs reasoned that if Israel's ground and air forces could be contained, placed on the defensive, and worn away by meatgrinder tactics, she might well be unable to hold out.

With considerable insight the Arab strategists recognized that the key to victory lay in carefully limiting their objectives. However attractive might be the prospect of exterminating the Israelis with a single crushing blow, the Arabs were intelligent enough to see that the troop deployments necessary to deliver such a blow could expose them to precisely the kind of lightning counter-thrusts that had given Israel victory in the past. Better, they concluded, to play it safe. The Syrians would grind the Israelis down on the Golan front in the north; the Egyptians, in the Sinai in the south. The *Chel Ha'Avir* would be lured into destroying itself in futile efforts to eliminate the two missile belts. If this strategy eventually succeeded in producing a total Israeli collapse, so much the better. But if the end of it were no more than that the Israelis were compelled to negotiate an unfavorable peace, that too would be acceptable. Israel would be that much nearer to ultimate destruction, and the Arabs had learned patience.

On the afternoon of October 6 the Israeli lines on the Golan Heights, held by the Barak Brigade to the south and the 7th Brigade on the north, were hit by 5th, 7th and 9th Syrian Divisions supported by 1st and 3rd Syrian armored Divisions. With 1,500 tanks—many of them the brand-new Soviet T-62 main battle tank—the Syrians had a crushing advantage in armor. They also had the element of surprise in their favor. Israeli ground forces, after years of neglect, were deficient in anti-tank missiles, artillery, flame throwers, and nightfighting equipment.

The blow struck by the Egyptians in the Sinai was no less severe than on the Syrian front. Using modern Soviet fording equipment, the Egyptians stormed over the Suez Canal and quickly overran most, though not all, of the Bar Lev Line fortifications. Israeli tanks stormed to the counterattack . . . only to be destroyed by a blizzard of Soviet-supplied Sagger and Snapper anti-tank missiles.

Israeli forces tried to mobilize as quickly as possible. Tank units were committed piecemeal to stem the tide of the invading forces, only to fall prey to the anti-tank missiles. The Israel Defence Force/Air Force went into action. Skyhawks and Phantoms swept toward the

Golan Heights—and were shot out of the sky, some by SAM-6 missiles, some by SAM-7s, others by the quadruple 23-mm cannon and even SAM-2s and SAM-3s. Under these missile umbrellas, the Arab armies moved relentlessly forward.

Elsewhere, North Vietnamese missile experts manned the SAM defenses guarding Damascus. These were the veterans who had exacted so heavy a toll of American aircraft during the Vietnamese war. Other allies from afar included North Korean pilots who flew MiG-21s on the Egyptian front, as well as pilots from Cuba and Pakistan flying with the Arab air forces.

Caught unprepared, the Israel Defence Forces needed at least 48 hours to mobilize and only the *Chel Ha'Avir* could buy them the time. Repeated attacks were launched against the pontoon bridges over which the Egyptian army was streaming into the Sinai and overwhelming the Bar Lev Line. This was precisely the scenario the Arab planners had foreseen.

Many of the bridges spanning the Suez Canal were destroyed in the face of bristling anti-aircraft defenses. But the effort was wasted, for the Israelis had not counted on the modern vehicle-mounted fording equipment which allowed the Egyptians to repair or replace a span in little more than an hour.

Meanwhile, also according to plan, in the early stages of the war the Egyptians and Syrians refrained from large-scale commitment of their air forces, remaining instead content to pick off Israeli combat aircraft with their missiles. At this stage the Arabs used their air power mainly to make hit-and-run attacks by the Egyptian air force against Israeli air bases. Egyptian commandos in large numbers were ferried by helicopter behind the Israeli lines to disrupt communications and cause as much damage as possible. The majority of these helicopters were shot out of the sky by the *Chel Ha'Avir*, but some got through. A specially trained group, called *Saiyeret*, "the unit," mopped up the Egyptian squads, but there was nevertheless some damage to installations, particularly at the Abu Rudeis oil fields.

By the end of the third day of fighting, it appeared that the Arab strategy had been brilliantly successful. The Egyptians were firmly established on the east bank of the Canal and the Syrians had seized part of the Golan Heights. The *Chel Ha'Avir*, irresistibly drawn into the killing ground of the missile belts, had lost at least 50 first-line combat aircraft, more than half of which had been downed by SAM-6s.

During the next five days the fronts remained relatively stable. The Syrians, under the pressure of increasing Israeli counterattacks and air strikes, drew back a little to consolidate their lines. The 70,000

Egyptian troops in the Sinai prudently refrained from advancing until their missile umbrella could be brought forward. Meanwhile the *Chel Ha'Avir*'s costly attacks on the SAM batteries, both north and south, were slowly beginning to show results; despite reinforcement, the total number of active batteries was starting to dwindle. Moreover, determined IDF/AF attacks on Syrian and Egyptian airfields were beginning to undermine the Arabs' resolution to avoid aerial combat with the Israelis. Dogfights became larger and more frequent and Arab aircraft losses began to mount.

But the basic Arab strategy nonetheless remained intact. On Saturday, Day 8 of the war, the big Egyptian armored forces in the south commenced their next lunge forward into the vital Sinai passes. Israel, by her own estimates, had only enough war material on hand for four more days of full-scale fighting. Once again, the future of the Jewish state seemed to be hanging by a thread.

It was at this crucial moment—the first of the war's two turning points—that the United States elected to intervene. The Russians, immoderate as usual, helped the Americans to come to this politically difficult decision. It is possible that if the Russians had been less blatant in their efforts to resupply their Arab clients, the American decision to aid Israel might have come too late. But since at least Day 5, the Soviets had been operating a regular large-scale airlift to Egypt and Syria; and this challenge (the Soviets refusing all American requests to desist), coupled with photographic evidence of the desperate situation of the Israeli ground forces provided by high-flying U.S. Lockheed SR-71 spy planes, prompted the Americans to take timely action.

Giant C-5A Galaxy transports, the largest in the world, began flying in tanks and infantry weapons. Phantoms were taken from U.S. Air Force units and, with in-flight refueling, were flown directly to Israel from their bases in Germany and the United States. Skyhawks were detached from Marine Corps squadrons and shipped to Israel aboard U.S. Navy aircraft carriers. Soon it became apparent that the American resupply effort would dwarf that of the Soviets. Only then did the Russians agree to call a halt to the emergency arms race.

On Day 9 (October 14), in a furious and bloody tank battle, the Israelis managed to contain the Egyptian armored drive toward the Sinai passes. Meanwhile, ever since the disastrous first three days, the *Chel Ha'Avir* had been enjoying increasing success.

Attacking again and again, the *Chel Ha'Avir* had carved a swath in the Syrian SAM defenses. Now it was Syria's turn to bleed. A large oil refinery was blasted. So was a radar station in Lebanon which had been supplying data to the Syrians. Several Cuban pilots were shot down. So were some Pakistanis. Three late-model Sukhoi Su-20 variable-sweep fighters were shot down near Mount Hermon. On the Egyptian front, some North Korean pilots were shot out of the sky. Six Libyan Mirages, on a raid against El Arish, were intercepted by Israeli Mirages. Three of the Libyan aircraft were downed. Two Tupolev Tu-16 Badgers of the Egyptian air force were shot out of the sky.

Syrian ground forces launched Frog surface-to-surface missiles against Israeli settlements and, in retaliation, the *Chel Ha'Avir* bombed Damascus. Two Sukhoi Su-20s were sent on a raid against Haifa. They never made it; one was shot down and the other escaped. Egyptian bombers launched 25 Kelt air-to-surface missiles against Israeli targets. The IDF/AF succeeded in shooting down twenty of these missiles. Only two struck their targets.

On October 16, the 11th day of the war, the Israelis managed to get a small detachment of tanks past the main body of Egyptian armor in the Sinai and to ferry them across the canal on rafts, thus creating a bridgehead near Deversoir on Egypt's now-ill-defended west bank. Although the Egyptian High Command seems to have failed to recognize it at the time, this was the second major turning point of the war. Little effort was made by the Egyptians on the ground to dislodge the Israeli tanks, and minor air attacks were mounted against them only about eighteen hours after their crossing.

In the days that followed, however, the full significance of the Israeli bridgehead became clear to both sides. The Israelis rushed more tanks to the scene and quickly built a bridge to hasten their passage across the canal. Somewhat tardily, the Egyptian air force responded with a furious effort to eliminate the threat. The *Chel Ha'Avir* flew to the counterattack and vast bloody air battles reeled through the skies above the enlarging Israeli enclave. The SAM batteries that lay in the path of the advancing Israeli armor were helpless to defend themselves, and by October 19 the Israelis were able to claim that ten of them had been overrun, thus opening a relatively SAM-free corridor through which IDF/AF aircraft could pass into Egypt.

By October 21, Day 16 of the war, the Israeli ground forces had effectively outflanked both the Egyptian troops in the Sinai and the Egyptian Third Corps in the vicinity of the town of Suez; the Syrians had been driven back to a defensive position on the Mt. Hermon line; and the *Chel Ha'Avir* had established definitive air superiority over both fronts. A U.N.-sponsored cease-fire was called on the 22nd. Fighting finally stopped on the 24th.

All told, the Arabs lost 514 aircraft, 334 in air-to-air combat. One *Chel Ha'Avir* fighter pilot downed 13 enemy aircraft in two days! The IDF/AF was aided somewhat by Arab SAM batteries which, in the course of the war, shot down 58 of their own aircraft. Israeli gunners also brought down some of their own Mirages, mistaking them for enemy Mirages (aircraft which were sold to Libya with the understanding that they would not be transferred, but which found their way to Egypt despite the pledge). As a result, large orange triangles bordered in black were painted on and under the wings and on the tailfins of all Israeli delta-winged aircraft as an aid to recognition.

Among the Arab aircraft losses were MiG-21, MiG-19, MiG-17, Su-7, Su-20 and Libyan-supplied Mirage fighters, Tu-16 bombers, and about forty Mi-8 helicopters. In air combat, *Chel Ha'Avir* pilots established a kill ratio in excess of 100 to one! One Skyhawk, attacked by MiG-21 fighters, jettisoned its bomb load and turned to meet its adversaries. The A-4 attack aircraft, while slow, is quite agile, and the pilot, using the little aircraft's maneuvering power to the fullest, managed to get behind one of the MiGs and, with a burst of 30-mm cannon fire (American Skyhawks are armed with smaller 20-mm cannon, whereas Israeli aircraft are fitted with the larger 30-mm with less ammunition) shot the MiG down. He then bagged a second MiG and was about to bag a third when two *Chel Ha'Avir* Mirages arrived on the scene and blasted the third MiG.

Once again Israel had won victory by the skin of her teeth. But this time the cost far exceeded anything she had had to pay before. In terms of the military establishment with which she had begun the war, Israel had lost 10 percent of her army, upwards of 30 percent of her tanks, and nearly 20 percent of her combat aircraft. Of the 102 aircraft lost by the *Chel Ha'Avir*, 53 had been Skyhawks; 33, Phantoms; 8, Mirages; and, 3, Super-Mystères. Forty percent of the IDF/AF losses were attributed to enemy missiles, but only 3 percent to enemy aircraft.

In the early days of the fighting, the IDF/AF had been so busy lending support to hard-pressed Israeli ground forces that it had had little time left over for attacks on the missile sites. "Instead of carrying out air defense suppression operations in an orderly manner," explained Major General Benjamin Peled, Commanding General of the IDF/AF, "we really preferred to break them up into small operations and try to do them in the periods in between other things more important at the time." Some Israeli officers, including former Commander General Ezer Weizman, subsequently suggested that this might have been a mistake and that knocking out the missiles should have been given a higher priority. Be that as it may, by the war's end the *Chel Ha'Avir* had succeeded in destroying no less than 44 of the 62 Egyptian missile batteries in the forward area.

Exactly how much the *Chel Ha'Avir* contributed to Israel's final victory is impossible to say, but certainly the contribution was very great. During the first 48 hours it gave crucial assistance to the beleaguered front-line troops until they could be reinforced by mobilized reservists. It was effective in thwarting the Egyptian campaign to bring helicopter-born commandos behind enemy lines. On several occasions it was given the primary credit for turning aside enemy armored attacks, both on the Golan and in the Sinai. It eventually overcame the enemy missiles, was supreme in air combat, and at all times kept the Israeli air space free of any major incursions by enemy aircraft.

Thus, while the *Chel Ha'Avir* might have had many things to reproach itself for, it had even more to be proud of. But above all, the Yom Kippur War had given the *Chel Ha'Avir*, like every other air force in the world, much to ponder. Many of the old pieties about how aerial warfare should be conducted suddenly looked obsolete. For example, missile and other anti-aircraft technology seemed to have made aerial blitzkriegs after the fashion of the Six Day War a thing of the past; in future, surface and air forces would probably have to effect levels of coordination beyond anything achieved before. But one thing was certain: the *Chel Ha'Avir* now knew that if it ever again made the mistake of preparing for the wrong war, it might never survive to fight another.

11

THE CHEL HA'AVIR TODAY

WHETHER ISRAEL AND THE *CHEL HA'AVIR* LEARNED THE LES-sons of the Yom Kippur War and are adequately prepared for a future conflict has not been tested as of this writing. But certainly many changes have taken place within the IDF/AF, and to all appearances it has never been more formidable or efficient.

On the night of July 3, 1976, it gave the world a dazzling display of this efficiency in a mission not of war, but of mercy. A few days earlier pro-Palestinian terrorists had hijacked a French airliner and forced it to land at Entebbe in Uganda. There, with the tacit coopera-tion of President Idi Amin, the hijackers held more than a hundred of the plane's passengers hostage in the airport building while demand-ing political concessions in exchange for their lives. The Israeli gov-ernment responded by giving overt indications that it was consider-ing the hijackers' demands. In reality it was planning a daring raid to set the hostages free.

In terms of equipment, the lynchpin of the operation was to be four of the huge Lockheed C-130 Hercules transports that Israel had acquired from the United States prior to the 1973 war, but in all, some twenty *Chel Ha'Avir* aircraft would participate. To begin with, RF-4Es, the reconnaissance version of the Phantom, overflew Entebbe, photographing the area to pinpoint the location of Ugandan MiGs and the disposition of the airport's defenses. On the basis of the information provided by the RF-4Es, the raid itself was begun.

Four C-130s—one of them outfitted as an aerial tanker—took off from Israel, escorted by eight F-4E Phantoms flying top cover. At the same time two Boeing 707s were launched. One went directly to Nairobi, Kenya, where it was used as a mobile hospital and where

131

emergency operations were performed on wounded soldiers and hostages; the other, with senior army and air force personnel on board, circled Entebbe Airport in the role of command ship, with a secondary role as backup communications aircraft. In order to avoid Egypt and Sudan, countries hostile to Israel, the aerial armada flew down the Gulf of Aqaba, almost skimming the water's surface—with Phantoms flying top cover—south along Northeast Africa, past Egypt and Sudan, and finally turning inland over Kenya and Uganda. The distance flown was almost 2,500 miles.

The raid itself was planned and carried out with almost surgical precision. Just prior to the arrival of the raiders, Israeli intelligence agents in Uganda cut communications lines between the airport and Uganda's capital, Kampala. The Hercules transports glided down silently, their turboprops idling. Instead of reversing the pitch of the propellers and applying power—an efficient, though noisy, means of stopping the big transports—the aircraft were stopped solely through the use of brakes. Then the three transports waddled to a darkened corner of the field. The fourth remained overhead ready to land and retrieve troops and hostages if one of the other ships was disabled.

In the dark shadows of the airfield, the first of the C-130 transports lowered its rear fuselage loading ramp. Out rolled a large black Mercedes limousine, followed by two buff-colored Land Rovers (Israelis use Jeeps which are khaki). The license plate of the Mercedes was the same as that on the car of the President of Uganda, Idi Amin. The escorting Land Rovers each contained five men dressed as Palestinian Arabs. (The Israelis had learned that Field Marshal Amin favored Palestinian Arabs as personal bodyguards, considering them to be more loyal than Ugandans.) Each of the "Palestinians," with the exception of the driver, carried a Soviet-made Kalashnikov AK-47 at the ready.

Ugandan soldiers viewed this procession approaching them. All snapped to attention and some saluted. There was nothing to cause suspicion. President Amin came to the airport daily. He had embraced the hijackers, used Palestinian guards, was driven about in a Mercedes limousine. The bodyguards were in Land Rovers and not Jeeps and were armed with Soviet weapons and not Israeli Uzis or Galils. Everything was in order.

While the three-car convoy approached the terminal unmolested, commandos from the other C-130s were not idle. Some placed explosive charges on the far side of the field to draw off the Ugandan soldiers. Some moved up under cover of darkness to protect the convoy. Others prepared to fire anti-tank rockets at the Ugandan MiG fighters.

Then everything happened at once. Charges went off and some of the Ugandan soldiers went to investigate. The MiG fighters then began to blow up, just as the "Palestinians" leaped from the Land Rovers and ran toward the terminal. Ugandan soldiers arriving by truck were cut down wholesale by an armored half-track that had emerged from the second C-130.

Israeli commandos rushed the terminal, shouted for the hostages to drop to the floor and, in a brief firefight, killed the seven terrorists. Ugandan fire came from the control tower and killed the Israeli commander of the operation—the sole Israeli military fatality—and was then effectively silenced by return fire.

The hostages were loaded aboard the C-130s and were then flown to nearby Kenya, where the transports refueled and the wounded were transferred to the Boeing 707 hospital plane. One of the C-130s had remained behind at the airport until the last of the raiding party could be loaded aboard. Elapsed ground time for the mission was 53 minutes.

It was a long night for the Ugandan army, which had at least twenty dead. Hours after the Israeli aircraft departed, Ugandan troops were still heard shooting at one another. William Scranton, American ambassador to the United Nations, in a speech before the Security Council on July 12, 1976, said of the raid to free the hostages that it was "a combination of guts and brains that has seldom if ever been surpassed." The raid, as it actually unfolded, would not have been possible without Hercules transports, whose range, payload, cargo-carrying capabilities, and landing field performance made the action feasible.

Prior to the raid, five Boeing 707 jetliners had been turned over by El Al to the IDF/AF, there now being a surplus in the world market of this type of aircraft. There had been some speculation as to what the Israeli military could do with this commercial aircraft. The Israeli raid on Entebbe partially answered this question.

Although Entebbe was a dramatic illustration of both the *Chel Ha'Avir*'s efficiency and its high state of readiness, the Yom Kippur War had been an equally dramatic illustration that something more than these two undoubted virtues was required. Having been taken by surprise by the coordinated blitz on both the Egyptian and Syrian fronts, IDF/AF planners had examined steps to be taken in order to avoid being caught off balance again. Negotiations were begun with the United States to acquire aircraft capable of providing Israel with an early-warning capability.

After examination of aircraft which could provide this capability, the aircraft decided upon were the Grumman E-2C Hawkeye (at $25 million per aircraft) for early warning, including low-level penetrations by strike aircraft, and the Grumman OV-1 Mohawk Elint aircraft. The Mohawks are intended for tactical reconnaissance, including detection of troop movements.

In order to carry out their missions, the Mohawks mount the following equipment:

> Two KA-60C 180-degree panoramic camera systems
> One KA-76 serial frame camera
> Infrared AN/AAS-24 surveillance system
> Alternative AN/APS-94D side-looking airborne radar (SLAR)

In addition, there are under-wing stations which allow the OV-1 to carry ECM pods and an LS-59A photo-flash unit. Deliveries of Mohawks to the *Chel Ha'Avir* commenced during the summer of 1976.

To counter ground-to-air missiles such as the SAM-6, Israel undoubtedly has procured advanced ECM gear from the United States, but any details relating to such equipment remains veiled in secrecy. It is, however, known that Israel acquired American Lance surface-to-surface missiles fitted with specially developed CBU cluster bomb warheads, and these are plainly intended for use against enemy missile batteries.

In order to help transport the Lance missiles to forward battle zones, Israel has also acquired eight Boeing CH-47C Chinook helicopters. These massive machines are capable of carrying seven-ton payloads on external slings, as well as 44 infantry troops or 24 stretchers or 27 paratroops in addition to their regular two-man crew. Somewhat smaller than the Chinooks are the dozen Sikorsky S-61 helicopters also recently obtained from the United States for troop transport, assault, and rescue roles.

With respect to fighters, the production of the *Kfir*—the indigenous J-79–powered version of the Mirage 5—has continued since its inception in 1972. As was indicated in an earlier chapter, the modifications required to marry the J-79 to the new Mirage's airframe went far beyond anything Israel's aircraft engineers had previously attempted, the *Barak* (Mirage III plus J-79) included. The aft fuselage had to be cut away because of the substantially shorter J-79 engine length. While this modification was destabilizing, the dorsal intake for the engine compartment cooling air restored the necessary stability. The wing leading edge was drooped to improve subsonic maneuverability, and altered trailing edge flaps were incorporated to improve take-off and landing characteristics. Because of increased engine weight and added external stores requirements, strengthened landing gear struts have been used to permit a higher all-up weight. *Kfirs* are armed with two 30-mm DEFA cannon with 125 rounds per gun.

Kfirs may be equipped with a small radome housing a radar similar to the Aida II for use in the ground-attack role. This radar is used solely for measurement of target range and the angular displacement to the line of sight. In addition, a navigation/attack system is fitted. For interception duties, a larger radome is fitted with a fire control system similar to the Cyrano II, which was manufactured under license in Israel for the Mirage III C. If the *Chel Ha'Avir* had had any reluctance about mass producing an indigenous fighter aircraft, this hesitation must have disappeared later when the United States State Department through withholding or delaying the finalization of agreements to sell the F-15 to Israel, attempted to apply pressure on Israel to adopt a "flexible" policy on concessions to Egypt.

If there was a basic flaw in the Mirage/*Kfir* concept, it was in the use of a pure delta configuration. Tailless deltas, while acceptable for bomber intercept, are not as maneuverable as more conventional fighter aircraft in the fighter-versus-fighter role. Much excess energy is lost because of trim drag at high angles of attack. While early production *Kfirs* were capable of level speed in the order of Mach 2.2, thanks to the additional thrust of the J-79 powerplant, the load-carrying limitations in the ground-attack role and the maneuvering limitations—both due to the tailless delta configuration—still remained.

A refinement of the basic version, known as the *Kfir*-C2, is a significant advance over the original. With greatly enhanced dogfight capabilities. the *Kfir*-C2 sports canard surfaces just aft of the air intakes and nose strakes. These changes, which have increased the basic weight by about 200 pounds, have resulted in an increase in maximum speed to over Mach 2.3.

The IDF/AF standardized on the *Kfir*-C2 for the air combat role to supplement the newer American fighter types destined for Israeli service. An export version of the C2 has been offered for $5 million, compared with $4.5 million for the original model. At that cost, the *Kfir* is among the most cost-effective aircraft in the world.

Among the squadrons of the *Chel Ha'Avir* now operating *Kfirs* is 101 Squadron, Israel's first fighter squadron, which had begun its operational career with Avia-Messerschmitts, then Spitfires, followed by Mustangs, Ouragons, Mystères, Super-Mystères, then Mirages. There are other new generation fighters which have come or will be coming along. And there may yet be another indigenous fighter which will serve with the IDF/AF in the future. But the *Kfir* is special. It was the first.

But good as the *Kfir* is, neither it nor the Phantom is advanced enough to cope easily with the newest Soviet threats to appear in Middle Eastern skies. The most prevalent of these aircraft, the MiG-23s (NATO-code-named "Flogger B") has already been delivered in considerable quantities to the air forces of Egypt, Syria, Iraq, and Libya. The Flogger is a swing-wing air superiority fighter with ground-attack capabilities. It is both faster and more maneuverable than the Phantom. A second fighter, the Sukhoi SU-20, is a more advanced version of the older SU-7 ground attacker.

The third, and most formidable, new Soviet plane is the famous MiG-25 ("Foxbat"), the world's fastest operational fighter. Although it is believed that no Foxbats have as yet been delivered to any Arab air forces, the threat that they may be at any time is clearly implicit. In any event, the *Chel Ha'Avir* has already had some dismaying encounters with Russian-piloted Foxbats. Since 1973 the Soviets have conducted a number of high altitude overflights of Israeli territory using Foxbats. Some of these flights ran along the Israeli coastline; others were made over Sinai. Phantoms which were scrambled to make interceptions failed even to get close to the intruders. Not even advance warning helped. In one case Israeli long-range detection devices picked up the sound of a Foxbat warming up its engines prior to take-off from the Damascus airport. The Israelis promptly scrambled a Phantom and positioned it so that it could attack the Foxbat with Sparrow air-to-air missiles when it entered Israeli air space. When the Foxbat finally arrived it was at 80,000 feet and going at an incredible Mach 3.2. Needless to say, the Phantom gave it no trouble whatsoever.

The fact is that the Phantom and, to some extent, the *Kfir*, do not really belong to the same generation of warplanes as the Flogger and the Foxbat, both of which incorporate the sophisticated technology of the mid-1970s. If the Israelis wanted anything comparable for the *Chel Ha'Avir*, the new equipment would not only have to come from America but have to be the very best the Americans could offer.

The Americans, on their own account, had been fretting about the Foxbat for some time and evolved two large fighters that they hoped might be able to cope with the Soviet threat: the two-place Grumman F-14 Tomcat and the single-place McDonnell Douglas F-15A Eagle. Neither plane is as fast as the Foxbat, but American planners believe them to be so much more maneuverable and sophisticated that the difference in speed is not crucial. Also in the works at the time that the Israelis began to express interest in new U.S. equipment was the General Dynamics F-16A, a lightweight single-place fighter.

The *Chel Ha'Avir* compared the F-14 and F-15. The Tomcat, though the slower of the two, could carry the long-range Phoenix missiles. But the Grumman aircraft had been dogged by technical problems, it was decidedly underpowered, and its cost—approximately $22 million each—decided the IDF/AF against it. After much negotiation, an order was placed for the F-15A. Initially, 48 of these Mach 2.5 fighters were ordered. But their size and cost still bothered the *Chel Ha'Avir*. "I don't want to be in the biggest target in the sky," commented one Israeli pilot. The order was cut back to 25, with a planned order of the cheaper, more agile F-16 to follow. Originally, deliveries were to begin in the spring of 1977, but the crisis situation in the Middle East was such that seven of the early F-15 test machines were sent back to McDonnell Douglas for refurbishing and were then ferried to Israel in the third quarter of 1976. The balance of the order was to be shipped in 1977. Then, the Ministry of Defence reversed itself and the original quantity was reinstated.

Perhaps even more attractive than the Eagle (at $15 million apiece) is the F-16A. Negotiations have been undertaken to add this agile little fighter to the IDF/AF in the future. At $4 million each, the F-16A offers great performance in an inexpensive package. The powerplant of the single-engine F-16A is identical to that in the larger twin-engine F-15A Eagle.

If a war were to break out now, what would the Israel Defence Force/Air Force have in operation? As of the beginning of 1978, the *Chel Ha'Avir* inventory, broadly, was as follows:

FIGHTER AND FIGHTER-BOMBERS

- 25 (approximately) F-15A Eagles—not all delivered—comprising one squadron (a second F-15A squadron will be formed upon delivery of the aircraft)
- 204 F-4E Phantom II fighter-bombers and 12 RF-4E reconnaissance fighters in six squadrons
- 50 Dassault Mirage III CJ interceptors in two squadrons
- 50 (approximately) *Neshers* (Israeli-built Mirages with the Atar engine) in two squadrons
- 50 (approximately) IAI *Kfirs* have been delivered in two squadrons; construction continues
- 25 Dassault Mystère IV fighters in storage
- 25 (approximately) Dassault Ouragons in storage

ATTACK AIRCRAFT

250+ A-4E/H/M/N Skyhawks and 24 two-seat TA-4H aircraft in
   six squadrons
10 Vautours in storage

TRAINERS

80 (approximately) IAI-built Fouga Magister twin-jet trainers
   armed with two light machine guns; these aircraft can also
   perform light ground-attack functions against lightly defended
   targets

TRANSPORT AIRCRAFT

12 Lockheed C-130E and 12 C-130H Hercules transports
2 Lockheed KC-130H aerial tankers
5 Boeing 707-320 transports variously configured for cargo, aerial
   refueling, and communications
12 Boeing C-97 Stratocruisers configured for aerial refueling,
   cargo, and electronic countermeasures (ECM) duties
20 Nord Noratlas transports
10 Douglas C-47 Dakotas

HELICOPTERS

12 Sud Super Frelons
15 Sikorsky S-65 C-3, and CH-53G
23 Bell 205 helicopters, used for medivac, communications, and,
   with TOW missiles, for anti-tank duties; these machines are
   actually Augusta-Bell aircraft, licensed and built in Italy
20+ Bell UH-1D; outwardly similar to the Augusta-Bell rotorcraft
a small number of Bell 206 Jet Rangers
12 Alouette II and III
12 Sikorsky S-61R
12 Boeing Vertol CH-47C Chinook missile transporters

LIGHT AIRCRAFT

20 Beech Model 80 Queen Air
12 Britten-Norman Islanders
10 Dornier Do 27
10 Dornier Do 28
14 IAI Arava 201
5 Cessna 206C Super Skywagon
3 IAI Westwind
20 Piper Super Cubs

EARLY WARNING AIRCRAFT

a small number of Grumman OV-1 Mohawks
4 Grumman E-2C Hawkeyes with an option for 2 more

MISCELLANEOUS

Ryan 124-1 reconnaissance drones

Israel will have, as first-line equipment for the foreseeable future, the F-15A Eagle, the *Kfir*-C2, the F-16, and the A-4 strike aircraft. To avoid being caught napping, as in 1973, Israel will depend on Elint equipment in helicopters, in E-2C Hawkeye and, possibly, OV-10 or EA-6B reconnaissance aircraft, supplemented by their force of some one dozen RF-4E Phantoms. There will probably also be increasing emphasis on the use of RPVs to interdict the SAM belts which took such a heavy toll of IDF/AF equipment in the past.

Is this force adequate to meet the challenges it might have to face if a Middle Eastern war were to erupt again in the near future? In some ways it is more difficult to answer this question now than at any time in the past. Not only is military technology evolving at such a rate that it tends to make even recent battlefield experience obsolete, but there have also been some dramatic shifts in the political and military situation within the Arab world. Notable among these has been the collapse of Russian influence in Egypt. By March 1976, Soviet-Egyptian relations had eroded to such a point that the Egyptians renounced their fifteen-year Treaty of Friendship with the Soviet Union, and the Russians, in retaliation, ceased all arms shipments to Egypt. One result of this has been a steady deterioration of equipment in all the Egyptian armed forces. Without spare parts or Russian maintenance, the Soviet-equipped Egyptian air force has largely fallen into disrepair, the unserviceability problem extending even to the most advanced aircraft now in Egyptian service—the twenty-odd MiG-23s delivered just prior to the Russian embargo. The United States has indicated that it might be willing to help the EAF out with deliveries of Northrop F-5E Tiger II lightweight fighters and other types, but it has proffered nothing on a par with the F-15 or F-16, and, as of this writing, has still not made any significant contribution to the EAF. Deliveries of small numbers of Saudi-supplied Mirage III E fighter-bombers and Mirage F-ICs directly from France have in the meantime eased Egypt's problem. A massive overhaul of Russian equipment by the United States and Great Britain is also in the offing.

Until its falling out with the Soviet Union, Egypt had always been Israel's most dangerous potential adversary. Now that dubious honor must go to Syria, the second largest Arab state on Israel's borders and still, insofar as weaponry is concerned, a Russian client. Since 1973 the Syrian Arab Air Force (SAAF) has taken delivery of approximately 140 late-model MiG-21s, 20 SU-20 tactical strike aircraft, and 45 MiG-23 and MiG-27 (the MiG-27 is essentially an advanced version of the MiG-23) interceptors. Additionally, Syria's SAM and anti-aircraft defenses have been greatly strengthened.

Iraq and Libya, though not immediate neighbors of Israel, have both continued to exhibit a high degree of hostility toward her. Both have recently received SAMs and MiG-23 and -27 aircraft from the Russians. The Libyans also have a strategic bombardment capability of sorts in the form of one squadron (probably Russian-manned) of three-jet Tupolev TU-22 bombers. (The fact that the Israeli F-15s also have limited strategic capabilities should be noted in this connection.) Algeria, though also very hostile and also Soviet-supplied, is probably both too far away and too weak militarily to be of immediate concern to Israel. Of the remaining major Arab states, none, including Saudi Arabia, maintains a very large military establishment and the majority—again including the Saudis—have pursued a relatively moderate policy toward Israel.

Thus, while Israel still has plenty of enemies, the temporary decline of Egyptian military power has made a vast improvement in Israel's position in the Middle East's ever-changing power balance. This ephemeral advantage could easily be offset if United States foreign policy were to assume a more pro-Arab orientation or if Egypt were once again to become a Soviet client, but for the time being, Israel's military position has probably never been more secure.

For nearly thirty years Israel's best hope of survival has always lain in her ability to win the next war. Now perhaps—just perhaps— her best hope may lie in her ability to avoid it. Egyptian President Anwar el-Sadat's unprecedented visit to Israel in November 1977 offered the possibility that for the first time since the War of Independence Israel and her most formidable enemy might at last find a way of composing their differences. If this were to happen, not only the Middle East but the whole world would take an enormous step toward achieving that goal of peace for which Israel has spent so much treasure and blood.

If the current negotiations fail—if again it is to be war—the *Chel Ha'Avir* will be ready. But if the peacemakers succeed, the men of the *Chel Ha'Avir*, past and present, can take pride in knowing that but for them Israel might never have endured to see a day when war would no longer be the condition of her survival.

APPENDIX I

HISTORICAL SUMMARY

CHRONOLOGY OF THE ISRAEL
DEFENCE FORCE/AIR FORCE (*CHEL HA'AVIR*)

November 1947	*Sherut Avir* ("Air Service") was formed.
May 14, 1948	The British mandate for Palestine was ended and the State of Israel was proclaimed. At midnight, Israel was invaded by the armies of Egypt, Syria, Jordan, and Lebanon, as well as contingents from Iraq and an "irregular" army led by Fawzi el Kaukji.
May 15, 1948	Tel Aviv was attacked by Egyptian Spitfires.
May 20, 1948	The Israeli Air Force attacked Arab forces near Samakh in the east. Tel Aviv was again bombed by the Egyptian Air Force.
May 29, 1948	Israeli fighter aircraft undertook their first mission when four Avia S-199 fighters (code-named *Sakhinim* or "knives") attacked an Egyptian armored column at Ashdod.
June 11, 1948	A truce was arranged by the United Nations. The cessation of hostilities, the first of the War of Independence, lasted until July 9.
July 18, 1948	A second truce was arranged, this one lasting until October 10.
October 15, 1948	Israeli forces launched "Operation *Yoav*." For the first time in the War of Independence, an Israeli offensive began with an aerial assault. Israeli aircraft bombed and strafed aircraft of the Egyptian air force stationed at El Arish.
December 27, 1948	Egypt staged air raids against Tel Aviv and Haifa. Israeli aircraft attacked El Arish and Rafah.
January 7, 1949	Israeli Spitfires intercepted RAF Spitfires operating in support of Egyptian forces. Four of the RAF fighters were downed. Later in the day, an RAF Tempest was shot down when four Tempests and a

143

	Mosquito were intercepted while searching for the downed RAF Spitfires.
February 24, 1949	An armistice agreement between Israel and Egypt was signed on the Island of Rhodes.
October 27, 1955	Abdul Gamal Nasser, Prime Minister of Egypt, announced an arms deal with Czechoslovakia. In exchange for cotton and rice, Egypt was to receive 530 armored vehicles, including 230 tanks, 500 pieces of artillery, 150 MiG-15 jet fighters, 50 Ilyushin Il-28 twin-jet bombers, many hundreds of transport vehicles, submarines, destroyers, and smaller naval units. At the time of this transaction, Israel and Egypt each possessed about 200 tanks. Egypt had about 80 jet fighters, while Israel had about 50 jet aircraft.
November 1, 1955	Jordan announced her intention of acquiring heavy modern weapons and forming an efficient air force.
July 1956	France agreed to supply Israel with modern jet fighters, including Ouragons and Mystère IVs, the latter becoming the first swept-wing jet to enter service with Israel.
October 25, 1956	Egypt, Syria, and Jordan announced the signing of a tripartite military agreement aimed at establishing a joint Arab command.
October 29, 1956	Outbreak of the Suez War. Sixteen IDF/AF Dakotas dropped a battalion of parachute troops at the Mitla Pass, 45 miles from the Suez Canal. Israeli Mustangs flew throughout the Sinai, cutting telephone lines with their propellers and wings to disrupt communications. During this short campaign, the IDF/AF shot down four MiGs and four de Havilland Vampires, while losing nine aircraft, eight of them to ground fire. The ninth, a Piper Super Cub, was brought down by a MiG-15. A cease-fire went into effect on November 6.
August 16, 1966	An Iraqi air force pilot defected to Israel in a MiG-21F fighter. *Chel Ha'Avir* pilots, by flying this aircraft, became familiar with the characteristics of the "Fishbed," the standard air combat fighter of Syria, Iraq, and Egypt.
April 7, 1967	A major air battle developed over the Sea of Galilee between Syrian MiG-21 fighters and Israeli Mirages. During the course of the battle, seven MiG-21s were shot down without loss to the *Chel Ha'Avir*.
June 5, 1967	Outbreak of the Six Day War. On the first day, the IDF/AF destroyed 350 Arab aircraft, 300 of them

Egyptian, including the entire inventory of Tupolev Tu-16 heavy bombers.

By the close of this brief war, the Arab air forces had lost 452 aircraft, 79 of them in air combat. Israel lost a total of 50 aircraft, mostly to ground fire, with 20 pilots killed. This victory was the greatest ever achieved by any air force in history.

March 1969 to August, 1970
The War of Attrition, fought on and over the banks of the Suez Canal, saw Egyptian artillery, protected by SAMS, hammering at Israeli positions. For its part, the IDF/AF flew repeated sorties against the SAMs and the Egyptian artillery. The fighting ended with the acceptance by both sides of an American-sponsored cease-fire.

September 6, 1969
Israel announced the arrival of the first McDonnell Douglas F-4E Phantom II from the United States.

July 30, 1970
In a large-scale engagement between Mirages and Phantoms of the *Chel Ha'Avir* and Soviet-piloted MiG-21 Fishbed-J fighters, five Russians were shot down, without loss to the IDF/AF. Three of the Russian pilots were killed during this battle.

September 13, 1973
Thirteen Syrian MiG-21 fighters and one Israeli Mirage were lost in combat over the Mediterranean Sea. The battle began when sixteen MiG-21s intercepted twelve Mirages in international waters about 150 miles north of Haifa. More MiGs later joined the battle. After the battle, IDF/AF helicopters rescued the Israeli pilot and one of the Syrian airmen. From the end of the 1967 Six Day War to this date, some 60 Syrian aircraft had been shot down for a loss of four *Chel Ha'Avir* fighters.

October 6, 1973
Outbreak of the Yom Kippur War. This war saw the employment by all sides of 6,000 modern tanks and 1,500 combat aircraft. Egypt and Syria began the fighting by launching a simultaneous two-front assault against the Golan Heights and across the Suez Canal. The forces were bolstered by contingents from Jordan, Saudi Arabia, Iraq, Algeria, Sudan, and Kuwait. Pakistani, North Korean, and Libyan pilots also were engaged in the fighting. Israel lost a total of 2,521 soldiers in the war. Syria had 1,100 tanks destroyed, while Israel lost 104 aircraft—almost one-quarter of her force—primarily to SAMS. Some 450 Arab aircraft were also destroyed in combat.

While Syria and Egypt were being resupplied on a

massive scale by the Soviet Union, the United States began a resupply operation to Israel. About 23,000 tons of arms and ammunition were flown in. A total of 670 transport missions were flown, many of them with C-5A galaxy transports. Even M-48 tanks were flown in to replace the heavy losses in tanks suffered by Israel. TOW anti-tank missiles and ECM equipment were also airlifted. Including replacement F-4 Phantoms and A-4 Skyhawks, the American aid amounted to $800 million.

July 4, 1976

The *Chel Ha'Avir*, using four C-130H Hercules transports, flew commando units almost 2,500 miles to Entebbe Airport, Uganda, to rescue 103 hostages, many of then Israelis, held by hijackers who threatened to kill them. A *Chel Ha'Avir* Boeing 707 acted as a command and communications ship, while a second Boeing 707, outfitted as a mobile hospital, was flown to nearby Kenya to await the arrival of the rescued hostages and to treat any wounded. The transports were escorted for most of the journey by F-4E Phantom escorts. The hostages were freed, with seven hijackers, three hostages, one Israeli officer, and at least twenty Ugandan soldiers being killed in the brief battle which took place at the airport. To cover their escape, Israeli soldiers blew up seven Ugandan MiG-21 and four MiG-17 fighters.

APPENDIX II

THE EVOLUTION OF ISRAELI AIRCRAFT ARMAMENT

MACHINE GUNS AND CANNON

During the earliest period of the Israel Defence Force/Air Force, aircraft armament was, at best, a haphazard thing. The Boeing B-17G aircraft arrived in Israel without guns of any sort. The .50-inch Browning machine guns which were the normal armament of the B-17G Flying Fortress were unavailable, so .30-inch machine guns were used instead. Spitfires were armed with 20-mm cannon and Mustangs had .50-inch machine guns. Aircraft were not rearmed, but fought with whatever weapons were either standard equipment or available at the time.

Immediately after the 1948 War of Independence, large numbers of Mosquito fighter-bombers, armed with .303-inch machine guns and 20-mm cannon, were obtained. They served alongside Mustangs and Spitfires, so that the logistics of maintaining so many different types of ammunition was a real problem.

By the time the 1956 Suez War broke out, the Spitfires and Mosquitos were no longer in service. Gloster Meteors and Dassault Ouragons, both armed with 20-mm cannon, were used along with the machine-gun-armed Mustangs. The Mystère IVA fighters, however, were armed with 30-mm cannon, the first of this size in *Chel Ha'Avir* service.

Immediately after the Suez War, Vautour attack bombers were obtained from the French and these, as well as the Super Mystère, and later the Mirage III CJ, were armed with the hard-hitting 30-mm DEFA cannon. One of the few aircraft to buck this trend was the little Magister trainer/ground-attack aircraft which, because of its diminutive size, was able to carry nothing more potent than a pair of 7.62-mm machine guns.

When Israel began taking delivery of the McDonnell Douglas A-4 Skyhawk, two 30-mm DEFA were specified as standard armament in place of the pair of 20-mm cannon which were the Skyhawk's normal armament.

The IDF/AF has been overjoyed with the 30-mm gun. It has destroyed tanks and has been lethal against enemy aircraft, often destroying the foe with no more than one or two hits. The air force has been critical of the smaller 20-mm round, considering that shell to lack the killing power of the larger round. *Chel Ha'Avir* pilots realize that in combat with such agile opponents as the MiG-21 Fishbed or the Sukhoi Su-7 Fitter, it is difficult to keep one's sights on the enemy for more than a very few seconds. Either the adversary is knocked out with a short burst or it survives. There is no other alternative. And an enemy that survives your attack may shortly turn the tables on you.

The McDonnell Douglas F-4E is armed with the 20-mm M61 rotary cannon. Although the round fired by the "Gatling" is not as large as desired by the *Chel Ha'Avir*, the rate of fire of 100 rounds per second compensates for its lower weight. Nevertheless, at least one Phantom has been fitted experimentally with a pair of 30-mm DEFAs in place of the M61.

AIR-TO-AIR MISSILES

The IDF/AF took a lot of convincing regarding AAMs. Nor did their early experiences with these guided weapons lessen this bias. At the time that the *Chel Ha'Avir* acquired their Dassault Mirage interceptors from the French government, they also purchased Matra R.530 missiles. These weapons, with a 60-pound warhead and a range of 3.7 miles, had a launch weight of 429 pounds. They were heavy, reducing the performance of the Mirages considerably. Also they were expensive. And even worse, they were not as effective as the cannon armament in the Israeli fighters.

At a time when the United States was relying solely on AAM armament on such aircraft as the early Phantoms (not to mention the F-86D with unguided rockets), Israel held fast to the belief that its cannon-armed fighters were superior for air combat. Nor did the arrival of the missile-armed Fishbed-D into the Middle East arena shake their faith in automatic cannon.

When the *Chel Ha'Avir* purchased the cannon-armed F-4E, they also acquired Sparrow and Sidewinder missiles for use with this Phantom variant. With a launch weight of 400 pounds and a warhead containing 60 pounds of high explosives, the Sparrow was similar to the Matra R.530 in size. However, the Sparrow, with semi-active radar homing, had a range of 13.8 miles, approximately four times that of the French missile. The Sparrow has not figured prominently in Middle Eastern air battles, though.

The Sidewinder is a different story altogether. It is a much smaller missile than the Sparrow. Depending on model, it has a launch weight slightly under 200 pounds, with an H.E. warhead weighing in at about 10 pounds. The Sidewinder has infrared guidance.

If there was any drawback to the Sidewinder, it was the fact that the price was somewhat high. This led to Israel's developing the *Shafrir* ("Dragonfly"), a reliable, simplified infrared guided AAM. The *Shafrir* was first blooded in the 1973 Yom Kippur War. It was in this conflict that the Israeli AAM, with a cost about one-quarter that of the Sidewinder, had the highest ratio of kills to firings of any of the guided missiles used during that war.

Since the 1973 war, the *Shafrir* has been revealed publicly and has been offered for export. An improved *Shafrir* with dogfight capability is already in development.

AIR-TO-SURFACE WEAPONS

During the War of Independence, the *Chel Ha'Avir*'s bombs were decidedly ersatz. Hand grenades were dropped from Austers, large egg-shaped cannisters were rolled and shoved and manhandled through Dakota and Commando hatches. With the end of the war, *Tass*, the Israeli arms industry, produced weapons of a more conventional nature. Bombs and unguided surface-to-air rockets were largely patterned after weapons of British, French, and American manufacture.

While most of the bombs and surface-to-air rockets in the IDF/AF inventory of the Fifties and Sixties were conventional, one decidedly was not. This was the "dibber."

Of French design, the dibber was a bomb designed by the French and adopted by Israel for the purpose of rendering airfield runways inoperative. Upon release, a retro-rocket slowed the bomb, which assumed a vertical position. Then, another rocket motor accelerated the bomb and drove it through the concrete runways. A delayed-action fuse allowed the dibber to drive all the way through the runway before the bomb exploded. This left a large crater which required considerable repair before the runway could again be used.

In the 1967 Six Day War, Egyptian military runways were knocked out by dibbers. Some had fuses with longer delays, so that the runways were kept out of action for long periods, giving the *Chel Ha'Avir* ample time to destroy the aircraft, which could neither go into action or escape. Many of these were destroyed by French Nord AS-30 surface-to-air missiles with infrared homing devices. These homed in on aircraft warming up on the fields below.

After the French embargo of weapons to Israel after the Six Day War, war material from the United States began to supplement the output from the Israeli armaments industry. In the interests of standardization, *Tass* began to manufacture bombs and rockets of American rather than French design. These included the following:

> M-118 3,000-pound bomb
> Mk.84 2,000-pound bomb
> Mk. 83 1,000-pound bomb
> M-117 750-pound bomb

Mk. 82 500-pound bomb
Mk. 81 250-pound bomb
LAU-51 rocket launchers, each containing nineteen
    70-mm rockets
LAU-10 rocket launchers, each containing four
    127-mm ZUNI rockets

In addition, there are the specialized bombs and rockets of Israeli design and manufacture. Another external store (which, strictly speaking, does not belong in this section) is the American-designed SUU-23 pod containing a 20-mm Vulcan cannon. It is deployed on pylons in much the same way as are fuel tanks, bombs, or rockets.

During the 1969–1970 War of Attrition, heavy losses to Soviet-supplied SA-2 missiles prompted the *Chel Ha'Avir* to request Shrike anti-radiation missiles which homed in on radar emanations from the SAM guidance equipment. These were furnished by the United States government and, together with American-furnished ECM (electronic countermeasures) equipment, reduced aircraft losses.

After the cease-fire which marked the close of the War of Attrition, Israel retained a large measure of the complacency founded on the lightning victory of the Six Day War. That war, and the War of Attrition on the banks of the Suez, had convinced the Israeli high command that there was little to fear from the SA-2 missile. Consequently, in the early 1970s, when the option of developing an RPV anti-SAM arose, it was rejected on the grounds that the *Chel Ha'Avir* could penetrate and destroy SAM belts with minimal losses. Their calculations, however, did not include the deadly SA-6 mobile SAM which was supplied to Syria and Egypt in vast quantities by the Soviet Union.

To combat the deadly array of Soviet-supplied SAMs and anti-aircraft guns as well as the latest radar units which supplied data to these weapons, the United States airlift to Israel, during the October Yom Kippur War, included large numbers of air-to-surface missiles as well as ECM pods.

Among the missiles airlifted in were advanced Shrike anti-radiation missiles. These weapons homed in on ground radar signals and destroyed the tracking equipment. Rockeye cluster bombs which the United States first deployed in Vietnam, were anti-personnel weapons and, in this case, were intended to cut down the personnel manning the SAM batteries. In no small measure, they were responsible for cutting a great gap in the Syrian missile belt.

Walleye "smart" bombs, both television- and laser-guided models, were supplied in large numbers. The HOBOS television-guided rockets and the highly advanced Maverick stand-off weapon also began to appear in the arsenal of the *Chel Ha'Avir*. The American weapons introduced during the 1973 war turned the tide. With the destruction of the SAM batteries, the Arab military were forced to commit their air forces to battle. Even the thirty North Korean pilots who flew with the Egyptian air force could not bolster that air force's abilities to any extent. In the one-sided battles which followed, battles which saw forty and fifty fighters on each side battling in old-fashioned dogfights, the Arab forces were badly mauled.

Although after the Yom Kippur War the IDF/AF continued to maintain in their inventory the Mavericks, Shrikes, and other air-to-surface weapons supplied by the United States, research continued aimed at the development of an indigenous weapon. This search has paid off. In 1977 the *Chel Ha'Avir* began to deploy their "home-grown" answer to the SAMs in the form of the *Luz*-1. Modifications were introduced on both the Phantoms and the *Kfir*-C2 fighter-bombers to allow them to carry this weapon.

The *Luz*-1 is a long-range (about 50 miles) television-guided missile with a 440-pound warhead. This missile, designed primarily to knock out SAMs, is said to be impervious to jamming. The *Luz*-1 has many components in common with the Gabriel surface-to-surface missile used successfully by Israel's navy during the 1973 war.

APPENDIX III

AIRCRAFT
SPECIFICATIONS

AEROSPATIALE SA 321K SUPER FRELON

Type: Medium transport helicopter
Crew: Two
Rotor diameter: 62 feet
Fuselage length: 63 feet, 7¾ inches
Height: 16 feet, 2 inches
Powerplant: three 1,550 shaft horsepower Turbomeca Turmo III C6
  turboshafts
Armament: none

Performance
Maximum speed: 149 mph at sea level
Cruising speed: 143 mph
Range: 404 miles (with a 2,500-kilogram payload)
Maximum climb: 1,372 feet per minute
Hovering ceiling: 7,380 feet in ground effect; 1,804 feet out of ground
  effect

Weights
Empty: 14,420 pounds
Maximum loaded: 27,557 pounds

AIRSPEED A.S. 65 CONSUL

Type: trainer and light cargo transport
Crew: Two
Span: 53 feet, 4 inches
Length: 35 feet, 4 inches
Height: 10 feet, 1½ inches
Powerplant: two 395 horsepower Armstrong Siddeley Cheetah 10
  air-cooled, radial engines
Armament: none

Performance
Cruising speed: 156 mph
Range: 900 miles

Weights
Empty: 6,047 pounds
Loaded: 8,250 pounds

AUSTER A.O.P. 5

Type: observation plane (pressed into service as a bomber in the 1948
    War)
Crew: two (or one with bomb load)
Span: 36 feet
Length: 22 feet, 5 inches
Height: 6 feet, 8 inches
Powerplant: one 130-horsepower Lycoming 0-290 four-cylinder
    horizontally opposed air-cooled engine
Armament: grenades, or one homemade 125-pound bomb known as a
    "pushkin" (It was in the cabin beside the pilot and was pushed out by
    hand, hence the name.)

Performance
Maximum speed: 130 mph
Cruising speed: 112 mph
Rate of climb: 800 feet per minute
Range: 220 miles
Service ceiling: 15,000 feet

Weights
Empty: 1,050 pounds
Maximum loaded: 1,920 pounds

AUSTER J/1 AUTOCRAT

Type: light cabin monoplane (pressed into service as a
    reconnaissance/bomber aircraft)
Crew: normally three; in military operation, one or two
Span: 36 feet
Length: 23 feet, 5 inches
Height: 6 feet, 6 inches
Powerplant: one 100-horsepower Cirrus Minor II four-cylinder in-line
    air-cooled engine
Armament: normally none; adapted for armament by Israel; for
    armaments carried, see Auster A.O.P. 5

Performance
Maximum speed: 120 mph
Cruising speed: 100 mph
Rate of climb: 568 feet per minute
Service ceiling: 15,000 feet
Range: 270 miles

Weights
Empty: 1,052 pounds
Loaded:1,850 pounds

AVIA S-199

Type: fighter
Crew: one
Span: 32 feet, 6½ inches
Length: 29 feet, 10¼ inches
Height: 8 feet, 6 inches
Powerplant: one Junkers Jumo Ju 211F; 1,350 horsepower at 2,600 rpm
Armament: two 12.7-mm MG 131 machine guns above the engine and
    two 20-mm MG 151 cannon in underwing gondolas

Performance

Maximum speed: 366 mph
Cruising speed: 287 mph
Rate of climb: 2,165 feet per minute initial rate
Range: 528 miles at 248 mph
Service ceiling: 31,170 feet

Weights
Empty: 5,730 pounds
Normal loaded: 7,714 pounds

AVRO ANSON

Type: twin-engine advanced trainer and light transport
Crew: two
Span: 56 feet, 6 inches
Length: 42 feet, 3 inches
Height: 13 feet, 6 inches
Powerplant: two 420-horsepower Armstrong Siddeley Cheetah 15 radial
    air-cooled engines
Armament: none normally mounted in this version

Performance
Maximum speed: 190 mph at sea level
Cruising speed: 175 mph
Range: 600 miles
Rate of climb: 750 feet per minute
Service ceiling: 18,750 feet

Weights
Empty: 6,114 pounds
Loaded: 9,770 pounds

BEECH MODEL 80 QUEEN AIR

Type: light utility transport
Crew: one or two
Span: 45 feet, 10½ inches
Length: 35 feet, 3 inches
Height: 14 feet, 8 inches

Powerplant: two 380-horsepower Lycoming IGSO-540-A1A six-cylinder
    horizontally opposed air-cooled engines
Armament: none

Performance
Maximum speed: 252 mph at 11,500 feet
Cruising speed: 230 mph at 15,000 feet (70 percent power)
Range: 1,330 miles
Rate of climb: 1,600 feet per minute
Service ceiling: 29,100 feet

Weights
Empty: 4,800 pounds
Loaded:8,000 pounds

BEECHCRAFT MODEL 35 BONANZA

Type: all metal cabin monoplane
Crew: one; accommodations for four
Span: 33 feet, 5½ inches
Length: 25 feet, 1 inch
Height: 6 feet, 6½ inches
Powerplant: one 185-horsepower Continental E-185-1 air-cooled
    horizontally opposed piston engine
Armament: none; during the War of Independence, it was used to drop
    homemade bombs and, at various times, hand-held automatic and
    semi-automatic weapons fired from within the cabin

Performance
Maximum speed: 184 mph
Cruising speed: 172 mph
Rate of climb: 950 feet, per minute
Range: 750 statute miles (maximum)
Service ceiling: 17,100 feet
Note: It has, at various times, been stated that this aircraft was a Model B
    35 Bonanza. Inasmuch as the Model B 35 did not appear on the Beech
    assembly line until 1950, it is safe to assume that the craft was, in
    truth, the first production model built in 1947 and 1948.

Weights
Empty: 1,580 pounds
Loaded: 2,650 pounds

BELL AH-1G HUEYCOBRA

Type: attack helicopter
Crew: two
Rotor diameter: 44 feet
Fuselage length: 44 feet, 5 inches
Powerplant: one 1,400 shaft horsepower Lycoming T53-L-13B turboshaft
Armament: one turret-mounted XM-197 three-barrel 20-mm cannon plus
    four attachment points for Minigun pods or rockets

Performance
Maximum speed: 219 mph
Range: 357 miles
Rate of climb: 1,230 feet per minute

Weights
Empty: 6,096 pounds
Maximum take-off weight: 9,500 pounds

BELL MODEL 47G-3B

Type: three-seat utility helicopter
Rotary diameter: 37 feet, 1½ inches
Fuselage length: 31 feet, 7 inches
Height: 9 feet, 3½ inches
Powerplant: one 260-horsepower Lycoming TVO-435 six-cylinder
    horizontally opposed piston engine
Armament: none

Performance
Maximum speed: 105 mph at sea level
Cruising speed: 92 mph at 5,000 feet
Range: 204 miles (maximum)
Rate of climb: 1,075 feet per minute
Hovering Ceiling: 19,400 feet in ground effect

Weights
Empty: 1,713 pounds
Maximum loaded: 2,850 pounds

BELL MODEL 206A JET RANGER

Type: five-seat utility helicopter
Rotor diameter: 33 feet, 4 inches
Fuselage length: 31 feet, 2 inches
Powerplant: one 317 shaft horsepower Allison 250-C18 turboshaft

Performance
Maximum speed: 150 mph at sea level
Cruising speed: 131 mph
Range: 460 miles
Rate of climb: 1,450 feet per minute
Hovering ceiling: 7,900 feet in ground effect; 3,350 feet out of ground
    effect

Weights
Empty: 1,425 pounds
Maximum take-off weight: 3,000 pounds

BELL MODEL 212 TWIN TWO-TWELVE

Type: 15-seat utility helicopter
Rotar diameter: 48 feet, 2½ inches

Powerplant: One 1,800 shaft horsepower Pratt & Whitney PT6T-3 coupled
    turboshaft (two turboshaft engines coupled to a single output shaft)
Armament: none

Performance
Maximum speed: 121 mph at sea level
Range: 296 miles at sea level
Rate of climb: 1,090 feet per minute
Hovering Ceiling: 17,100 feet in ground effect, 9,900 feet out of ground
    effect

Weights
Empty: 5,500 pounds
Maximum take-off weight: 10,000 pounds

BELL UH-1D IROQUOIS (AUGUSTA-BELL 205A)

Type: fifteen-seat utility helicopter
Rotor diameter: 48 feet
Fuselage length: 41 feet, 6 inches
Height: 13 feet, 4 inches
Powerplant: one 1,400 shaft horsepower Lycoming T53-L-13 turboshaft
Armament: none

Performance
Maximum speed: 127 mph at sea level
Cruising speed: 110 mph
Range: 392 miles
Rate of climb: 1,760 ft/min.
Hovering ceiling: 10,000 feet in ground effect; 4,500 feet out of ground
    effect

Weights
Empty: 4,667 pounds
Maximum take-off weight: 9,500 pounds

BOEING B-17G FLYING FORTRESS

Type: bomber
Crew: ten
Span: 103 feet, 9 inches
Length: 74 feet, 4 inches
Height: 19 feet, 1 inch
Powerplant: four 1,200 horsepower Wright R-1820-97 air-cooled engines
Armament: thirteen .50-inch machine guns

Performance
Maximum speed: 287 mph at 25,000 feet
Cruising speed: 182 mph
Range: 1,800 miles at 160 mph at 25,000 feet with a 4,000-pound bomb
    load
Rate of climb: 900 feet per minute
Service ceiling: 35,000 feet

Weights
Empty: 36,135 pounds
Equipped: 44,560 pounds
Normal take-off weight: 55,000 pounds
Maximum take-off weight: 72,000 pounds

BOEING C-97 STRATOCRUISER

Type: long-range military transport and flight-refueling tanker
Crew: four
Span: 141 feet, 3 inches
Length: 110 feet, 4 inches
Height: 38 feet, 3 inches
Powerplant: four 3,500-horsepower Pratt & Whitney R-4360 four-bank
    radial air-cooled engines
Armament: none

Performance
Maximum speed: 375 mph at 25,000 feet
Cruising speed: 300 mph
Range: 4,300 miles
Rate of climb: 1,100 feet per minute
Service ceiling: 35,000 feet

Weights
Empty: 82,490 pounds
Normal loaded: 153,000 pounds
Maximum loaded: 175,000 pounds

BOEING-STEARMAN PT-17 KAYDET

Type: two-seat primary trainer and general-purpose biplane
Span: 32 feet, 2 inches
Length: 25 feet
Height: 9 feet, 2 inches
Powerplant: one 220-horsepower Continental W-670 air-cooled radial
    (other engines also used)
Armament: none

Performance
Maximum speed: 124 mph
Cruising speed: 106 mph
Range: 505 miles
Rate of climb: 840 feet per minute
Service ceiling: 11,300 feet

Weights
Empty: 1,936 pounds
Loaded: 2,717 pounds

BOEING VERTOL CH-47C CHINOOK

Type: medium-transport helicopter
Crew: two or three

Rotor diameter: 60 feet
Fuselage length: 51 feet
Height: 18 feet 6½ inches
Powerplant: two 3,750 shaft horsepower Lycoming T55-L-11 turboshafts
Armament: none

Performance
Maximum speed: 190 mph at sea level
Cruising speed: 158 mph
Rate of climb: 3,275 feet per minute
Hovering ceiling: 14,750 feet
Range: 250 miles

Weights
Empty: 20,378 pounds
Maximum gross: 46,000 pounds

BOEING 707-320B

Type: long-range commercial transport
Crew: three to five
Span: 145 feet, 9½ inches
Length: 152 feet, 11 inches
Height: 42 feet, 5 inches
Powerplant: four Pratt & Whitney JT3D-3 turbofans each rated at
    18,000-pound static thrust (wet)
Armament: none

Performance
Maximum speed: 615 mph at 23,000 feet
Cruising speed: 597 mph at 23,000 feet
Range: 5,735 miles (8,070 miles with maximum fuel)
Rate of climb: 4,000 feet per minute
Service ceiling: 39,000 feet

Weights
Empty: 137,500 pounds
Maximum loaded: 328,000 pounds

BRISTOL BEAUFIGHTER Mk. 10

Type: twin-engine attack aircraft
Crew: two
Span: 57 feet, 10 inches
Length: 41 feet, 4 inches
Height: 15 feet, 10 inches
Powerplant: two 1,600-horsepower Bristol Hercules XVII
    fourteen-cylinder radial air-cooled engines
Armament: four 20-mm cannon mounted in the lower portion of the nose
    and six .303-inch machine guns in the wings

Performance
Maximum speed: 320 mph at 10,000 feet
Range: 1,750 miles
Rate of climb: 1,460 feet per minute
Service ceiling: 19,000 feet

Weights
Empty: 15,592 pounds
Normal loaded: 24,000 pounds
Maximum overload: 25,400 pounds

BRISTOL BEAUFIGHTER Mk. IIF

Type: twin-engine attack aircraft
Crew: two
Span: 57 feet, 10 inches
Length: 42 feet, 9 inches
Height: 15 feet, 10 inches
Powerplant: two 1,250-horsepower Rolls-Royce Merlin XX
    twelve-cylinder liquid-cooled engines
Armament: four 20-mm cannon mounted in the lower portion of the nose
    and six .303-inch machine guns in the wings

Performance
Maximum speed: 301 mph at 15,000 feet
Cruising speed: 177 mph
Range: 1,170 miles
Rate of climb: 1,960 feet per minute
Service ceiling: 26,500 feet

Weights
Empty: 13,800 pounds
Normal loaded: 21,000 pounds
Maximum overload: 25,400 pounds

BRITTEN-NORMAN BN-2A ISLANDER

Type: light utility transport
Crew: one or two and eight or nine passengers
Span: 49 feet
Length: 39 feet, 5¼ inches
Height: 13 feet, 8 inches
Powerplant: two 260-horsepower Lycoming 0-540-E4C5 six-cylinder
    horizontally opposed air-cooled engines
Armament: none

Performance
Maximum speed: 170 mph at sea level
Cruising speed: 160 mph at 7,000 feet (75 percent power)
Range: 717 miles
Rate of climb: 1,050 feet per minute
Service ceiling: 14,600 feet

Weights
Empty: 3,675 pounds
Maximum take-off weight: 6,600 pounds

CESSNA MODEL 207 SUPER SKYWAGON

Type: seven-seat light utility transport
Span: 36 feet, 7 inches
Length: 31 feet, 9 inches
Height: 9 feet, 5 inches
Powerplant: one 300-horsepower Continental I0-520-F six-cylinder
    horizontally opposed air-cooled engine
Armament: none

Performance
Maximum speed: 168 mph at sea level
Cruising speed: 158 mph at 6,500 feet (75 percent power)
Range: 695 miles
Rate of climb: 810 feet per minute
Service ceiling: 13,300 feet

Weights
Empty: 1,858 pounds
Maximum take-off weight: 3,800 pounds

CESSNA 185 SKYWAGON

Type: light utility transport
Crew: one
Span: 36 feet
Length: 26 feet, 2 inches
Height: 7 feet, 6½ inches
Powerplant: one 260-horsepower Continental I0-470-F six-cylinder
    horizontally opposed air-cooled engine
Armament: none

Performance
Maximum speed: 176 mph at sea level
Cruising speed: 165 mph at 8,000 feet at 70 percent power
Range: 885 miles (maximum)
Rate of climb: 1,000 feet per minute
Service ceiling: 17,300 feet

Weights
Empty: 1,520 pounds
Normal loaded: 3,200 pounds

CESSNA 205 SUPER SKYWAGON

Type: light utility transport
Crew: one
Span: 36 feet, 7 inches
Length: 27 feet, 9 inches
Height: 9 feet

Powerplant: one 260-horsepower Continental I0-470-S six-cylinder
    horizontally opposed air-cooled engine
Armament: none

Performance
Maximum speed: 173 mph at sea level
Cruising speed: 163 mph at 6,500 feet at 75 percent power
Range: 1,275 miles (maximum)
Rate of climb: 965 feet per minute
Service ceiling: 16,100 feet

Weights
Empty: 1,750 pounds
Normal loaded: 3,300 pounds

CESSNA 206C SUPER SKYWAGON

Type: light utility transport
Crew: one
Span: 36 feet, 7 inches
Length: 27 feet, 9 inches
Height: 9 feet
Powerplant: one 280-horsepower Continental I0-520-A six-cylinder
    air-cooled engine
Armament: none

Performance
Maximum speed: 177 mph at sea level
Cruising speed: 166 mph at 6,000 feet at 75 percent power
Range: 1,075 miles
Rate of climb: 1,075 feet per minute
Service ceiling: 16,700 feet

Weights
Empty: 1,780 pounds
Loaded: 3,300 pounds

CONSOLIDATED VULTEE PBY-5A CATALINA

Type: general-purpose amphibian flying boat
Crew: two
Span: 104 feet
Length: 63 feet, 10 inches
Height: 18 feet, 10 inches
Powerplant: two 1,200-horsepower Pratt & Whitney R-1830-92 air-cooled
    radial engine
Armament: none carried on Catalinas in Israeli service

Performance
Maximum speed: 196 mph at 7,500 feet
Cruising speed: 130 mph
Range: 2,520 miles
Rate of climb: 920 feet per minute
Service ceiling: 15,800 feet

Weights
Empty: 17,564 pounds
Normal loaded: 34,000 pounds

CURTISS C-46 COMMANDO

Type: medium-range transport
Crew: two
Span: 108 feet, 1 inch
Length: 76 feet, 4 inches
Height: 21 feet, 9 inches
Powerplant: two 2,000-horsepower Pratt & Whitney R-2800-51 or
    R-2800-75 air-cooled radial engines
Armament: none

Performance
Maximum speed: 265 mph at 13,000 feet
Cruising speed: 227 mph at 10,000 feet
Range: 1,600 miles
Rate of climb: 1,500 feet per minute
Service ceiling: 24,500 feet

Weights
Empty: 29,483 pounds
Normal loaded: 45,000 pounds
Maximum overload: 50,000 pounds

DASSAULT M.D. 450 OURAGON

Type: fighter-bomber
Crew: one
Span: 40 feet, 3¾ inches
Length: 35 feet, 2¾ inches
Height: 13 feet, 7 inches
Powerplant: one 5,004-pound static thrust Hispano Suiza Nene 104B
    turbojet
Armament: four 20-mm Hispano 404 Model 50 cannon (125 rounds per
    gun); 2 x 1,000-pound bombs; 2 napalm bombs; 2 x 500-pound bombs
    plus 2 x 106-gallon fuel tanks; 4 x 500-pound bombs

Performance
Maximum speed: 584 mph at sea level; 516 mph at 39,370 feet
Cruising speed: 460 mph
Rate of climb: 7,480 feet per minute at sea level
Time to 39,370 feet: 10 minutes
Range: 520 miles (570 miles maximum)
Service Ceiling: 42,650 feet

Weights
Empty: 9,132 pounds
Normal loaded: 13,646 pounds (15,230 pounds with two 625-liter tip
    tanks)
Maximum loaded: 17,416 pounds

DASSAULT MIRAGE III BJ

Type: trainer
Crew: two
Span: 26 feet, 11½ inches
Length: 47 feet, 4⅞ inches
Height: 13 feet, 9⅓inches
Powerplant: one SNECMA Atar 9B3 turbojet: 9,370-pound static thrust,
    13,225-pound static thrust with afterburner
Armament: 2 x 1,000-pound bombs; two Sidewinders plus two 137 Imp.
    gallon (165 U.S. gallon) fuel tanks

Performance
Maximum speed: 1,386 mph at 39,370 feet
Cruising speed: 576 mph (Mach 0.86) at 36,000 feet
Rate of climb: 29,000 feet per minute
Service ceiling: 58,000 feet
Range: 1,240 miles

Weights
Empty: 13,820 pounds
Maximum loaded: 26,455 pounds

DASSAULT MIRAGE III CJ

Type: fighter
Crew: one
Span: 26 feet, 11½ inches
Length: 45 feet, 5¼ inches
Height: 13 feet, 9⅓ inches
Powerplant: one SNECMA Atar 9 B turbojet; 9,370-pound static thrust,
    13,225-pound static thrust with afterburner
Armament: two 30-mm DEFA cannon; 2 x 1,000-pound bombs; two
    Sidewinders plus two 137 Imp. gallon (165 U.S. gallon) fuel tanks

Performance
Maximum speed: 1,386 mph at 39,370 feet
Rate of climb: 30,000 feet per minute
Range: 400 miles (820 miles maximum)
Service ceiling: 59,000 feet

Weights
Empty: 13,040 pounds
Normal loaded: 18,620 pounds
Maximum loaded: 26,015 pounds

DASSAULT MYSTÈRE IVA

Type: fighter (later, fighter-bomber)
Crew: one
Span: 36 feet, 5¾ inches
Length: 42 feet, 1¾ inches
Height: 15 feet, 1 inch

Powerplant: one Hispano-Suiza Verdun 350 turbojet; 7,710-pound static
    thrust
Armament: two 30-mm DEFA cannon; 72 x 37-mm rockets; 4 x 500
    pound bombs; 2 x 1,000-pound bombs; 2 x 500-pound bombs plus
    2 x 106-gallon tanks; 2 x napalm bombs

Performance
Maximum speed: 696 mph at sea level; 615 mph at 39,370 feet
Cruising speed: 510 mph
Rate of climb: 8,860 feet per minute
Range: 570 miles (820 miles maximum)
Service ceiling: 45,000 feet

Weights
Empty: 12,950 pounds
Normal loaded: 16,530 pounds
Maximum loaded: 20,050 pounds

DASSAULT SUPER-MYSTÈRE B.2

Type: fighter
Crew: one
Span: 34 feet, 5¾ inches
Length: 46 feet, 1¼ inches
Height: 14 feet, 10¾ inches
Powerplant: one SNECMA Atar 101G turbojet; 7,495-pound static thrust,
    9,920-pound static thrust with afterburner
Armament: two 30-mm DEFA cannon; 4 x 500-pound bombs;
    2 x 1,000-pound bombs; two napalm bombs; or 2 x 500-pound bombs
    plus 2 x 180 Imp. gallon fuel tanks

Performance
Maximum speed: 686 mph at sea level; 783 mph at 39,370 feet
Cruising speed: 560 mph normal, 610 mph maximum
Rate of climb: 17,500 feet per minute
Range: 540 miles (730 miles maximum)
Service Ceiling: 55,750 feet

Weights
Empty: 15,400 pounds
Normal loaded: 19,840 pounds
Maximum loaded: 22,046 pounds

DE HAVILLAND D.H. 82A TIGER MOTH

Type: light training biplane
Crew: two
Span: 29 feet, 4 inches
Length: 23 feet, 11 inches
Height: 8 feet, 9½ inches
Powerplant: one 130-horsepower Gipsy-Major four-cylinder in-line
    air-cooled engine
Armament: none

Performance
Maximum speed: 109 mph at sea level
Cruising speed: 93 mph
Rate of climb: 673 feet per minute at sea level
Service ceiling: 13,600 feet
Range: 302 miles

Weights
Empty: 1,280 pounds
Normal loaded: 1,770 pounds
Maximum loaded: 1,825 pounds

DE HAVILLAND D.H. 89 DRAGON RAPIDE

Type: light commercial transport
Crew: two
Span: 48 feet
Length: 34 feet, 6 inches
Height: 10 feet, 3 inches
Powerplant: two 200-horsepower de Havilland Gipsy 2 in-line air-cooled
    engines
Armament: none

Performance
Maximum speed: 150 mph
Cruising speed: 130 mph
Range: 520 miles
Rate of climb: 867 feet per minute
Service ceiling: 16,000 feet

Weights
Empty: 3,230 pounds
Normal loaded: 6,000 pounds

DE HAVILLAND DHC-1 CHIPMUNK

Type: two-seat primary trainer
Span: 34 feet, 4 inches
Length: 25 feet, 5 inches
Height: 7 feet
Powerplant: one Bristol Siddeley (de Havilland) Gipsy Major 8
    four-cylinder in-line air-cooled engine
Armament: none

Performance
Maximum speed: 138 mph at sea level
Cruising speed: 119 mph
Range: 280 miles
Rate of climb: 840 feet per minute
Service ceiling: 15,800 feet

Weights
Empty: 1,425 pounds
Normal loaded: 2,014 pounds

DE HAVILLAND MOSQUITO
(SPECIFICATIONS FOR THE FB VI)

Type: two-seat fighter-bomber
Span: 54 feet, 2 inches
Length: 40 feet, 6 inches
Height: 15 feet, 3 inches
Powerplant: two 1,230-horsepower Rolls-Royce Merlin XXI or two
    1,635-horsepower Rolls-Royce Merlin 25 liquid-cooled engines
Armament: four 20-mm cannon and four .303-inch machine guns
    (bomber versions were unarmed)

Performance
Maximum speed: 380 mph at 13,000 feet
Cruising speed: 325 mph at 15,000 feet
Range: 1,205 miles
Rate of climb: 1,870 feet per minute
Service ceiling: 36,000 feet

Weights
Empty: 14,300 pounds
Normal loaded: 22,300 pounds

DORNIER DO 27

Type: single-engine STOL utility aircraft
Crew: one
Span: 39 feet, 4½ inches
Length: 31 feet, 6 inches
Height: 8 feet, 10¾ inches
Powerplant: one 340-horsepower Lycoming GS0-480-B1B6 air-cooled
    engine
Armament: none

Performance
Maximum speed: 174 mph
Cruising speed: 146 mph at 8,200 feet
Range: 685 miles
Rate of climb: 550 feet per minute
Service ceiling: 10,800 feet

Weights
Empty: 2,596 pounds
Loaded: 4,070 pounds

DORNIER DO 28D

Type: twin-engine STOL utility aircraft
Crew: one
Span: 51 feet, 10¾ inches
Length: 37 feet, 5¼ inches
Height: 12 feet, 9½ inches

Powerplant: two 380-horsepower Lycoming IGS0-540-A1E air-cooled
   engines
Armament: none

Performance
Maximum speed: 199 mph at 10,000 feet
Cruising speed: 178 mph at 10,000 feet
Range: 1,143 miles
Rate of climb: 1,400 feet per minute
Service ceiling: 24,280 feet

Weights
Empty: 4,775 pounds
Loaded: 8,050 pounds

DOUGLAS C-47 DAKOTA (DC-3)

Type: short-to medium-range military transport
Crew: two
Span: 95 feet
Length: 64 feet, 5½ inches
Height: 16 feet, 11½ inches
Powerplant: two 1,200-horsepower Pratt & Whitney R-1830-92
   Twin-Wasp fourteen-cylinder air-cooled radial engines
Armament: none

Performance
Maximum speed: 229 mph at 7,500 feet
Cruising speed: 185 mph at 10,000 feet
Range: 1,500 miles
Rate of climb: 1,130 feet per minute
Service ceiling: 23,200 feet

Weights
Empty: 16,970 pounds
Normal loaded: 26,000 pounds

DOUGLAS C-54 (DC-4) SKYMASTER

Type: medium-range transport
Crew: three to five
Span: 117 feet, 6 inches
Length: 93 feet, 11 inches
Height: 27 feet, 6¼ inches
Powerplant: four 1,350-horsepower Pratt & Whitney R-2000-3 or R-2000-7
   air-cooled radial engines
Armament: none

Performance
Maximum speed: 274 mph at 14,000 feet
Cruising speed: 239 mph at 15,200 feet
Range: 3,300 miles
Rate of climb: 1,070 feet per minute
Service ceiling: 22,500 feet

Weights
Empty: 38,200 pounds
Maximum loaded: 73,000 pounds

DOUGLAS DC-5

Type: high-wing twin-engine transport
Crew: three
Cargo: 16 passengers or 3,530-pound payload
Span: 78 feet
Length: 62 feet, 2 inches
Height: 19 feet, 10 inches
Powerplant: two 900-horsepower Wright GR-1320-G102A radial engines
Armament: none

Performance
Maximum speed: 230 mph at 7,700 feet
Cruising speed: 202 mph at 10,000 feet (65 percent power)
Rate of climb: 1,585 feet per minute (take-off power)
Range: 1,600 miles (maximum)
Service ceiling: 23,700 feet
Absolute ceiling on one engine: 11,400 feet

Weights
Empty: 13,674 pounds
Useful load: 6,326 pounds
Gross: 20,000 pounds

FAIRCHILD F-24R ARGUS

Type: four-plane high-wing cabin monoplane
Crew: one
Span: 36 feet, 4 inches
Length: 24 feet, 10 inches
Height: 8 feet
Powerplant: one 165-horsepower Ranger 6-410B2 air-cooled engine
Armament: none

Performance
Maximum speed: 132 mph
Cruising speed: 117 mph
Rate of climb: 760 feet per minute
Service ceiling: 16,800 feet
Range: 640 miles

Weights
Empty: 1,495 pounds
Gross: 2,550 pounds

FOKKER S.11 INSTRUCTOR

Type: primary trainer
Crew: two or three

Span: 36 feet, 1 inch
Length: 26 feet, 10 inches
Height: 7 feet, 4 inches
Powerplant: one 190-horsepower Lycoming 0-435-A six-cylinder
    horizontally opposed air-cooled engine
Armament: none

Performance
Maximum speed: 130 mph at sea level
Cruising speed: 102 mph at sea level
Time to 3,300 feet: 4 minutes, 24 seconds
Range: 390 miles
Service ceiling: 13,100 feet

Weights
Empty: 1,806 pounds
Normal loaded: 2,422 pounds

FOUGA CM 170 MAGISTER

Type: two-seat jet trainer/ground-attack aircraft
Span: 37 feet, 7/8 inches
Length: 33 feet, 9½ inches
Height: 9 feet, 2¼ inches
Powerplant: two 836-pound static thrust Turbomeca Marboré II turbojets
Armament: two 7.62-mm machine guns

Performance
Maximum speed: 443 mph at 30,000 feet
Range: 576 miles
Service ceiling: 40,000 feet

Weights
Empty: 4,268 pounds
Maximum loaded: 6,978 pounds

GENERAL DYNAMICS F-16A

Type: single-seat air combat fighter
Span: 31 feet
Length: 47 feet, 7¾ inches
Height: 16 feet, 5¼ inches
Powerplant: one 25,000-pound static thrust reheat Pratt & Whitney
    F100-PW-100 turbofan
Armament: one 20-mm M-61A-1 Vulcan rotary cannon and up to 11,000
    pounds of external stores

Performance
Maximum speed: 1,255 mph (Mach 1.95) at 36,000 feet
Cruising speed: 924 mph (maximum continuous)
Ferry range: 2,300 miles
Service ceiling: 52,000 feet

Weights
Empty: 14,100 pounds
Maximum take-off weight: 33,000 pounds

GLOSTER METEOR T.7

Type: trainer
Crew: two
Span: 37 feet, 2 inches
Length: 43 feet, 6 inches
Height: 13 feet
Powerplant: Rolls-Royce, Derwent 8, 3,500-pound static thrust
Armament: none

Performance
Maximum speed: 585 mph at sea level (.78 Mach); 545 mph at 30,000 feet
    (.80 Mach)
Cruising speed: 391 mph at 30,000 feet
Rate of climb: 7,600 feet per minute at sea level (clean); 3,500 feet per
    minute at 30,000 feet
Range: 460 miles (750 miles maximum)
Service ceiling: 45,000 feet

Weights
Empty:10,935 pounds
Normal loaded: 15,800 pounds
Maximum take-off weight: 17,600 pounds

GLOSTER METEOR F.8

Type: fighter
Crew: one
Span: 37 feet, 2 inches
Length: 44 feet, 7 inches
Height: 13 feet
Powerplant: Rolls-Royce, Derwent 8, 3,500-pound static thrust
Armament: four 20-mm cannon in nose

Performance
Maximum speed: 592 mph at sea level (.78 Mach); 550 mph at 30,000 feet
    (.81 Mach); 530 mph at 40,000 feet (.80 Mach)
Cruising speed: 414 mph
Rate of climb: 7,000 feet per minute at sea level (clean); 1,700 feet per
    minute at 30,000 feet
Range: 600 miles (865 miles maximum)
Service ceiling: 40,000 feet

Weights
Empty: 11,381 pounds
Normal loaded: 15,700 pounds
Maximum take-off weight: 19,065 pounds

GLOSTER METEOR FR.9

Type: fighter-recon
Crew: one
Span: 37 feet, 2 inches
Length: 44 feet, 7 inches
Height: 13 feet
Powerplant: Rolls-Royce, Derwent 8, 3,500-pound static thrust
Armament: four 20-mm cannon in nose

Performance
Maximum speed: 592 mph at sea level (.78 Mach); 550 mph at 30,000 feet
    (.81 Mach); 540 mph at 40,000 feet (.80 Mach)
Cruising speed: 414 mph
Rate of climb: 7,000 feet per minute at sea level (clean); 2,700 feet per
    minute at 30,000 feet
Range: 600 miles (865 miles maximum)
Service ceiling: 44,000 feet

Weights
Empty: 11,565 pounds
Normal loaded: 15,770 pounds
Maximum take-off weight: —

GLOSTER METEOR NF.13

Type: all-weather interceptor
Crew: two
Span: 43 feet
Length: 48 feet, 6 inches
Height: 13 feet, 11 inches
Powerplant: Rolls-Royce, Derwent 8, 3,700-pound static thrust
Armament: four 20-mm cannon in wings

Performance
Maximum speed: 500 mph at sea level (.66 Mach); 535 mph at 30,000 feet
    (.79 Mach)
Rate of climb: 5,800 feet per minute at sea level (clean); 2,000 feet per
    minute at 30,000 feet
Range: 725 miles (950 miles maximum)
Service ceiling: 43,000 feet

Weights
Empty: 11,884 pounds
Normal loaded: 18,700 pounds
Maximum take-off weight: 20,490 pounds

GRUMMAN E-2C HAWKEYE

Type: Early warning, surface surveillance and strike-control aircraft
Crew: five
Span: 80 feet, 7 inches
Length: 57 feet, 7 inches

Height: 18 feet, 7 inches
Powerplant: two 4,910 equivalent shaft horsepower Allison T56-A-422
    turboprops
Armament: none

Performance
Maximum speed: 374 mph
Cruising speed: 310 mph
Mission endurance: 7 hours
Ferry range: 1,605 miles
Rate of climb: 2,515 feet per minute
Service ceiling: 30,800 feet

Weights
Empty: 37,678 pounds
Maximum take-off weight: 51,569 pounds

GRUMMAN OV-1 MOHAWK

Type: two-seat observation aircraft
Span: 48 feet
Length: 41 feet
Height: 12 feet, 8 inches
Powerplant: two 1,400 shaft horsepower Lycoming T53-L-701 turboprops
Armament: none

Performance
Maximum speed: 290 mph with SLAR pod
Cruising speed: 230 mph
Range: 944 miles (maximum)
Service ceiling: 25,000 feet

Weights
Empty: 10,000 pounds
Maximum take-off weight: 18,109 pounds

GRUMMAN WIDGEON

Type: four/five-seat commercial amphibian
Span: 40 feet
Length: 31 feet, 1 inch
Height: 11 feet, 5 inches
Powerplant: two 200-horsepower Ranger L-440-5 six-cylinder in-line
    inverted air-cooled engines
Armament: none

Performance
Maximum speed: 153 mph
Cruising speed: 138 mph
Range: 920 miles
Rate of climb: 1,000 feet per minute
Service ceiling: 14,600 feet

Weights
Empty: 3,250 pounds
Normal loaded: 4,525 pounds

HELIOPOLIS GOMHOURIA

Type: two-seat primary trainer
Span: 34 feet, 9 inches
Length: 25 feet, 5 inches
Height: 6 feet, 5 inches
Powerplant: one 140-horsepower Continental C 145 six-cylinder
    horizontally opposed air-cooled engine
Armament: none

Performance
Maximum speed: 150 mph
Cruising speed: 121 mph
Rate of climb: 785 feet per minute
Service ceiling: 16,400 feet
Range: 620 miles

Weights
Empty: 1,056 pounds
Loaded: 1,650 pounds

HILLER UH-12E

Type: three-seat utility helicopter
Rotor diameter: 35 feet, 5 inches
Fuselage length: 27 feet, 11¼ inches
Powerplant: one 305-horsepower Lycoming VO-540-A1B six-cylinder
    horizontally opposed air-cooled engine
Armament: none

Performance
Maximum speed: 95 mph at sea level
Cruising speed: 82 mph
Hovering ceiling: 5,200 feet (in ground effect)
Service ceiling: 13,200 feet
Range: 500 miles

Weights
Empty: 1,816 pounds
Loaded: 2,700 pounds

IAI ARAVA 201

Type: STOL light utility transport
Crew: two
Span: 68 feet, 6 inches
Length: 42 feet, 6 inches
Height: 17 feet, 1 inch

Powerplant: two 783 equivalent shaft horsepower Pratt & Whitney
   PT6A-34 turboprops
Armament: two fixed and one flexibly mounted .50-inch Browning
   machine guns

Performance
Maximum speed: 203 mph at 10,000 feet
Cruising speed: 198 mph at 10,000 feet
Range: 650 miles
Service ceiling: 24,000 feet

Weights
Empty: 8,300 pounds
Maximum take-off weight: 15,000 pounds

IAI KFIR-C2

Type: single-seat ground-attack and air superiority fighter
Span: 26 feet, 11½ inches
Length: 50 feet, 10 inches
Height: 13 feet, 11 inches
Powerplant: one General Electric J79-GE-17 turbojet rated at
   17,900-pound thrust with afterburner
Armament: two 30-mm DEFA cannon with 125 rounds per gun plus
   external stores consisting of various combinations of air-to-air missiles
   (*Shafrir*, Sidewinder), bombs, rockets, and external fuel tanks

Performance
Maximum speed: Mach 2.3+
Cruising speed: 630 mph
Rate of climb: 50,000 feet per minute
Service ceiling: 55,000 feet
Range: 1,500 miles

Weights
Combat weight: 20,660 pounds (with 50 percent internal fuel plus two
   Shafrir air-to-air missiles)
Maximum take-off weight: 32,120 pounds

IAI MODEL 1123 WESTWIND

Type: light jet transport
Accommodations: crew of two plus up to ten passengers
Span: 44 feet, 9½ inches
Length: 52 feet, 3 inches
Height: 15 feet, 9½ inches
Powerplant: two 3,100-pound static thrust General Electric CJ610-9
   turbojets
Armament: none

Performance
Maximum speed: 541 mph at 19,500 feet

Cruising speed: 420 mph at 41,000 feet
Range: 2,120 miles
Service ceiling: 45,000 feet

Weights
Empty: 11,070 pounds equipped
Maximum take-off weight: 20,800 pounds

LOCKHEED C-130E and C-130H HERCULES

Type: multi-purpose medium transport
Accommodations: crew of four plus 92 troops or cargo
Span: 132 feet, 7¼ inches
Length: 97 feet, 8½ inches
Height: 38 feet
Powerplant: four 4,050 shaft horsepower Allison T56-A-7A turboprops
Armament: none

Performance
Maximum speed: 380 mph (C-130E); 384 mph (C-130H)
Cruising speed: 368 mph
Range: 2,420–4,700 miles, depending on cargo
Service ceiling: 22,600 feet

Weights
Empty: 72,892 pounds
Normal gross: 155,000 pounds

LOCKHEED HUDSON

Type: general-purpose transport
Crew: two
Span: 65 feet, 6 inches
Length: 44 feet, 4 inches
Height: 11 feet, 10½ inches
Powerplant: two 1,200 horsepower Wright Cyclone GR-1820-G205A
   air-cooled radial engines
Armament: none

Performance
Maximum speed: 250 mph
Cruising speed: 180 mph
Range: 2,160 miles
Service ceiling: 24,500 feet

Weights
Empty: 12,929 pounds
Normal loaded: 18,500 pounds

LOCKHEED LODESTAR

Type: commercial transport
Span: 65 feet, 6 inches

Length: 49 feet, 9⅞ inches
Height: 11 feet, 10½ inches
Powerplant: two 1,200-horsepower Wright Cyclone GR-1820-G205A
    air-cooled radial engines
Armament: none

Performance
Maximum speed: 271 mph
Cruising speed: 246 mph
Range: 1,660 miles
Service ceiling: 30,000 feet

Weights
Empty: 11,790 pounds
Normal loaded: 18,500 pounds

LOCKHEED MODEL 049 CONSTELLATION

Type: long-range transport
Crew: three
Span: 123 feet
Length: 95 feet, 1²/₁₆ inches
Height: 23 feet, 8 inches
Powerplant: four 2,200-horsepower Wright R-3350 air-cooled radial
    engines
Armament: none

Performance
Maximum speed: 330 mph
Cruising speed: 255 mph
Range: 2,400 miles
Time to 10,000 feet: 7 minutes, 6 seconds
Service ceiling: 25,000 feet

Weights
Empty: 50,500 pounds
Normal gross: 72,000 pounds
Maximum overload: 86,250 pounds

McDONNELL DOUGLAS SKYHAWK A-4E

Type: single seat light attack bomber
Span: 27 feet, 6 inches
Length: 42 feet, 10¾ inches
Height: 15 feet, 2 inches
Powerplant: one Pratt & Whitney J-52-P-6A turbojet rated at 8,500
    pounds static thrust
Armament: Two 20-mm cannon and an external ordinance load of 8,200
    pounds

Performance
Maximum speed: 685 mph at sea level
Cruising speed: 550 mph

Range: 1,800 miles
Service ceiling: 49,000 feet (clean)

Weights
Empty: 9,284 pounds
Normal loaded: 14,647 pounds (clean)
Maximum take-off weight: 24,500 pounds

McDONNELL DOUGLAS SKYHAWK A-4H

Type: single seat light attack bomber
Span: 27 feet, 6 inches
Length: 42 feet, 10¾ inches
Height: 15 feet, 2 inches
Powerplant: one Pratt & Whitney J52-P-8A turbojet rated at 9,300 pounds
    static thrust
Armament: two 30-mm DEFA cannon and up to 11,800 pounds of
    external stores

Performance
Maximum speed: 675 mph at sea level
Cruising speed: 550 mph
Range: 2,440 miles (maximum)
Service ceiling: 47,900 feet

Weights
Empty: 9,940 pounds
Normal loaded: 16,300 pounds (clean)
Maximum take-off weight: 27,420 pounds

McDONNELL DOUGLAS SKYHAWK A-4N

Type: single seat light attack bomber
Span: 27 feet, 6 inches
Length: 40 feet, 3¼ inches
Height: 15 feet
Powerplant: one Pratt & Whitney J52-P-408A turbojet rated at 11,200
    pounds static thrust
Armament: two 30-mm DEFA cannon and up to 8,200 pounds of external
    stores

Performance
Maximum speed: 685 mph at sea level
Cruising speed: 560 mph
Range: 2,200 miles
Rate of climb: 15,850 feet per minute
Service ceiling:

Weights
Empty: 10,600 pounds
Maximum take-off weight: 24,500 pounds

McDONNELL DOUGLAS F-4E PHANTOM II

Type: two-seat tactical strike fighter
Span: 38 feet, 4¾ inches
Length: 62 feet, 10½ inches
Height: 16 feet, 3⅓ inches
Powerplant: two 11,870 pound dry and 17,900 pound reheat General
    Electric J79-GE-17 turbojets
Armament: one 20-mm M61A-1 rotary cannon and four to six AIM-7E
    Sparrow III, with options of four Sidewinders or various external
    stores, such as gun pods, bombs, fuel tanks

Performance
Maximum speed: 1,500 mph (Mach 2.27) at 40,000 feet
Cruising speed: 585 mph
Range: 2,300 miles (maximum)
Rate of climb: 30,000 feet per minute
Service ceiling: 58,000 feet

Weights
Empty: 30,425 pounds
Maximum loaded: 60,630 pounds

McDONNELL DOUGLAS RF-4E PHANTOM II

Type: tactical reconnaissance aircraft
Span: 38 feet, 4¾ inches
Length: 62 feet, 10½ inches
Height: 16 feet, 3⅓ inches
Powerplant: two 11,870 pound dry and 17,900 pound reheat General
    Electric J79-GE-17 turbojets

Performance
Maximum speed: 1,500 mph (Mach 2.27) at 40,000 feet
Cruising speed: 585 mph
Range: 2,300 miles (maximum)
Rate of climb: 30,000 feet per minute
Service ceiling: 58,000 feet

Weights
Empty: 30,425 pounds
Maximum loaded: 57,320 pounds

McDONNELL DOUGLAS F-15A EAGLE

Type: single-seat air superiority fighter
Span: 42 feet, 9¾ inches
Length: 63 feet, 9 inches
Height: 13 feet, 5½ inches
Powerplant: two 25,000 pound thrust reheat Pratt & Whitney
    F100-PW-100 turbofans
Armament: one 20-mm M61A-1 rotary cannon, four AIM-9L Sidewinder
    and four AIM-7F Sparrow AAMs

Performance
Maximum speed: 1,650 mph (Mach 2.5) at 36,000 feet
Cruising speed: 625 mph
Ferry range: 2,980 miles
Rate of climb: 60,000+ feet per minute
Service ceiling: over 60,000 feet

Weights
Empty: 26,147 pounds
Normal loaded: 38,250 pounds
Maximum take-off weight: 54,123 pounds

MIKOYAN MiG-17

Type: fighter
Crew: one
Span: 31 feet, 6 inches
Length: 37 feet, 3¼ inches
Height: 11 feet
Powerplant: one Klimov VK-1A turbojet rated at 5,952-pound static thrust
    and 6,990-pound static thrust with afterburning
Armament: one 37-mm and two 23-mm cannon

Performance
Maximum speed: 692 mph at sea level; 635 mph at 39,370 feet
Cruising speed: 570 mph
Rate of climb: 12,795 feet per minute at sea level
Range: 870 miles (maximum)
Service ceiling: 54,468 feet

Weights
Empty: 9,850 pounds
Normal loaded: 11,465 pounds
Maximum loaded: 14,000 pounds (approximately)

MIKOYAN MiG-21F

Type: day interceptor
Crew: one
Span: 23 feet, 5½ inches
Length: 44 feet, 2 inches (51 feet, 8½ inches to tip of nose boom)
Height: 14 feet, 9 inches
Powerplant: one Tumansky RD-11 two-spool turbojet, rated at
    9,500-pound static thrust and 12,500-pound static thrust with
    afterburner
Armament: one 30-mm NR-30 cannon and two K-13 Atoll air-to-air
    missiles

Performance
Maximum speed: 1,340 mph at 40,000 feet (Mach 2)
Cruise speed: 625 mph
Rate of climb: 35,000 feet per minute at sea level

Service ceiling: approximately 60,000 feet
Range: 680 miles

Weights
Empty: 12,000 pounds
Normal loaded: 15,500 pounds (clean)
Maximum loaded: 17,000 pounds (two K-13 Atoll AAMs and one
    centerline 165 U.S. gallon fuel tank)

MIKOYAN MiG-23E

Type: interceptor
Crew: one
Span: 46 feet, 9 inches (at 21° sweep); 26 feet, 9½ inches (at 72° sweep)
Length: 55 feet, 1½ inches
Height: 15 feet, 9 inches
Powerplant: one unidentified turbojet, estimated at 24,250-pound static
    thrust with afterburning
Armament: one 23-mm twin-barrel type cannon; five pylons for
    external stores

Performance
Estimated maximum speed: Mach 2.3 at altitude (1,540 mph)
Estimated cruise speed: 625 mph
Estimated ceiling: 60,000+ feet
Range: 2,000 miles
Rate of climb: 50,000 feet per minute

Weights
Empty: 18,000 pounds (approximately)
Normal loaded: 34,600 pounds
Maximum take-off: 39,130 pounds

MILES M-57 AEROVAN

Type: light-twin-engined cargo or passenger aircraft
Crew: two
Span: 50 feet
Length: 36 feet
Height: 13 feet, 6 inches
Powerplant: two 150-horsepower Cirrus Major four-cylinder in-line
    air-cooled engines
Armament: none

Performance
Cruising speed: 110 mph
Range: 450 miles

Weights
Empty equipped: 3,000 pounds
Loaded: 5,300 pounds

MILES M-65 GEMINI 1A

Type: four-seat cabin monoplane
Span: 36 feet, 2 inches
Length: 22 feet, 3 inches
Height: 7 feet, 6 inches
Powerplant: two 100-horsepower Blackburn Cirrus Minor 2 in-line
    air-cooled engines
Armament: none

Performance
Maximum speed: 145 mph
Cruising speed: 135 mph
Range: 820 miles
Rate of climb: 650 feet per minute
Service ceiling: 13,500 feet

Weights
Empty: 1,910 pounds
Normal loaded: 3,000 pounds

NOORDUYN NORSEMAN

Type: general-purpose light transport
Crew: two; bench type seats could be fitted for eight passengers
Span: 51 feet, 8 inches
Length: 32 feet, 4 inches
Height: 10 feet, 1 inch
Powerplant: one Pratt & Whitney R-1340-S3H1 nine-cylinder air-cooled
    radial engine
Armament: none

Performance
Maximum speed: 155 mph
Cruising speed: 141 mph
Range: 484 miles
Time to 5,000 feet: 7 minutes
Service ceiling: 17,000 feet

Weights
Empty: 4,240 pounds
Loaded: 7,400 pounds

NORD 1203/II NORÉCRIN

Type: three-seat cabin monoplane
Span: 33 feet, 6¼ inches
Length: 23 feet, 8 inches
Height: 9 feet, 6 inches
Powerplant: one 135-horsepower Regnier 4LO engine
Armament: none

Performance
Maximum speed: 174 mph
Cruising speed: 137 mph
Range: 560 miles
Rate of climb: 985 feet per minute
Service ceiling: 16,400 feet

Weights
Empty: 1,437 pounds
Loaded: 2,313 pounds

NORD 2501 NORATLAS

Type: medium-range tactical transport
Crew: 4 (extra crew are carried on long-range flights)
Span: 106 feet, 7½ inches
Length: 72 feet, ⅔ inches
Height: 19 feet, 8¼ inches
Powerplant: two 2,040-horsepower SNECMA (license-built Bristol) 738
    radial air-cooled engines
Armament: none

Performance
Maximum speed: 252 mph at 5,000 feet; 273 mph at 9,840 feet
Cruising speed: 201 mph
Range: 1,740 miles
Service ceiling: 28,210 feet

Weights
Empty: 29,424 pounds
Normal loaded: 45,423 pounds
Maximum overload: 47,850 pounds

NORTH AMERICAN AT-6 TEXAN (OR HARVARD)

Type: basic trainer
Crew: two; some aircraft in Israeli service modified to three-seat
    configuration
Span: 12 feet ¼ inches
Length: 20 feet, 8 inches
Height: 11 feet, 8½ inches
Powerplant: one 600-horsepower Pratt & Whitney air-cooled radial
    engine
Armament: at various times, from one to three .30-inch machine guns,
    including one flexibly mounted gun for the observer; sometimes no
    armament; aircraft in Israeli service normally did not mount the
    flexibly mounted gun

Performance
Maximum speed: 212 mph
Cruising speed: 146 mph
Range: 629 miles (870 miles maximum)
Rate of climb: 1,643 feet per minute
Service ceiling: 24,000 feet

Weights
Empty: 3,900 pounds
Normal loaded: 5,200 pounds
Maximum loaded: 5,017 pounds

NORTH AMERICAN P-51D MUSTANG

Type: single-seat fighter
Span: 37 feet
Length: 32 feet, 3 inches
Height: 12 feet, 2 inches
Powerplant: one 1,490-horsepower Packard V-1650-7 liquid-cooled
    engine
Armament: six .50-inch Browning machine guns

Performance
Maximum speed: 437 mph at 25,000 feet
Cruising speed: 362 mph
Range: 950 miles
Rate of climb: 3,320 feet per minute
Service ceiling: 41,900 feet

Weights
Empty: 7,125 pounds
Gross: 11,600 pounds

PILATUS PC-6A TURBO-PORTER

Type: light STOL utility transport
Crew: one
Span: 49 feet, 10½ inches
Length: 36 feet, 1 inch
Height: 10 feet, 6 inches
Powerplant: one Turboméca Astazou IIE or IIG turboprop rated at 523
    shaft horsepower
Armament: none

Performance
Maximum speed: 174 mph
Cruising speed: 155 mph at 10,000 feet
Range: 500 miles
Service ceiling: 28,000 feet

Weights
Empty: 2,270 pounds
Normal loaded: 4,444 pounds
Maximum loaded: 4,850 pounds

PIPER CUB

Type: liaison and general purpose
Crew: one
Span: 35 feet, 3½ inches

Length: 22 feet
Height: 6 feet, 8 inches
Powerplant: one 65-horsepower air-cooled Continental 0-170-3
Armament: none

Performance
Maximum speed: 85 mph
Cruising speed: 75 mph
Range: 206 miles
Rate of climb: 514 feet per minute
Service ceiling: 14,500 feet

Weights
Empty: 865 pounds
Loaded: 1,400 pounds

PIPER SUPER CUB

Type: liaison and general purpose
Crew: one
Span: 35 feet, 3½ inches
Length: 22 feet, 6 inches
Height: 6 feet, 8½ inches
Powerplant: one 150-horsepower air-cooled Lycoming 0-320
Armament: none

Performance
Maximum speed: 130 mph
Cruising speed: 115 mph
Range: 770 miles
Rate of climb: 960 feet per minute
Service ceiling: 19,000 feet

Weights
Empty: 930 pounds
Loaded: 1,750 pounds

REPUBLIC RC-3 SEABEE

Type: four seat amphibian flying boat
Span: 37 feet, 8 inches
Length: 27 feet, 11 inches
Height: 10 feet, 1 inch
Powerplant: one 215-horsepower Franklin 6A8-215-B7F air-cooled engine
Armament: none

Performance
Maximum speed: 120 mph
Cruising speed: 103 mph
Range: 560 miles
Rate of climb: 700 feet per minute
Service ceiling: 12,000 feet

Weights
Empty: 1,950 pounds
Normal loaded: 3,000 pounds

RWD-13

Type: private and commercial aircraft
Accommodations: crew of one plus two passengers
Span: 37 feet, 8 inches
Length: 25 feet, 9 inches
Height: 6 feet, 8½ inches
Powerplant: one 120-horsepower PZI "Junior" air-cooled piston engine
Armament: none

Performance
Maximum speed: 135.4 mph
Cruising speed: 112 mph
Rate of climb: 1,116 feet per minute
Ceiling: 19,680 feet
Range: 560 miles

Weights
Empty: 1,166 pounds
Gross: 1,958 pounds

SIKORSKY S-55

Type: twelve-seat utility helicopter
Rotor diameter: 53 feet
Fuselage length: 42 feet, 2 inches
Height: 13 feet, 4 inches
Powerplant: one Wright R-1300-3 seven-cylinder radial air-cooled engine
    rated at 700 horsepower
Armament: none

Performance
Maximum speed: 115 mph at sea level
Cruising speed: 93 mph
Range: 400 miles
Rate of climb: 1,020 feet per minute
Hovering ceiling: 8,600 feet (in ground effect)

Weights
Empty: 5,045 pounds
Loaded: 7,500 pounds

SIKORSKY S-58

Type: sixteen-seat transport and general-purpose helicopter
Rotor diameter: 56 feet
Fuselage length: 46 feet, 9 inches
Height: 15 feet, 10 inches

Powerplant: one Wright R-1820-84 nine-cylinder radial air-cooled engine
    rated at 1,525 horsepower
Armament: none

Performance
Maximum speed: 134 mph at sea level
Cruising speed: 101 mph
Range: 225 miles
Rate of climb: 1,100 feet per minute
Hovering ceiling: 4,000 feet (in ground effect)

Weights
Empty: 7,560 pounds
Loaded: 12,700 pounds

SIKORSKY S-61R

Type: troop transport, assault, and rescue helicopter
Rotor diameter: 62 feet
Fuselage length: 57 feet, 3 inches
Height: 17 feet
Powerplant: two 1,500 shaft horsepower General Electric T58-GE5
    turboshafts
Armament: none

Performance
Maximum speed: 162 mph at sea level
Cruising speed: 144 mph
Range: 465 miles
Rate of climb: 1,300 feet per minute
Hovering ceiling: 4,100 feet (in ground effect)

Weights
Empty: 13,255 pounds
Normal loaded: 22,050 pounds

SIKORSKY CH-53G

Type: heavy assault transport helicopter
Crew: three
Rotor diameter: 72 feet, 3 inches
Fuselage length: 67 feet, 2 inches
Height: 22 feet
Powerplant: two General Electric 3,925 shaft horsepower T64-GE-413
    turboshafts
Armament: none

Performance
Maximum speed: 196 mph at sea level
Cruising speed: 173 mph
Range: 257 miles
Rate of climb: 2,180 feet per minute
Service ceiling: 21,000 feet

Weights
Empty: 23,485 pounds
Normal loaded: 36,400 pounds
Maximum loaded: 42,000 pounds

SIKORSKY S-65 C-3

Type: heavy assault transport helicopter
Crew: three
Rotor diameter: 72 feet, 3 inches
Fuselage length: 67 feet, 2 inches
Height: 22 feet
Powerplant: two General Electric 3,435 shaft horsepower T64-GE-7
    turboshafts
Armament: none

Performance
Maximum speed: 186 mph
Cruising speed: 172 mph
Range: 257 miles
Rate of climb: 2,180 feet per minute
Service ceiling: 21,000 feet

Weights
Empty: 23,324 pounds
Normal loaded: 37,399 pounds
Maximum loaded: 42,000 pounds

SOCATA RALLY E

Type: three-seat light cabin monoplane
Span: 31 feet, 4⅓ inches
Length: 22 feet, 9 inches
Height: 8 feet, 10⅓ inches
Powerplant: one 145-horsepower Continental 0-300-A six-cylinder
    horizontally opposed air-cooled engine
Armament: none

Performance
Maximum speed: 136 mph at sea level
Cruising speed: 124 mph at 4,920 feet
Range: 594 miles (maximum)
Rate of climb: 770 feet per minute
Service ceiling: 11,800 feet

Weights
Empty: 1,113 pounds
Normal loaded: 1,874 pounds

SUD-AVIATION SE-3130 ALOUETTE II

Type: seven-seat general-purpose helicopter
Rotor diameter: 33 feet, 6 inches

Fuselage length: 31 feet, 10 inches
Height: 9 feet
Powerplant: one 400 shaft horsepower Turbomeca Artouste II shaft
  turbine
Armament: none

Performance
Maximum speed: 109 mph at sea level
Cruising speed: 106 mph
Range: 330 miles
Rate of climb: 880 feet per minute
Ceiling: 6,560 feet in ground effect

Weights
Empty: 1,875 pounds
Maximum loaded: 3,527 pounds

SUD-AVIATION SA-3160 ALOUETTE III

Type: seven-seat general-purpose helicopter
Rotor diameter: 26 feet, 1 inch
Fuselage length: 32 feet, 8¾ inches
Height: 10 feet 1½ inches
Powerplant: one 550 shaft horsepower Turbomeca Artouste IIIB
  turboshaft
Armament: none

Performance
Maximum speed: 130 mph
Cruising speed: 121 mph
Range: 278 miles (345 miles maximum)
Rate of climb: 1,082 feet per minute
Service ceiling: 17,200 feet

Weights
Empty: 2,436 pounds
Normal loaded: 4,630 pounds

SUD-AVIATION S0-4050 VAUTOUR IIA

Type: attack bomber
Crew: one
Span: 49 feet, 6¾ inches
Length: 54 feet, 1 inch
Height: 14 feet, 1¾ inches
Powerplant: two 7,716 pound thrust SNECMA Atar 101-3 turbojets
Armament: Four 30-mm DEFA cannon

Performance

Maximum speed: 685 mph at sea level
Cruising speed: 550 mph
Range: 3,700 miles
Rate of climb: 12,000 feet per minute
Service ceiling: 49,000 feet

Weights
Empty: 22,500 pounds
Normal loaded: 33,000 pounds

SUD-AVIATION S0-4050 VAUTOUR IIB

Type: bomber
Crew: two
Span: 49 feet, 6¾ inches
Length: 54 feet, 1 inch
Height: 14 feet, 1¾ inches
Powerplant: two 7,716 pound thrust SNECMA Atar 101-3 turbojets
Armament: none

Performance
Maximum speed: 685 mph at sea level
Cruising speed: 550 mph
Range: 1,600 miles
Rate of climb: 11,200 feet per minute
Service ceiling: 49,000 feet

Weights
Empty: 21,780 pounds
Normal loaded: 33,100 pounds

SUD-AVIATION SI-4050 VAUTOUR IIN

Type: all-weather fighter
Crew: two
Span: 49 feet, 6¾ inches
Length: 54 feet, 1 inch
Height: 14 feet, 1¾ inches
Powerplant: two 7,716 pound thrust SNECMA Atar 101-3 turbojets
Armament: four 30-mm DEFA cannon

Performance
Maximum speed: 686 mph at sea level
Cruising speed: 550 mph
Range: 3,700 miles
Rate of climb: 11,820 feet per minute
Service ceiling: 49,000 feet

Weights
Empty: 23,150 pounds
Normal loaded: 33,069 pounds
Maximum: 45,635 pounds

SUKHOI SU-7 FITTER

Type: ground support fighter
Crew: one

Span: 31 feet, 2 inches
Length: 55 feet, 9 inches
Height: 15 feet, 5 inches
Powerplant: one Lyulka AL-7F-1 turbojet rated at 22,050-pound static
    thrust with afterburner
Armament: two 30-mm cannon

Performance
Maximum speed: 1,085 mph at 36,000 feet
Rate of climb: 29,500 feet per minute (without stores)
Range: 900 miles
Service ceiling: 49,700 feet

Weights
Normal loaded: 26,455 pounds
Maximum overload: 30,865 pounds

SUPERMARINE SPITFIRE Mk. 16

Type: single-seat fighter
Span: 36 feet, 10 inches (some had clipped wings with a 32 foot, 8-inch
    span)
Length: 31 feet, 4 inches
Height: 12 feet, 7¾ inches
Powerplant: one 1,720-horsepower Packard-Merlin 286 liquid-cooled
    engine
Armament: two 20-mm cannon and two .50-inch machine guns

Performance
Maximum speed: 405 mph at 22,000 feet
Cruising speed: 324 mph at 20,000 feet
Range: 434 miles (980 miles maximum)
Rate of climb: 4,530 feet per minute
Service ceiling: 43,000 feet

Weights
Empty: 5,610 pounds
Maximum loaded: 9,500 pounds

TAYLORCRAFT MODEL C

Type: light cabin monoplane
Crew: two
Span: 36 feet
Length: 22 feet
Height: 6 feet, 8 inches
Powerplant: one 55-horsepower Lycoming 0-145-A2 four-cylinder
    horizontally opposed air-cooled engine
Armament: none

Performance
Maximum speed: 110 mph
Cruising speed: 90 mph

Rate of climb: 550 feet per minute
Absolute ceiling: 17,000 feet
Range: 275 miles

Weights
Empty: 720 pounds
Normal loaded: 1,200 pounds

TEMCO TE-1A BUCKAROO

Type: two-seat primary trainer
Span: 29 feet, 2 inches
Length: 21 feet, 8 inches
Height: 6 feet, 1½ inches
Powerplant: one 145-horsepower Continental C145-2H six-cylinder
    air-cooled horizontally opposed engine
Armament: none

Performance
Maximum speed: 160 mph
Cruising speed: 145 mph
Range: 470 miles (maximum)
Service ceiling: 14,000 feet

Weights
Empty: 1,250 pounds
Loaded: 1,840 pounds

VULTEE BT-13

Type: two-seat basic trainer
Span: 42 feet
Length: 28 feet, 7 inches
Height: 9 feet, 1 inch
Powerplant: one 450-horsepower Pratt & Whitney T2B2 "Wasp Junior"
    radial air-cooled engine
Armament: none-fitted (as designed)

Performance
Maximum speed: 182 mph at sea level
Cruising speed: 170 mph at 5,000 feet
Range: 1,050 miles (maximum)
Service ceiling: 21,000 feet

Weights
Empty: 2,966 pounds
Loaded: 3,981 pounds

YAK-11

Type: basic trainer
Crew: two
Span: 30 feet, 10 inches

Length: 27 feet, 10¾ inches
Height: 10 feet, 9¼ inches
Powerplant: one 730-horsepower Shvetsov ASh-21 radial engine
Armament: none

Performance
Maximum speed: 264 mph at sea level; 286 mph at 7,380 feet
Cruising speed: 205 mph
Range: 795 miles
Service ceiling: 23,300 feet

Weights
Empty: 4,410 pounds
Loaded: 5,512 pounds

APPENDIX IV

FLIGHT LOG
OF
JOSEPH JOHN DOYLE

In 1948 a pilot arrived to aid in the War of Independence. His name was Joseph Doyle and he was a Canadian ace of the Second World War. Doyle, who was not Jewish, was typical of *Mahal*—foreign volunteers—who were committed to the survival of Israel. They fought, and many died, during that first grim period in Israel's existence.

Joseph John Doyle was assigned to 101 Squadron and served in that unit through the war, not leaving until after the end of hostilities. His work done, he returned to Canada. On the following pages his log book is reproduced, with explanatory comments in parentheses.

There have been many attempts to explain "how it was" during the War of Independence. Many books, both fiction and nonfiction, have sought to capture that time, a period in history when adventurers, soldiers of fortune, mercenaries, former ghetto fighters, kibbutzniks, and former concentration camp victims with numbers still tatooed on their arms stood together against a common enemy.

There was little discipline at that time. This is clearly shown in the log book entries. There would be time enough for discipline once an uneasy peace was established, when a "real" army coalesced. But that was in the future. Doyle's log book portrays a period not unlike the era of the Flying Tigers. The simple entries, more than almost any book or film of that period, succeed in informing us how it was.

201

DATE	AIRCRAFT		FIRST PILOT	CREW OR PASSENGERS	PURPOSE OF FLIGHT AND REMARKS	FLIGHT TIME
	Type	No.				
Sept. 20, 1948	Dakota	18	Wolf Canter	self	Tel Aviv to Ramat David	:30
Oct. 10	Commando	46	Art Ford	self	Aquir to Ruhamah	:30
					Flying in supplies to the Negev settlements and kibbutzes in occupied territories.	
Oct. 10	Commando	46	Art Ford	self	Ruhamah to Aquir	:30
Oct. 10	Commando	84	"Red" Nott	self	Aquir to El-Imara	:40
Oct. 10	Commando	84	"Red" Nott	self	El-Imara to Aquir	:40
Oct. 10	Commando	84	"Red" Nott	self	El-Imar	:40
Oct. 11	Commando	26	Art Ford	self	Aquir to Ruhamah	:30
					Air shaky too late in morning.	
Oct. 11	Commando	26	Art Ford	self	Ruhamah to Aquir	:30
Oct. 11	Vultee Valiant					:30
				101 Squadron at Herzliya		
Oct. 18	Vultee Valiant	BT-13	Auergarten	self	Circuits and bumps	:25
					First flight on squadron.	
Oct. 18	Vultee	BT-13	self		Circuits and bumps	:30
					Airborne alone.	
Oct. 18	Piper Cub	59	self	pass.	Herzliya to Tel Aviv	:20
Oct. 18	Piper Cub	59	self	—	Tel Aviv to Herzliya	:20
				—	Nice little puddle jumper.	

DATE	AIRCRAFT		FIRST PILOT	CREW OR PASSENGERS	PURPOSE OF FLIGHT AND REMARKS	FLIGHT TIME
	Type	*No.*				
Oct. 18	Vultee	BT-13	self	Axelrod	Herzliya to Aquir	:10
Oct. 18	Vultee	BT-13	self	Axelrod	Aquir to Herzliya	:10
					Flying Harry to see about Giddy's pranged Me 109.	
Oct. 19	Spitfire IX	133	self	—	Escort B-17s to Huligat	:50
					Bombing good. Flak accurate for height.	
Oct. 20	Spitfire IX	132	self	—	Photo reconnaissance escort to El Arish	1:15
					Aircraft on dromes. Flak quite good.	
Oct. 21	Spitfire IX	132	self	—	Patrol Beersheba–El Arish	1:35
					Rudy [Auergarten] and I bounced 4 Egyptian "Spits." Destroyed 1, damaged 2. ("Confirmed. Intelligence Officer W. Reiter")	
Oct. 21	Piper	59	self	Axelrod	Herzliya to Lydda	:20
					Met "Dan" Samuels again. He's in charge of a tank outfit.	
Oct. 21	Piper	59	self	Axelrod	Lydda to Herzliya	:20
Oct. 22	Spitfire	131	self	—	Scramble base	1:20
					Iraqi Mosquito over field. Could not intercept.	
Oct. 22	Piper	59	self	pass.	Herzliya to Tel Aviv	:10
Oct. 22	Piper	59	self	pass.	Tel Aviv to Herzliya	:10
Oct. 23	Spitfire	132	self	—	Patrol area Majdal	1:30
					Nothing around. Just a stooge.	

DATE	AIRCRAFT		FIRST PILOT	CREW OR PASSENGERS	PURPOSE OF FLIGHT AND REMARKS		FLIGHT TIME
	Type	No.					
Oct. 24	Spitfire IX	133	self	—	Visual recce of Faluja	Aborted. Boris had engine trouble	:15
Oct. 24	Seabee	61	self	Wilson	Checked out in Seabee	What a bloody aircraft.	:20
Oct. 25	Seabee	61	self	Lionel	Herzliya to Aquir		:20
Oct. 25	Seabee	61	self	Lionel	Aquir to Herzliya	Paddy the Irishman at Flying Control	:20
Oct. 25	Spitfire (?) (This was the Spitfire built from scrap using parts from different marks)	130	self	—	Photo recce Ramallah area	Aborted when film jammed in camera.	:45
Oct. 26	Spitfire (?)	130	self	—	Photo recce Latrun area	Photos of Latrun and area. Nothing around.	1:05
Oct. 29	Spitfire IX	132	self	—	Escort B-17s to Tarshisha	Hits on target. Not much flak.	1:15
Oct. 31	Spitfire IX	133	self	—	Test	A/C (aircraft) still u/s [unserviceable].	:20
Nov. 1	Spitfire IX	131	self	—	Patrol Gaza and roads	Nothing doing.	:55

DATE	AIRCRAFT Type	No.	FIRST PILOT	CREW OR PASSENGERS	PURPOSE OF FLIGHT AND REMARKS		FLIGHT TIME
Nov. 9	Spitfire IX	132	self	—	Patrol roads and Gaza area	Movement on roads to south.	1:10
Nov. 9	Spitfire IX	133	self	—	Ferrying to new base	Squadron move to Qastina, new base in Negev.	:20
Nov. 11	Seabee	61	self	—	Qastina to Herzliya	Rudy and Boris shot down "Gypo" Dak [Dakota].	:20
Nov. 11	Seabee	61	self	—	Herzliya to Qastina		:20
Nov. 12	Seabee	61	self	pass.	Qastina to Herzlia		:20
Nov. 12	Seabee	61	self	pass.	Herzliya to Qastina		:20
Nov. 12	Vultee	BT-13	self	—	Area recce		:15
Nov. 12	Piper	59	self	—	Local flying	Pissing along seafront. Fun!	:25
Nov. 13	Seabee	61	self	pass.	Qastina to Herzlia		:20
					(Incomplete records on hand)		:25
						Faluja burning. Shelling Iraqui El Manshiya.	:55
						Bomb hits straight across town.	1:15

DATE	AIRCRAFT Type	No.	FIRST PILOT	CREW OR PASSENGERS	PURPOSE OF FLIGHT AND REMARKS	FLIGHT TIME
						:20
					Rudy shot down Gypo Spit over Faluja area.	:20
			(Incomplete records on hand)			
						:40
						:20
					Damascus—Beirut.	1:50
						:20
						:20
						:20
					Landed at Ramat David.	:40
					Flak too accurate. Driven off target twice.	
						:10
					[Wayne] Peake shot down "Mossie." Thinks it was a "Hallie." [This was an RAF reconnaissance Mosquito from Cyprus which overflew Israel. It crashed in the Mediterranean. Peake thought he had downed a Halifax bomber.]	:10
						:20
			(Incomplete records on hand)			
						:20
						:25

DATE	AIRCRAFT Type	No.	FIRST PILOT	CREW OR PASSENGERS	PURPOSE OF FLIGHT AND REMARKS	FLIGHT TIME
					Shooting up jackals.	:20
						:25
					Transport on road. Sighted E/a.c. [enemy aircraft]. Lost him.	1:00
					El Auja, El Arish and enemy airfields	1:20
Dec. 2	Vultee	99	self	pass.	Qastina to Tel Aviv	:15
Dec. 2	Vultee	99	self	pass.	Tel Aviv to Qastina	:15
Dec. 2	Spitfire (?)	130	self	—	Photo recce Amman, Mafraq dromes	1:30
Dec. 2	Spitfire(?)	130	self	—	Photo recce	:20
					Weather over area very bad.	
Dec. 3	Spitfire IX	132	self	—	Escort to Mafraq, Amman	1:30
					Mafraq contains Ansons, Dakotas.	
Dec. 5	Vultee	99	self	pass.	Tel Aviv to Base 4	:15
Dec. 5	Vultee	99	self	pass.	Base 4 to Aquir	:10
					Bye-bye Vultee.	
Dec. 10	Seabee	61	self	Peake	Base 4 to Tel Aviv	:15
Dec. 10	Seabee	61	self	Ide Lovici	Aquir to Base 4	:10
Dec. 11	Seabee	61	self	Kroll	Tel Aviv to Base 4	:20
					No airspeed or altimeter. Cloudy.	
Dec. 15	Spitfire(?)	130	self	—	Photo recce to Negev	:50
					Nothing much observed.	

DATE	AIRCRAFT Type	No.	FIRST PILOT	CREW OR PASSENGERS	PURPOSE OF FLIGHT AND REMARKS	FLIGHT TIME
Dec. 15	Seabee	61	self	pass.	Qastina to Tel Aviv	:25
Dec. 15	Seabee	61	self	pass.	Tel Aviv to Qastina — Peake crashed in Me 109 on take-off.	:25
Dec. 16	Spitfire IX	132	self	—	Visual recce of Rafa—Gaza — Observed 2 trains and M.T. [motor transport]. Flak heavy.	1:25
Dec. 16	Seabee	61	self	photographer	Base 4 to Aquir	:10
Dec. 16	Seabee	61	self	photographer	Aquir to Tel Aviv — Checked out "Dick."	:20
Dec. 16	Seabee	61	self	Dick	Tel Aviv to Aquir	:20
Dec. 16	Seabee	61	self	—	Aquir to Qastina	:10
Dec. 16	Piper Cub	68	self	Eskenezy	Local flying	:25
Dec. 16	Piper Cub	68	self	Shlomo	Local flying — Shooting up countryside.	:25
Dec. 18	Piper Cub	68	self	Eskenezy	Base 4 to Aquir	:10
Dec. 18	Piper Cub	68	self	Eskenezy	Aquir to Base 4 — Mail pickup.	:10
Dec. 18	Seabee	61	self	3 pass.	Base 4 to Aquir	:10
Dec. 18	Seabee	61	self	Feldman	Aquir to Base 4 — Check out "Cy."	:10
Dec. 18	Seabee	61	self	Peake	Base 4 to Tel Aviv	:20
Dec. 18	Seabee	61	self	armoreur	Tel Aviv to Haifa — Leave for Peake.	:40
Dec. 18	Seabee	61	self	—	Haifa to Base 4 — Stormovik airgunned.	:55
Dec. 20	Mustang	191	self	—	Recce Hebron, Bethlehem — [Arab] Legion on roads.	1:05

DATE	AIRCRAFT Type	No.	FIRST PILOT	CREW OR PASSENGERS	PURPOSE OF FLIGHT AND REMARKS		FLIGHT TIME
Dec. 21	Piper Cub	68	self	photographer	Photographic trip	Beit Darras—Qastina—Kaazor	:25
Dec. 21	Seabee	61	self	pass.	Base 4 to Tel Aviv		:20
Dec. 21	Seabee	61	self	—	Tel Aviv to Base 4		:25
Dec. 22	Spitfire	133	self	—	Scramble	No joy. Rudy damaged Fiat G-50 [actually a Fiat G-55B].	:30
Dec. 23	Mustang	191	self	—	Escort "Spits"	Escorting Spits from abroad.	:25
Dec. 24	Spitfire	131	self	—	Escort "B-17s" Rafah	Bombs dropped in sea.	1:15
Dec. 27	Mustang	41	self	—	Visual shipping recce	Strafed trucks, armored cars, gun 105 mm, shot up airfield. Searching for enemy corvettes.	1:30
Dec. 28	Spitfire	11	self	—	Escort Harvards to Faluja	Jumped 8 Fiats. I destroyed 1, damaged 1; Levett damaged 2. ("Confirmed. Intelligence Officer W. Reiter.")	1:15
Dec. 28	Spitfire	14	self	—	Strafing El Arish Road	Damaged 2 trucks. Shot up armored car and M.T. [motor transport].	1:20
Dec. 29	Mustang	41	self	—	Recce Abuweigila, El-Arish	Visual recce. Dove to deck to avoid flak!	:50

DATE	AIRCRAFT		FIRST PILOT	CREW OR PASSENGERS	PURPOSE OF FLIGHT AND REMARKS	FLIGHT TIME
	Type	No.				
Dec. 30	Spitfire	14	self	—	Recce Bur-Hamma	"Mac" and I jumped 2 Fiats strafing. 1 destroyed for me, 1 for "Mac." ("Confirmed. Intelligence Officer W. Reiter")	1:20
Dec. 31	Piper Cub	68	self	pass.	Base 4 to Tel Aviv		:20
Dec. 31	Piper Cub	68	self	—	Tel Aviv to Base 4		:20
Jan. 1, 1949	Spitfire	16	self	—	Dive bombing railroad junction	Cut railroad. "Red" shot up by flak.	:55
						Cy shot down a Fiat and Boris damaged 2 on Jan 5.	
Jan. 6	Piper Cub	68	self	—	Local flying. Three landings	Joy-riding mechanics.	:55
Jan. 6	Piper Cub	68	self	—	Base 4 to Ekron		:10
Jan. 6	Piper Cub	68	self	—	Ekron to Qastina		:10
Jan. 7	Spitfire	12	self	—	Escort to Khan Yunis	Damned good bombing. Flak good.	:50
Jan. 7	Mustang	41	self	—	Escort Harvards to Deir-El-Ballah	Jumped 8 enemy aircraft. I destroyed 1, damaged another 1. Later on "Mac" shot down 1 "Spit." "Slick" [Goodlin, USAF test pilot] 1, Bill 1 and "Denny" and Ezer [Weizman] each damaged 1. "Turkey shoot."	1:35

DATE	Type	No.	FIRST PILOT	CREW OR PASSENGERS	PURPOSE OF FLIGHT AND REMARKS	FLIGHT TIME
	AIRCRAFT					
Jan. 10	Spitfire	12	self	—	Flypast for "Sam's wife [Sam Pomerantz, an American engineer and pilot, killed on a delivery flight of Spitfire].	:10
Jan. 11	Piper Cub	68	self	Axelrod	Base 4 to Ekron	:10
Jan. 11	Piper Cub	68	self	Wilson	Aquir to Qastina	:10
Jan. 12	Vultee	99	self	Chester	Ekron to Base 4	:10
Jan. 13	Seabee	61	self	Axelrod	Air test	A/C serviceable.	:30
Jan. 15	Seabee	61	self	pass.	Base 4 to Tel Aviv	:20
Jan. 15	Seabee	61	self	pass.	Tel Aviv to Base 4	:20
Jan. 21	Piper Cub	68	self	passengers	Local flying	:45
Jan. 22	Piper Cub	68	self	passengers	Local flying	:45
Jan. 23	Seabee	61	self	Arnold	Qastina to Tel Aviv	Taxi service.	:20
Jan. 23	Seabee	61	self	Arnold	Tel Aviv to Ramat David	Off to get liquor.	:40
Jan. 23	Seabee	61	self	Arnold	Ramat David to Haifa	To pick up Ezer [Weizman].	:15
Jan. 23	Seabee	61	self	Ezer	Haifa to Ein Shemer	Force landed due to engine trouble.	:40
Jan. 24	Piper Cub	68	self	pass.	Local flying	:10
Jan. 25	Piper Cub	68	self	pass.	Base 4 to Aquir	:20
Jan. 25	Piper Cub	68	self	—	Aquir to Base 4	:15

Flying mechs around.

DATE	AIRCRAFT Type	No.	FIRST PILOT	CREW OR PASSENGERS	PURPOSE OF FLIGHT AND REMARKS	FLIGHT TIME
Jan. 26	Piper Cub	68	self	—	Local flying	:10
Jan. 27	Piper Cub	68	self	pass.	Qastina to Ekron	:15
Jan. 27	Piper Cub	68	self	—	Ekron to Base 4	:15
Jan. 28	Piper Cub	68	self	pass.	Base 4 to Tel Aviv	:20
Jan. 28	Piper Cub	68	self	pass.	Tel Aviv to Qastina	:20
Jan. 29	Piper Cub	68	self	—	Base 4 to Tel Aviv	:20
Jan. 29	Piper Cub	68	self	—	Tel Aviv to Ekron	:20
Jan. 29	Piper Cub	68	self	—	Ekron to Qastina	:10
Feb. 1	Spitfire	17	self	—	Practice flying	:40
Feb. 2	Harvard	1105	self	Baher	Aquir from Base 4. Long time no Harvard.	1:15
Feb. 2	Spitfire	204	self		Test, ferry from Aquir A/C O.K.	:15
Feb. 3	Piper Cub	0419	self	Arnold	Base 4 to Tel Aviv Off to pick up "Supplies."	:20
Feb. 3	Piper Cub	0419	self	Arnold	Tel Aviv to Ramat David Gave lecture and picked up liquor.	:30
Feb. 3	Piper Cub	0419	self	Arnold	Ramat David to Base 4 Night flying with "full load" of spirits.	:55
Feb. 4	Piper Cub	68	self	Lilli and Denny	Qastina to Tel Aviv Denny off to town.	:20

DATE	AIRCRAFT Type	AIRCRAFT No.	FIRST PILOT	CREW OR PASSENGERS	PURPOSE OF FLIGHT AND REMARKS		FLIGHT TIME
Feb. 4	Piper Cub	68	self	Lilli	Tel Aviv to Herzliya		1:10
Feb. 4	Piper Cub	68	self	Lilli	Herzliya to Base 4	Night flying.	:20
Feb. 22	Spitfire	15	self	—	Test hop and practice	A/C O.K. Pilot rusty.	:40
Feb. 23	Spitfire	21	self	—	Formation flying	Sweep round country with Bill George.	1:00
Mar. 1	Harvard	1105	self	Stern	Instruments instruction		1:00
Mar. 3	Spitfire	17	self	—	Training formation		1:10
Mar. 8	Spitfire	21	self	—	Escort to C46s	To Avraham.	1:00
Mar. 12	Spitfire	17	self	—	Training formation		:45
Mar. 13	Spitfire	20	self	—	Training formation		:20
Mar. 14	Spitfire	25	self	—	Training formation		:25
Mar. 27	Spitfire	17	self	—	Training formation		1:05
Mar. 28	Harvard	1108	self	Wilson	Base 4 to Tel Aviv		:15
Mar. 28	Harvard	1108	self	Dangott	Tel Aviv to Base 4		:15
Mar. 28	Norseman	0802	self	John	Training	Check out.	:10
Mar. 28	Norseman	0802	self	John	Practice		:25
Mar. 29	Harvard	1108	self	Arnold	To Tel Aviv from Base 4		:15

DATE	AIRCRAFT Type	No.	FIRST PILOT	CREW OR PASSENGERS	PURPOSE OF FLIGHT AND REMARKS	FLIGHT TIME
Mar. 29	Harvard	1108	self	Sinclair	Base 4 from Tel Aviv	:25
April 1	Mustang	2303	self	—	From B.O.D. to base	New kite. 1:10
April 3	Spitfire	41	self	—	Experiment	With napalm. :20
April 11	Spitfire	23	self	—	Training pupils	:55
April 18	Spitfire	16	self	—	A/C test	Engine trouble. 1:05
April 24	Spitfire	17	self	—	Base 4 to Ramat David	:25
April 24	Spitfire	17	self	—	Bomber affiliation	1:00
April 24	Spitfire	17	self	—	Ramad David to Base 4	:30
April 25	Spitfire	17	self	—	Base 4 to Ramat David	:30
April 25	Spitfire	17	self	—	Bomber affiliation	1:05
April 25	Spitfire	17	self	—	Ramat David to Base 4	:30
April 27	Spitfire	10	self	—	Formation	1:10
April 27	Spitfire	10	self	—	Formation	1:05
April 28	Spitfire	12	self	—	Formation	1:15
April 28	Spitfire	10	self	—	Formation	1:10
April 29	Spitfire	19	self	—	Formation	:50
May 2	Spitfire	12	self	—	Formation	:40

DATE	AIRCRAFT		FIRST PILOT	CREW OR PASSENGERS	PURPOSE OF FLIGHT AND REMARKS	FLIGHT TIME
	Type	*No.*				
May 2	Spitfire	12	self	—	Formation 12 ship [i.e., 12 aircraft]	1:05
May 6	Spitfire	19	self	—	Formation 12 ship	:40
					Parade over Tel Aviv "The Day" [May 6, 1949, Independence Day, Israel's 1st Anniversary].	
May 9	Piper Cub	0420	self	"Cy"	Recce of Mt. Carmel area. Aquir—return	1:55
May 12	Spitfire	23	self	—	Army cooperation Strafing in front of army. Last flight in 101 squadron	

"Thank you for everything and always welcome back.
    Shalom. Ezer"
        O.C. [Officer in Command]
        101 Squadron

APPENDIX V

CAMOUFLAGE OF CHEL HA'AVIR AIRCRAFT

There has been a wealth of misinformation given about the camouflage of the aircraft of the Israel Defence Force/Air Force. The faded paint of aircraft on a scrap heap, airplanes which have developed strange and gaudy tints under a merciless tropical sun, have been taken as the basis of camouflage of service aircraft. Perhaps it is time to dispel some of the myths and cast some light on what is (and was) found on aircraft in service with the *Chel Ha'Avir*.

During the War of Independence, Israel fought for its existence. When an aircraft arrived, it was pressed into service, camouflage be damned! There were Dakotas and Commandos in service in olive drab—because their previous owners had kept them in that color. Spitfires could be found in brown and green as well as natural metal. The Messerschmitts from Czechoslovakia arrived in an olive or gray-green and that is the color they fought in. Stan Miller, a veteran of 101 Squadron in 1948, described the Messerschmitt camouflage as follows: "The aircraft later on had striped tails (red and white) and the Star of David. I think at the beginning all they had was the Star of David, though. They had gray colors painted on them, but I don't think they were properly camouflaged. The basic color was that grayish-green color. It's almost a khaki color." When asked whether they had some rough attempts at camouflage atop the grayish-green, he replied, "I think so."

Questions regarding the camouflage of Israeli aircraft were put to Maurice Commanday, another veteran of the 1948 war. His letter of response stated:

> Quite frankly, despite my colorblindness (without which I might
> have become a pilot in WW II and subsequently become "unavail-
> able" for service in Israel in '48) any interest in the painting of

our few aircraft would have been minimized by the priorities of repairing aircraft without spares, tools, trained personnel, and technical literature.

My wife, who was nurse at our base, advises me that our aircraft were painted camouflage brown and green (which colors I do not differentiate between) and reference to one or two faded photographs from those days more or less confirms. Whether these "paint jobs" were organized by higher authorities or what, I don't have the faintest idea. As far as I was concerned they were there as part of the scenery and were accomplished by "painters" I suppose. I can assure you that aircraft are not much affected by the pigment and binders they carry and one cannot consider paint in any way part of an airplane's structure. Whether or not the camouflage was "taped off," "chalked off" or sprayed on with Chinese laundry spray I have no idea.

As for the Beaufighters, they were a troublesome lot of junk for the most part. Only one survived to do much fighting out of six which left R.A.F. Abingdon sometime in May or June [1948]. That five actually reached Israel was a miracle and, as I say, four were wiped out, most through a combination of war-weariness and pilot incompetence and inexperience. The remaining specimen was fitted with two 20-mm cannon which, in turn, were dependent upon worn-out snail magazines which were resurrected from the local RAF junk pile. As a consequence they would generally fire two rounds and jam. The only known usefulness, at least as far as my memory is concerned, was a surprise attack on the Egyptian base at El Arish during which the last remaining Beaufighter flipped a napalm bomb into a hangar which seemed to annoy a few Egyptians. It finally made a forced landing near the famous police fortress at Faluja where the aircrew plus one passenger were killed by the Egyptians. Whether or not the landing was due to enemy action or what was never revealed to me.

I would be unhappy to see that collection of war-weary junk romanticized as I would the Englishman who smuggled them out of England. It is my understanding that he subsequently took up safecracking as a vocation and is still languishing in Dartmoor Gaol, or had been to a few years ago. His motivation, in my view, did not merit accolades, by any means. He was strictly a mercenary and was available, I believe, to anyone for a price.

To answer your questions further, I don't remember any identity bands or stripes [such as were used during the D-day invasion] and didn't know there was a "103 Squadron" insignia. In fact I had forgotten there even was such a squadron. "Squadrons" were not much of an identity in those days. We had an air base of some sort with various aircraft and people who flew them from time to time between which time we struggled to achieve some degree of airworthiness. To assume any degree of unit identity, in my view, is unwarranted romanticism.

Your question . . . presupposes a degree of organization that simply did not nor could not exist at that time. If anyone approached me with a written order to paint or camouflage or otherwise decorate an aircraft I'm afraid that he would have left my presence feet first. In the circumstances we found ourselves, very little in the way of written orders were in fact executed.

We had aircraft flying on combat missions without armament to protect themselves against enemy aircraft! We had homemade bombs which were more hazardous to the giver than the recipient! Most of us spoke languages unknown to one another. Paint? Camouflage? Squadron markings? Trivia!

Very truly yours,
Maurice R. Commanday

Commanday's views about the airworthiness of Israeli aircraft were confirmed by Majdal, a veteran of the three B-17 69th Squadron, who said: "I'll be frank with you. In the American air force I would have . . . put them out of action. There were none of them fit to fly, not fit to go on a mission—there's no question in my mind because, as far as I'm concerned, they were held together with chewing gum."

So, under the circumstances, there was little consideration of camouflage. Nor was there any standardization at that time. One of the three B-17s was left in bare metal, while the other two were camouflaged. One had a coat of faded olive drab, the other had a camouflage of faded tan with green mottling over it.

At Herzliya, a fuel storage tank was painted in a contour camouflage to blend with the hillside and a pilot went aloft to view the camouflage from the air. When he came down, he was asked how the fuel tank looked from the air. "Like a camouflaged fuel tank," he replied.

With the end of the War of Independence, rules for the application of camouflage to their aircraft were developed by the Israel Defence Force/Air Force. Because of the nature of the terrain, particularly in the Negev Desert in the south, the colors used through the Fifties and mid-Sixties were a light rust brown and navy blue on upper surfaces and light gray on under surfaces. Because of the tropical sun, the dark blue, in time, faded to a light purple. When some Israeli aircraft were encountered by visitors on a scrap heap, the paint was usually bleached by the sun. This has led some to conclude that there was a standard Israeli camouflage of light purple and brown.

There were significant exceptions to this general rule of color. Helicopters were often painted brown and green. Some military aircraft were left in natural metal. To the uninitiated, these variations may have seemed whimsical, but there were rules governing the application of camouflage.

First-line aircraft were, almost without exception, left in bare metal until they were considered to be superseded by aircraft with superior performance. If the aircraft were intended mainly for ground-support duties, they were camouflaged. This held until the end of the Sixties. Let's examine several aircraft to see how the rule applied.

When Mustangs were purchased from Sweden in 1951, they were left in bare metal. Since they were at that time the premier fighter plane in the country, the addition of paint would have resulted in a loss of performance. The arrival of Meteors two years later signaled the beginning of camouflage paint for the Mustangs since they were no longer first line aircraft. By the time the 1956 war was fought, some Mustangs were camouflaged while others had yet to receive their war paint.

Mosquitos served in a silver finish (they were made of wood, so it was a silver dope that was used) and went out of service so fast that they were never camouflaged. Dassault Ouragons were almost all camouflaged right from the beginning of their service career. An exception? Not actually. They were obsolete when purchased and their service career almost paralleled that of the swept-wing Mystère IVA, which had made the unswept Ouragon obsolete almost before the latter entered service.

Some Noratlas transports were camouflaged, while others were left in natural metal. In addition to paratroop and cargo duties within Israel, the Nord transport was called on to make long-distance flights out of the country, so there was a rationale for leaving some without camouflage—although long-distance flights by service aircraft were made by camouflaged aircraft with as much frequency as flights by Noratlas in bare metal.

Mystères began their service careers in bare metal and donned camouflage when the supersonic Dassault Super Mystère arrived on the scene. The Super Mystère stayed with natural metal until the uncamouflaged Dassault Mirages entered service. Mirages remained in bare metal right through the Six Day War and beyond.

A notable exception to the camouflage of this period is the Boeing Stratocruiser, which has retained the original Pan American commercial scheme of blue markings on natural metal, with the addition of the Israeli Star of David. In the early Seventies the United States delivered KC-97 (military tanker versions of the Stratocruiser) aircraft in bare metal. It is believed that at least some of these have since been camouflaged.

There was one Nord Noratlas which departed from the conventional scheme of the period. Instead of the two-tone rust brown and slate blue upper surface, this aircraft was camouflaged in a dark gray and medium gray upper surface in conventional wave pattern with a light gray undersurface. This particular aircraft was intended for use as a transport for commandos on clandestine raids into Syria to seek out infiltrator bases.

In the mid-Sixties the basic camouflage colors and patterns underwent a significant change. Upper surfaces went from a two-color to a three-color pattern. As with the earlier camouflage, patterns were masked off and sprayed, so there was a sharp demarcation between colors. Upper surface colors consisted of tan (Federal Color Card No. 33531), brown (Federal Color Card No. 30219), and green (Federal Color Card No. 34227). Undersurfaces were finished in pale blue (Federal Color Card No. 35622). The polyurethane enamel was applied over a single coat of epoxy primer. In the late Sixties, first McDonnell Douglas A-4 Skyhawks and then the F-4E Phantoms made their appearance in the skies over Israel. These aircraft were camouflaged in the now-standard three-tone upper surface pattern.

With the arrival of the Phantoms, Mirages were painted in the new camouflage scheme instead of the previous bare metal. Although camouflaged, the Mirage was hardly considered a second-line aircraft at this point, since it was retained in the intercept role, the Phantoms being used as fighter-bombers. While using the same three-tone camouflage, Mirages had a larger proportion of tan in the camouflage, since the aircraft was operated from forward air bases in desert regions.

Although all aircraft camouflaged in Israel had sharp demarcations between colors, as did new American aircraft intended for Israel, some refurbished aircraft from the Vietnamese War broke all the rules. They were rushed to Israel to fill the gap until factory-fresh aircraft could arrive on the scene. Such aircraft usually had a spray camouflage without the sharp demarcation of paint found on factory-supplied ships. A number of them retained a light gray undersurface (Federal Color Card No. 36622). The upper surface brown of refurbished aircraft was retained, since this was the same color as that found on Israeli aircraft. Some retained the Vietnamese green (either Federal Color Card No. 34079 or 34102), adding the tan over the alternate green.

Israel received Lockheed C-130 transports from the United States late in 1971. These aircraft were delivered in Vietnamese-style camouflage, but were quickly repainted to conform to the standard three-tone Israeli colors.

A distinctly nonstandard scheme was applied to the MiG-21F which was flown to Israel in August 1966 by a defecting Iraqi pilot. The aircraft had its Iraqi camouflage removed and was flown in bare metal with garish red markings. As a whimsical touch, the code number "007" was added, recalling Ian Fleming's fictional character, James Bond. In 1967 some MiG-17s that were pressed into Israeli service (they had come down in Israel) had the then-standard rust brown and dark blue with a pair of bright yellow stripes around each wing tip and around the fuselage midsection.

It is uncertain how long Israel will retain the present camouflage scheme. The present pattern and colors have now been retained for as long a period as any previous scheme in IDF/AF history.